# DISCOURSES OF DOMINATION: RACIAL BIAS IN THE CANADIAN ENGLISH-LANGUAGE PRESS

*Discourses of Domination* explores the issue of racial bias in the Canadian English-language press. Applying critical discourse analysis as their principal methodology, Frances Henry and Carol Tator investigate the way in which the media produce, reproduce, and disseminate racist thinking through language and discourse.

The core of the text consists of a series of case studies, including several high-profile cases involving the alleged criminality of persons of colour. Using these case studies as a springboard, Henry and Tator demonstrate how the media construct people of colour, immigrants, refugees, and First Nations peoples as 'others' – those who live outside the 'imagined community' of Canada. Their analysis ultimately points to the tension between democratic liberalism as a defining characteristic of Canadian society and the collective racist ideology that is embedded in the dominant culture. *Discourses of Domination* thus provides a greater understanding of newer forms of racism, located within systems of cultural production and representation.

FRANCES HENRY is Professor Emerita, Department of Anthropology, York University. She is one of Canada's leading experts in the study of racism and anti-racism.

CAROL TATOR is a Course Director in the Department of Anthropology, York University. She has worked on the front lines of the anti-racism movement for over two decades, assisting public sector institutions to respond to racism in their systems and structures.

# Discourses of Domination

Racial Bias in the Canadian
English-Language Press

FRANCES HENRY AND CAROL TATOR
With a chapter by
Sean Hier and Joshua Grenberg

UNIVERSITY OF TORONTO PRESS
Toronto Buffalo London

ISBN: 0-8020-3600-7 (cloth)
ISBN: 0-8020-8457-5 (paper)

Printed on acid-free paper

---

**National Library of Canada Cataloguing in Publication Data**

Henry, Frances, 1931–
  Discourses of domination : racial bias in the Canadian
  English-language press

  Includes bibliographical references and index.
  ISBN 0-8020-3600-7 (bound).     ISBN 0-8020-8457-5 (pbk.)

  1. Racism in the press – Canada – Case studies.   2. Canadian
  newspapers (English)   3. Discourse analysis.   I. Tator, Carol
  II. Title.

  PN 4914.R29H45 2002     302.23'22'080971     C2002-900907-3

---

This book has been published with the help of a grant from the Humanities
and Social Sciences Federation of Canada, using funds provided by the Social
Sciences and Humanities Research Council of Canada.

The University of Toronto Press acknowledges the financial assistance to its
publishing program of the Canada Council for the Arts and the Ontario Arts
Council.

University of Toronto Press acknowledges the financial support for its publishing activites of the Government of Canada through the Book Publishing
Industry Development Program (BPIDP).

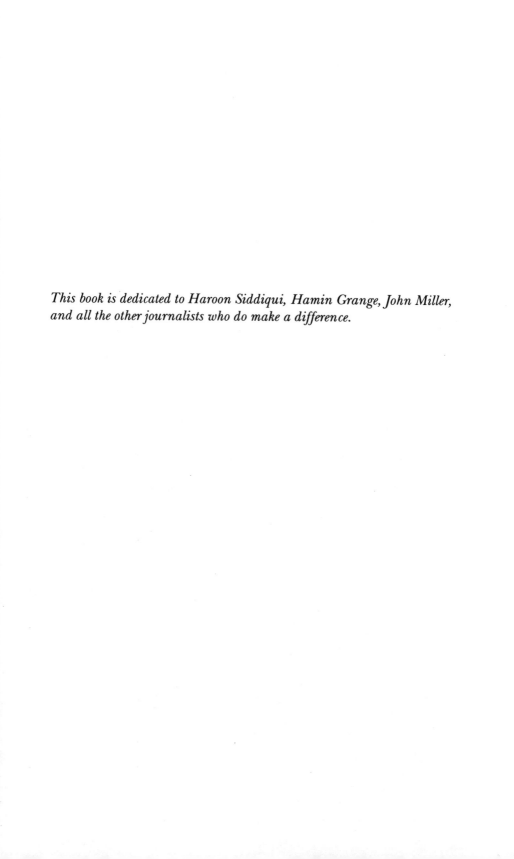

*This book is dedicated to Haroon Siddiqui, Hamin Grange, John Miller, and all the other journalists who do make a difference.*

# Contents

# Acknowledgments

Many people and several organizations were instrumental in bringing this book to fruition. We thank the Canadian Race Relations Foundation for funding this project. The School of Journalism of Ryerson Polytechnic University supported the case study on the racialization of crime. Marnie Bjornson played an instrumental role in the discourse analysis of this case study. Kirk Moss demonstrated creativity and persistence in his interviews with journalists and broadcasters. We greatly appreciate the generosity with which these individuals shared their experiences and reflections. We are also very indebted to our research assistant, Karen Snider, who helped with the data collection. Karen's computer knowledge was invaluable. We would especially like to note the significant contribution of journalists such as Haroon Siddiqui, editor emeritus of the *Toronto Star*, and Hamlin Grange, journalist and broadcaster, and many other journalists of colour, whose passion for their work and commitment to a more just and equitable society are an inspiration. We are especially grateful to the Canadian Association of Black Journalists for their contributions in supporting this initiative.

*Discourses of Domination: Racial Bias in the English-Language Press* is the second book to be published by the University of Toronto Press on the subject of racism in cultural production, and we are grateful to Virgil Duff, senior editor at the press, for his support and assistance. Once again, Matthew Kudelka's fine copy editing made an invaluable contribution to our final manuscript.

Finally, we would like to thank our husbands, Jeff Henry and Charles Tator, and our children, Terrence and Miriam Henry and Ira, Michael, and Julie Tator, for their love and support, which has sustained our lives and our work.

# DISCOURSES OF DOMINATION: RACIAL BIAS IN THE CANADIAN ENGLISH-LANGUAGE PRESS

# Introduction

Unemployed Ontarians would be well advised to ferret out that ancestor who claimed native roots or a history on an African slaveship. Or they might even consider inventing such a relative.

Editorial, Globe and Mail, 1 September 1994

In not reporting on the unusual pathologies of [ethnic groups other than aboriginals], we are failing in our duty to inform society of significant social facts.

William Thorsell, Globe and Mail, 9 April 1994

Our sponsored immigration policy has 'ended up putting grandmas and grandpas or nieces and nephews on our welfare rolls by the hundreds of thousands.'

Diane Francis, National Post, 4 January 2000

Send them back. That's the opinion of the majority of callers who responded to Friday's *Times-Colonist* phone poll on the 123 *Chinese* migrants who arrived here last week. And 44% indicated that they should be allowed to stay.

Victoria Times Colonist, 12 July 1999

Unfortunately, these days most of the murderers seem to be Black ... Given the society we live in, racial conflict is often the result of when there is Black-and-White crime ... Are we a society of racists? Certainly not. It's just that White Canadians are understandably fed up with people they see as outsiders, coming into their country and beating and killing them.

Maharaj, Toronto Sun, 15 April 1994

Quotes such as the ones cited above, laced with negative images and meanings, can be found almost every day in Canada's newspapers. We contend that these kinds of discourse are not isolated aberrations, but reflect a set of core assumptions, hypotheses, and world views held by many of those who work in the mass media. In this book we hope to shows how some members of the Canadian press give voice to racism, and how the media marginalize, denigrate, and silence ethnoracial minorities. When we speak of 'the media' as a collective institution, we do not mean to suggest that all of the media are guilty of racist discourse all of the time. But we will be selecting particular examples of media discourse that misrepresents or distorts the images of people of colour. In doing so, we recognize that there are also examples of the media exhibiting temperance, moderation and fairness in their treatment of issues involving people of colour. That being said, our intent is to demonstrate where they go wrong rather than what they do right.

Though racism in Canada's social systems and public institutions takes many forms, racism in the media is one of the most important areas of inquiry if we hope to develop effective strategies and mechanisms for dismantling racism in Canadian society. The media are one of the most powerful institutions in a democratic society because they help transmit its central cultural images, ideas, and symbols, as well as a nation's narratives and myths. Media discourse plays a large part in reproducing the collective belief system of the dominant society and the core values of society (Hall et al., 1975; van Dijk, 1988).

Supposedly, the media allow for the free flow and exchange of knowledge, opinions, and information. To the extent they do, media organizations are among the most important instruments a liberal democratic state has for producing and disseminating its ideals. The media are expected to reflect alternative viewpoints, to remain neutral and objective, and to provide free and equitable access to all groups, irrespective of their sociocultural identity, and irrespective of gender, social class, racial or ethnic background, religious beliefs, sexual orientation, and so on.

The print and electronic media have a strong effect on the everyday lives of individuals and communities. Radio, television, the print media, and other systems of representation (e.g., academia, school curricula, film, art, literature, films, theatre, music) are the elements out of which we form our identities. These vehicles of cultural production help shape our sense of self, our understanding of what it means to be male/female, and our sense of ethnicity, class, race, and national identity. They help us understand who is *us* who is *them*. This often has the effect of organizing Canadians into sharply opposed camps. This process can deeply affect our lives, depending on which meanings are assigned to the categories in play, and under what circumstances (Kellner, 1995; Hall, 1997).

The media hold up a mirror in which society can see itself reflected. As we demonstrate in this book, that mirror's reflections are sometimes severely distorted. The media do not objectively record and describe reality, nor do they neutrally report facts and stories. Rather, some media practitioners socially reconstruct reality based on their professional and personal ideologies, corporate interests, and cultural and organizational norms and values (van Dijk, 1988a: 91; Fiske, 1994; Hackett and Zhao, 1998).

For many people the mass media are a crucial source of the beliefs and values from which they develop their pictures of their social worlds. People turn to their newspaper or the evening broadcast news to learn about the events, issues, and stories that are unfolding in their immediate social world and beyond. They turn to the news to gain an understanding of not only events but also people, especially those belonging to groups with whom they rarely interact. Thus, the media play a critical role in the 'construction of reality,' acting as a 'filter, gatekeeper or agenda setter' (Hackett and Zhao, 1998). Media images and stories carry powerful but coded meanings and messages. Although we subscribe to the view that the media produce and reproduce meanings, ideas, values, and norms, we do not believe that the media produce only one dominant discourse or that audiences are mere passive receptacles.

In the past two-and-a-half decades, we the authors of this book have been deeply involved with the mass media – the print media in particular. Together, over that time, we have monitored the Toronto print media on almost a daily basis. We have analysed media discourse and written about racism in the press in earlier works (see Henry et al., 2000; Tator et al., 1998). We have worked with many journalists covering stories that relate to people of colour and to issues of critical importance in a racially diverse society. Our recent research is central to our work as both scholars and antiracism activists.

In this book, whenever possible we try to present a national perspective on racism in the media. We have included citations from both national newspapers, the *Globe and Mail* and the *National Post* in an attempt to present as much national coverage of issues as possible. But, it is important to note that for the past several decades, Ontario has been one of the main sites of antiracism struggles in Canada. It also has the greatest number of people of colour in its population Moreover, its minority communities, especially in Toronto, have for decades been profoundly concerned about racism in the media and have been trying to mediate a more constructive relationship with both the print and electronic media. This book, and our many other studies of racism in Canadian society, are strongly influenced by our commitment to both social justice and social action. Our perspective is congruous with the outlook of writers such as bell hooks, who sees the airing of diverse perspectives as a means for us to educate one another and acquire a sense of 'critical consciousness' (1990: 6). It is also shaped by the work of Michel Foucault, who argued for the necessity 'to question over and over again what is postulated as self evident, to disturb people's mental habits, ... to dissipate what is familiar and accepted, to re-examine rules and institutions ... to participate in the formation of a political will in which citizens have a role to play' (1980: 258).

We hope this book offers a constructive critique of the media and their systems of representation. It is not our intention to label as racist any particular newspaper, journalist, or editor, and we do not see ourselves as agents of the 'cultural thought police.' We believe that journalists often operate within discursive spaces that transcend them, and we agree with Hall (1981) and Riggins (1997) when they contend that the media's offerings flow out of a set of complex and often contradictory system of structures, practices, and discourses, and not the personal inclinations of any of its practitioners. As we demonstrate throughout this book, journalists and editors contribute whether consciously or not to the marginalization and denigration of people of colour and other minorities; however, our concern is not with individual prejudicial attitudes. By focusing on this narrow aspect of racism we would be deflecting the problem of media representation away from the ideological centres and the historical, political, cultural, and institutional contexts within which racism in some of the media has functioned.

Our approach, then, involves examining 'codes of meaning' (Hebdige, 1993) – that is, the unquestioned assumptions, values, norms, and practices that are rooted in the dominant culture's ideology and in the subcultures of media organizations. We wish to help uncover and critically examine what passes as 'everyday commonsense' (Essed, 1990) – what mainstream culture defines as 'truth,' and accepts as 'fact,' and views as 'reality' (Foucault, 1980).

At this point we must situate ourselves in regard to a critical question in media studies: Do the media reflect reality and do so fairly accurately, or do they 'misrepresent' – that is show bias and unequal treatment – in their texts and images? If, for example, the *Globe and Mail* maintains a consistent campaign against employment equity legislation, is it reflecting fairly and accurately the views of its readers, or those of its owners and managers, or both? When the *National Post* repeatedly targets the Tamils and their alleged terrorist activities, is it presenting an accurate picture of the real world, or is it constructing an image that is consistent with the ideological position of its publishers and editors? Does the dominant cultural, economic, and politic elite – the presumed readers of the *Post* – influence their point of view? These are complex questions that cannot be avoided in any analysis of media text; in this book we cannot provide definitive answers. However, our position on these issues is that generally speaking, the media – especially the print media – reflect the ideological positions of their elite owners; their editorials, features, and even news stories replicate the assumptions, beliefs, and values of those owners. In other words, the discourses and representations in many newspapers founded on conservative ideologies are 'accurate' to the extent that they reproduce the hegemonic perspectives of their owners. Moreover, a newspaper will select a style of discourse that is consistent with its own purposes. Thus, the tabloid format of the *Toronto Sun* – large numbers of photos and short news articles, as well as many advertisements – influences its discourse. (The same can be said of all newspapers in the Sun chain.) Also, the *Sun*'s choices of news to cover, and the commentary of its columnists, are consistent with an ideology that rarely if ever challenges the status quo.

Media consumers cannot be regarded as a homogeneous, passive, and uncritical mass; at the same time, we cannot ignore the media's crucial role in influencing and reinforcing attitudes and opinions. Readers of a given newspaper usually subscribe to that paper's ideological positions, and the relationship between a particular medium and its audience is interactive. Thus, media constructions – especially of ethnoracial groups – are not strictly speaking 'misrepresentations,' because they reflect the values and belief systems of the media owners and their audiences. Often, however, these constructions are inaccurate, biased, unbalanced, and unfair, and do not reflect the real lives and activities of real people – in this case, people of colour and First Nations peoples.

We hope this book will help clarify some of the conditions necessary to bring about meaningful change in the relationship between the mainstream, White-dominated media and Canada's ethnoracial and First Nations communities, which often feel marginalized, excluded, and powerless to change how they are portrayed. We also hope this book will encourage a re-examination of existing paradigms relating to public discourse in the media and other sociocultural and political systems. It is time to recast the principle of freedom of expression so as to incorporate the discourses, experiences, contributions, stories, issues, and voices of racial minorities and other communities that have, historically and currently, been marked and marginalized as 'others.'

Power is at the centre of cultural politics. Cultural practices and systems of representation involve relations of power, and 'social power manifests itself in competing discourses' (Jordan and Weedon, 1995: 14). Power both enables and disables; it allows or denies individuals opportunities for self-realization, and groups opportunities for recognition. Power also involves challenging the authority of mainstream media authorities and media institutions. The struggle for power should be in the context of empowering individuals and communities, rather than 'power over' any group. This is a crucial distinction. Ethnoracial minorities are searching for ways to preserve control over their own lives and the lives of their communities. They are no longer content to stand outside the doors of print media organizations, radio and television stations, and advertising agencies and corporate organizations. They are demanding the opportunity to enter the public culture and to play a role in transforming it. Their ultimate goal is to affirm racial and cultural difference and integrate that difference into the core of Canada's social, cultural, and political life (Kulyk Keefer, 1996; Mackey, 1995).

Our research has focused on some of the print media – in particular, on the four Toronto newspapers. This is not to suggest that racism in the electronic media is less important. However, the study of racism in the electronic media is extremely complex, and resources have not allowed us to pursue this important area of inquiry in this book. However, in our review of the literature we do refer to some of the findings of studies on the electronic media. Also, we have incorporated the findings of an empirical study documenting some of the experiences of people of colour working in the Toronto print and electronic media. As well, we have included a case study on Avery Haines, a broadcaster with CTV who was fired for making on-air pejorative remarks against minorities. Soon after, she was hired by CityTV.

**Terminology**

In almost all our earlier work, we began with a discussion of the importance of language for analysing and understanding racism and other forms of bias and discrimination. The language of this field of inquiry is constantly evolving as the phenomenon of racism mutates into diverse forms and manifestations. New terms emerge, and historical context affects how 'old' words are used and understood. Concepts that arise repeatedly in this book such as race, culture, truth, liberal values, tolerance, freedom of expression, equal opportunity, immigrants and refugees, and White and Black, are coded with different meanings; they exist as part of diverse social and interpretative frameworks. Powerful currents alter interpretations, depending on the social context, the particular situation, the speaker, and the reader or audience.

This point is mostly dramatically illustrated by the multiple meanings embedded in the notion of *colour* – a term that remains the nucleus of the race classification system. Paradoxically, colour as a signifier bears little relation to the actual skin tones of human beings. No White person is truly white, nor is any Black individual completely devoid of colour. Whites do not consider themselves part of the colour spectrum; rather, they identify themselves as the universal norm. However, the gradations of colour from white to black associated with various racial groups have economic, social, and cultural consequences. The ideology that defines Whites as superior renders people of different colours inferior.

In Canadian society, skin colour has an important relationship to status and position. Sherene Razack (1998) argues that the language of colour delineates the politics of domination and subordination, observing that 'White ... is the colour of domination' (11). There is nothing socially or politically neutral about skin colour. People of a given (non-white) colour are assigned certain cultural traits, which have meanings attached to them – meanings that are in turn incorporated into everyday language and the discursive practices of politicians, bureaucrats, institutional authorities, the media, and other opinion shapers (Shohat and Stam, 1994). The assertion that 'Blacks are prone to commit crimes' thus signifies that members of a racial group, identified by their skin colour, have a propensity for certain kinds of behaviour.

There is a growing body of research analysing the power of the term *whiteness*, both as a description and as symbol, experience, and ideology (see Frankenberg, 1993; Gabriel, 1998). As the authors of *Off White* (Fine et al., 1997) point out: 'Rarely is it acknowledged that Whiteness demands and constitutes hierarchy, exclusion and deprivation' (viii). However, Whiteness is invisible to those who possess it. Most White people perceive themselves as colourless and therefore without privileges and subjectivities (Roman, 1993). White culture is the hidden norm against which the 'differences' of all other subordinate groups are evaluated. For those who have inherited its mantle, Whiteness suggests normality, truth, objectivity, and merit.

It is for these reasons that references to colour in this book are used in their political sense. We capitalize the terms 'Black' and 'White' to reflect this. The reader will note that references citing British literature or experiences use the term Black inclusively when referring to people of colour. However, in all other discussions, Black refers specifically to people of African descent.

We use the terms 'mainstream,' 'Anglo,' and 'the dominant group' interchangeably throughout this book when referring to the group in Canadian society that maintains the power to define itself and its culture as the norm. We note here that labelling people as White can be as problematic as classifying other people as Blacks, or people of colour, or visible minorities. Even within the category of Whiteness, there are important differences in terms of patterns of racialization. For example, 'Anglo-ness' does not necessarily confer a monolithic state of privilege: Jews in North America have also experienced marginalization and racialization, and so have the Irish, Italians, Poles, Ukrainians, and Germans, among others.

We use the phrases 'racial minorities' and 'people of colour' often in this book, but we do so cautiously. Referring to groups of people as minorities is, at the very least, inaccurate, when one considers that they represent four-fifths of the world's population. Furthermore, huge distinctions exist among racial minorities or people of colour. For example, within each of the groups examined in this book there are significant differences relating to class and gender. The experiences of recent affluent immigrants from Hong Kong, who have come to Canada with significant resources and business skills, bear little resemblance to those of unskilled workers who are a third-generation Chinese Canadian, or to those Chinese refugees fleeing from political persecution.

We use the phrases 'racial minorities' and 'people of colour' when referring to groups of people who because of their physical characteristics have been subjected to differential and unequal treatment in Canada. Their minority status is the result of their lack of access to power, privilege, and prestige relative to Whites. Although there are significant differences among 'racial minorities' or 'people of colour' – as there are within any ethnoracial group – members of these diverse communities share a history of exposure to racial bias and discriminatory barriers based on the colour of their skin. So for the purposes of this book, we have grouped them together. We use the term First Nations in this book although there are also references to Aboriginals and indigenous peoples. Again, this term refers to an extremely heterogeneous population.

Finally, what do we mean by 'race' and 'racism'? From our perspective, race is a socially constructed phenomenon based on the false assumption that physical differences such as skin colour, facial features, and hair colour and texture are related to intellectual, moral, or cultural superiority. The concept of race has no basis in biological realities and, it follows, no meaning independent of its social definitions. But as a social construction, race has significantly affected the lives of people of color (Banton, 1977; Miles, 1989; Rex, 1983).

Racism (more correctly, 'social racism') refers to the assumptions, attitudes, beliefs, and behaviours of individuals and to the institutional policies, processes, and practices that flow from those understandings. Racism as racialized language or discourse manifests itself in euphemisms, metaphors, and omissions that support given ideologies and policies. It is reflected in the collective belief systems of the dominant culture, and it is woven into the laws, languages, rules, and norms of Canadian society.

Another term we use often in this book, 'racialization,' regularly appears in studies on racism produced in the United Kingdom – especially those which take a political economy perspective. In our analysis we use the terms 'racialized' and 'racist' interchangeably when referring to discourse (as both language and social practice). The term racialized, which is less familiar to North American readers, has been defined as 'processes by which meanings are attributed to particular objects, features and processes, in such a way that the latter are given special significance and carry or are embodied with a set of additional meanings' (Miles, 1989: 70).

Ideological racialization refers to the ways in which discourse can become imbued with racial dimensions. It is part of the processes by which populations of people are constructed, differentiated, 'inferiorized,' and excluded (Anthias, 1998). The concept of racialization is useful because it moves us away from the construct of race relations that assumes that races exist, and helps us try to understand the relations between them. Racialization focuses on how groups not previously defined as 'races' have come to be redefined in this way, and assesses the factors that are part of such processes (Small, 1994).

For example, in Canada, the debate about immigration has become racialized because substantial numbers of immigrants are now people of colour. Restricting immigration thus becomes a means of excluding these groups. The racialization of crime results in the stigmatization of certain groups. For example, racialization in the media results in news stories and editorials in which Blacks figure prominently in crimes that are also committed by members of other groups in society.

In a series of case studies, using critical discourse analysis (see chapter 4) as our analytical approach, we show how journalists, editors, and publishers filter the news through a White, Western, male, and middle-class perspective. We examine how the media construct racist discourse; to this purpose we closely consider the main rhetorical arguments and strategies and the global themes and topics that appear in new stories, editorials, and feature columns. We then analyse news discourse at the micro-level of analysis, considering overall schematic forms, style, and rhetoric and the meanings underlying the actual words and sentences (van Dijk, 1991). Several case studies comprise the core content of this book. Each of these illustrates how the media articulate and transmit powerful and negative messages about ethnoracial minorities, which in turn pass into the collective psyche of Canadian society. Generations of deleterious projections of a group can inflict, and have inflicted, harmful wounds on individuals and communities. They also make it more difficult to develop a healthy democratic society (Pieterse, 1992).

One of our goals in this book is to demonstrate the subtle and overt ways in which the media produce, reproduce, and disseminate racist ideology and racialized discourse. We also hope to provide readers with tools for better understanding the various linguistic and rhetorical strategies employed by the media, wittingly or unwittingly, to create discourses that marginalize, misrepresent, and disadvantage minorities in a number of significant ways. In this study we examine how racism in the media is linked to forms of racialized discourse within other institutions and systems such as government, law enforcement, and the justice system.

Racialized discourse in the media consists of that repertoire of words, images, texts, explanations, and everyday practices which, when threaded together, produce an understanding of the world and the position and status of people of colour in that world (Fiske, 1994). We share the view of van Dijk (1988a) who contends that discourse is not just a symptom of the problem of racism. Essentially, it reinforces individual beliefs and behaviours, collective ideologies, public policies and programs, organizational planning processes, practices, and decision making. Discourse is language put to social use, and it is often invisible to those who use it (Fiske, 1994).

Our analysis of racism in the media reflects a fundamental tension that we have explored in earlier books (see Henry et al., 2000; Tator et al., 1998) – that is, the tension between democratic liberalism as a defining characteristic of Canadian society and the collective racist ideology embedded in the dominant culture both historically and in modern times. This conflict creates a fundamental and constant moral tension between the everyday experiences of people of colour and the perceptions of those who have the power to redefine that reality such as journalists and editors, broadcasters, producers, and advertisers, as well as politicians and bureaucrats, police and judges, teachers and academics, curators and filmmakers, and the corporate elite. One of the subjects of this study is the multiplicity of ways in which this value conflict is expressed in the institutional spaces of the media in their everyday discursive practices.

**Outline of the Book**

The chapters in Part I provide a framework and context for the case studies that follow. In chapter 1 we examine the study's theoretical foundation. We discuss the concepts of ideology, racist ideology, and racialized discourse. We highlight some of the fundamental tensions and conflicts that characterize a democratic liberal society in which racist discourse is a pervasive and systemic reality. We identify some of the diverse approaches to the study of racism in the media. We follow all this with a discussion of the approach that we have chosen to guide our study, which is based on a cultural studies orientation. Our theoretical centre is embedded in the broader notion that the discursive reproduction of racism reinforces the power of the dominant culture and legitimizes systems of inequality. In this chapter we also briefly introduce the reader to the concept of critical discourse analysis, a research method that analyses how dominance and inequality are enacted through systems of representation and, more specifically, through the everyday 'talk' and 'text' of the media. We conclude with an examination of the discourses of dominance associated with our theory of democratic racism (explored in earlier works – see Henry et al., 2000, and Tator et al., 1998).

In chapter 2 we review the body of Canadian literature relating to racism in the media. The findings of two decades of research on this subject demonstrate a consistent pattern of racialized discourse in the print media; they also signal the importance of the issues. The research points to the pressing need for Canadians to continue to seek strategies to address the everyday racism that is so systemic in press coverage.

In chapter 3 we take up the theme of how minorities working in the media are represented. We begin with a brief comparative analysis of the quantitative data as they relate to people of colour working in the print media in the United States, the United Kingdom, and Canada. We then present the findings of our empirical study on the experiences of journalists and reporters working in Toronto print and electronic media organizations.

In the first chapter of Part II we introduce the reader to critical discourse analysis, which is the methodology that underlies all our case studies. We review some of the main elements of newsmaking and refer to some of the more important tools and techniques used in this analytic methodology. We offer two case studies in this section. Both relate to the theme of how minorities are marginalized in the workplace.

The case study in chapter 5 is based on an incident that occurred in the electronic media in January 2000. A CTV broadcaster, Avery Haines, made some highly prejudicial remarks that were inadvertently aired on television, and was subsequently fired by the station for 'unprofessional behaviour.' We show how the mainstream media responded with almost unanimous support for their colleague. Drawing from the extensive media coverage of the incident, we examine the some of the discourses that were used by journalists and editors, who claimed that Haines was a victim of 'political correctness,' 'reverse racism,' and 'special interest groups.' The case study exposes many of the issues and personal challenges that respondents identified in our empirical study on representation in chapter 3. It also highlights the values and norms that are deeply embedded in the corporate culture of many if not most media workplaces – values and norms that are usually invisible to those who identify with the dominant culture.

In chapter 6 continue the theme of media workplace representation that was reflected in the preceding case study, but also go well beyond it. The case study examines the discourse on the policy of employment equity reflected in the *Globe and Mail* between 1993 and 1995. At the time, the issue was high on the public agenda in Ontario. As part of their 1995 election platform, the provincial Conservatives promised to rid the province of employment equity legislation, which had been brought in by an earlier NDP government. After Mike Harris's Conservatives won the election, almost their first action was to rescind that legislation. In our discourse analysis for this case study, we focus on editorials written during this period; we also include two opinion pieces written by William Thorsell, the *Globe*'s editor-in-chief at the time.

In Part III we introduce the theme of dominant discourses on immigrants and immigration. In chapter 7 we consider how immigrants and refugees are racialized, using the columns of one journalist, Diane Francis who writes for the *National Post* and other periodicals, including *Maclean's*. This case study presents a concrete example of a particular columnist using a subject such as immigration and refugee policies to create a racialized discourse that homogenizes, essentializes, and maligns all immigrants and refugees. We then analyze the *National Post*'s coverage of the Tamil community and how the newspaper constructed a racist discourse that disparaged an entire population with a deluge of negative representations.

In chapter 8, Sean Hier and Joshua Greenberg contribute a powerful case study about how Canada's press covered the sudden appearance of 600 Chinese migrants on the coast of British Columbia between July and September 1999. Drawing on the theory of 'moral panic,' the authors examine how the news discourse about these migrants was constructed and reproduced; how their 'illegal entry' was problematized; and how the arrival of these migrants became transformed into a discursive crisis focusing on national security. The authors link their findings to the almost unique position of the Chinese in Canada, arguing that this latest episode has reinforced their traditionally marginalized position in Canadian society.

In chapter 9 we continue to look at how the media racializes ethnoracial minorities. As an example, we use the Just Desserts incident, in which a White woman was shot and killed by Black assailants in a Toronto restaurant. We include another case study on the racialization of crime, relating to a killing at a Chinese restaurant in downtown Toronto, which led to a stream of racialized discourse centring on the Asian community.

In Part IV we discuss conflicts between First Nations people and the mainstream media. In chapter 10 we present two case studies. The first of these examines the *National Post*'s coverage of a story involving a First Nations woman and her community, Pelican Narrows in Saskatchewan. A Reform MP from Saskatchewan was accused (and later found guilty) of sexually assaulting a teenager from a First Nations reserve while he was an RCMP officer there many years before. We compare the *Globe and Mail*'s discourse with the coverage found in two Saskatchewan newspapers, the *Saskatoon Star Phoenix* and the *Regina Leader Post*. The second case study deals with the controversy surrounding Aboriginal fishing rights in New Brunswick, which culminated in the violence at Burnt Church. Here we analyse several editorials about the issue in the *National Post*.

In the conclusion we revisit some of the main findings of our study, and then review the discourses of dominance constructed by Canada's press in the context of 'democratic racism.' We argue that the everyday discourse in Canada's press reinforces racial inequalities in Canadian society. We critique journalism's claims to 'objectivity,' 'detachment,' and neutrality, arguing that everyday media discourse operates in counterpoint to these ideals. We conclude by discussing the need for greater reflexivity in the profession of journalism.

Our study of racialized discourse in the Canadian print media points to fact that media discourses are a terrain of struggle. The kinds of dominant representations we have uncovered are difficult to overturn. They provide a deep reservoir of familiar myths, unexamined assumptions, and reassuring stereotypes. The mass media reaffirm dominant ideologies and legitimize inequalities. All of our findings underscore the fact that every discursive community interprets words, images, and ideas in its own way, and then constructs meanings that make sense in relation to its particular social, cultural, and historical context. However, only dominant discourses find their way into the public domain; oppositional or alternative discourses are routinely silenced. Many of our case studies provide examples of how individuals and communities are attempting to challenge racialized discourse in the mainstream media.

Our analysis of the English print media in Canada indicates that as a methodology, critical discourse analysis offers a powerful weapon in the struggle to understand, expose, and resist oppressive forms of discourse in the media. Our analysis also establishes the interrelationship between racialized media discourse and other expressions of racialized inequality in other sectors of Canadian society. We share the view of many other scholars, such as Fiske (1994), Fairclough and Wodak (1997), Hall (1997), and the theoretician who has most inspired and informed our work, Teun van Dijk (1991), that altering the everyday discursive practices embedded in systems of representation such as the media is crucial to social change.

PART I
ESTABLISHING A SOCIAL CONTEXT

# 1

# Theoretical Framework

Theory is always a (necessary) detour on the way to something more important.

Hall, 1991

This book and its engagement with theory is directed toward that critical goal of understanding the ways in which relations between communication and race can be transformed in ways that are enabling, rather than limiting.

Gandy, 1998

The theoretical orientation we employ in this book on the (mis)representation of people of colour in the media is multidisciplinary. It is influenced by the model of analysis of Teun van Dijk (1988a; 1991; 1993; 1998), by the seminal work of Hall and his colleagues at the Centre for Contemporary Cultural Studies, (1973; 1981; 1997), and by Wetherell and Potter (1992), among others[1]. The field of knowledge it incorporates includes cultural studies, communications studies, discourse analysis, critical race theory[2] and antiracist perspectives. The Centre for Contemporary Cultural Studies provided the framework for including media studies in the emerging field of cultural studies in that it conceptualized the media as part of popular culture. Van Dijk was one of the first scholars to apply critical discourse analysis to the study of the press.

In this chapter we analyse some of the complex links between everyday language and representations, public discourse in the media, and the construction and preservation of racism in Canadian society. The subject of how the media reproduce racial inequality begins with a consideration of ideology and Hall's premise that the media are critical sites for the production, reproduction, and transformation of ideologies. We agree with Stuart Hall that the media are part of the dominant culture's means of ideological production (1981).

At this point we must note that the study of media representation lends itself to many different theoretical and methodological approaches. As early as 1973, media studies were on the research agenda of the Centre for Contemporary Cultural Studies in the United Kingdom. The field of cultural studies opened the way to an approach that emphasized how 'reality' can be studied through language, discourse, representations, and images. Cultural studies – then and now – eschews the more traditional approaches to research, which rely solely on the empiricist tradition in the social sciences. Its emphasis is less on establishing the empirical 'facts' than on the shifting terrain – that is, language, text, and image – terrain that is open to many levels of interpretation. Cottle (2000) has recently commented on the many valid approaches to studying the media in contemporary society: 'Each of these areas of research and theorization are indispensable for an understanding of the interrelated complexities informing the interactions between media and ethnic minorities and changing cultural boundaries.' Our approach is informed by cultural studies, especially as we believe that its methods of analysis are conducive to engaged social action.

**The Nature of Ideology**

Ideology is those beliefs, perceptions, assumptions, and values that provide members of a group with an understanding and an explanation of their world. Hall defines ideology as 'the mental frameworks – the languages, the concepts, categories, imagery of thought, and the systems of representation – which different classes and social groups deploy in order to make sense of, figure out and render intelligible the way society works' (1996a: 26). However, ideology does not simply make sense of society; it also regulates social practices. Both Hall and van Dijk (1998b) support the view that ideologies organize, maintain, and stabilize particular forms of power and dominance. Ideology constitute a baseline that various groups in a heterogeneous society apply when framing their attitudes and organizing means and strategies to further their own ideals, goals, and interests. Ideology is *shared*; it operates at a collective level, rather than flowing out of individual cognition. Though individuals can communicate ideological statements, ideologies are not themselves the outcome of individual consciousness or intention (Hall, 1981).

Eurocentrism is an example of an ideology. It upholds the supremacy of Europe's values, ideas, and peoples as a core and shared belief system (see Shohat and Stam, 1994). Orientalism is a form of Eurocentrism: the European construction of the 'Orient' acts as a vehicle for expressing Eurocentric values, assumptions, and norms (see Said, 1978).

Ideology influences how people interpret social, cultural, political, and economic systems and structures; it is linked to their needs, hopes, and fears. But ideological formations are not static; rather, they are constantly evolving, often as a result of contradictory experiences (Hall, 1983). Ideologies are discursive constructions drawn from particular perspectives. They 'iron out' the contradictions, dilemmas, and antagonisms of practices in ways that are consistent with the interests and projects of domination (Chouliaraki and Fairclough, 1999).

In everyday ideological constructs, ideas about difference – race, ethnicity, gender, and class, among other classifications – are produced, preserved, and promoted. These ideas form the basis for social behaviour. Ideology defines 'difference' and, conversely, determines what is 'natural' and 'normal.' Ideology denotes a set of ideas and values that legitimate particular economic and social conditions. It penetrates and saturates everyday discourses in the form of common sense, and it provides codes of meaning (Hall, 1981; Hebdige, 1993). Ideology normalizes the status quo and presents as immutable certain aspects of the human condition that currently exist, such as racism.

**The Definition and Function of Racist Ideology**

Racist ideology provides the conceptual framework for the political, social, and cultural structures of inequality and for systems of dominance based on race. It also provides the processes for excluding and marginalizing people of colour that characterize Canadian society. Racism's cognitive dimensions are located in collective patterns of thought, knowledge, and beliefs, as well as in individual attitudes, perceptions, and behaviours: 'Racism as ideology includes the whole range of concepts, ideas, images and institutions that provide the framework of interpretation and meaning for racial thought in society' (Essed, 1990: 44).

In sum, racist ideology organizes, preserves, and perpetuates a society's power structures. It creates and preserves a system of dominance based on race, and it is communicated and reproduced through agencies of socialization and cultural transmission. These vehicles of socialization include the mass media and other vehicles of cultural production such as schools and universities; religious doctrines and practices; master narratives and images transmitted through art, music, and literature; and the justice system, which includes the police, the courts, and the prison system. Racist ideology is reflected and regenerated in the very language that people read, write, and speak (Goldberg, 1993).

Ideology is largely invisible to most people because it is deeply embedded in their 'commonsense,' everyday lived experience (Essed, 1991; van Dijk, 1998b). According to this view, racist thinking is natural – part of how ordinary people view the world. People do not need to have specialized knowledge about minority groups to be racist. 'Commonsense' racism is not based on theory, nor is it supported by a unified body of knowledge. It amounts to a 'storehouse of knowledge' that guides (Lawrence, 1982: 49): 'the practical struggle of everyday life of the popular masses' 'It is indeed a peculiarity of ideology that it imposes (without appearing to do so) obviousness as obviousness which we cannot fail to recognize and before which we have the inevitable and natural reaction of cry out (aloud or in the still small voice of conscience): "That's obvious! That's right! That's true!"' (Althusser, 1971a: 127).

The construct of common sense as a set of social beliefs and social representations is demonstrated most clearly in recent neoconservative arguments that denigrate and marginalize minorities. Ontario's Conservative government, during the election of 1995, which brought it to power, promised a 'Common Sense Revolution.' This was coded language that expressed neoconservatives' resistance to all public policies that offered the possibility of social change (see the case study on employment equity).

Racist ideology helps people 'understand' the increasingly complex and changing nature of the societies in which they live. Thus, recently unemployed people can easily blame new immigrants, whom they perceive as taking their jobs away. A corporate manager can justify refusing to hire those who are racially and often culturally 'different' on the basis of not wanting to disrupt workplace harmony. People who are fearful in their homes and on the streets can now blame all the Black or Asian people, in the belief that crime is something 'they' do. Teachers whose Black students are underachieving can believe it has nothing to do with their racial attitudes or classroom practices. In their selection of topics for news stories and in their reportage, editors and journalists can proclaim their 'neutrality,' 'objectivity,' and 'detachment' even while denigrating an entire community (see the case studies that form the core of this text).

These forms of everyday racism are part of what has been called the 'new racism,' which includes *aversive* (Gaertner and Dovidio, 1986) *symbolic* (McConahay and Hough, 1976), and *inferential* racism (Hall, 1981).[3] Hall distinguishes overt racism from inferential racism by describing the latter as manifested in 'apparently naturalised representations of events and situations relating to race, whether "factual" or "fictional," which have racist premises and propositions inscribed in them as a set of *unquestioned assumptions*' (10–11). The 'new racism' manifests itself in more subtle and insidious ways and is largely invisible to those who are part of the dominant culture. This form of racism is pervasive (see Henry et al., 2000) and is often expressed discursively through 'text and talk, expressed in board meetings, job interviews, policies, laws, parliamentary debates, political propaganda, textbooks, scholarly articles, movies, TV programs and news reports in the press, among hundreds of other genres' (van Dijk, 1993). The new racism rarely demonstrates itself in violence or overt racist behaviour, yet its consequences for minorities are just as severe: it limits and constrains their life chances.

The present authors have identified 'democratic racism' as a particular form of the new racism. This form constitutes both an ideology that emphasizes racism and a set of discursive policies and practices that regulate behaviour in specific institutions and settings.

### The Concept of Democratic Racism

Despite the ideological foundation of democratic liberalism, and despite a legislative state framework based on the policies of multiculturalism and employment equity, and despite the Canadian Human Rights Code, provincial human rights codes, and the Charter of Rights and Freedoms, racism continues to penetrate all levels of Canadian society (Henry et al., 2000; Li, 1999; Tator et al., 1998; Razack, 1998). This has created a fundamental tension in Canadian society – a dissonance between the ideology of Canada as a democratic liberal state and the racist ideology that is reflected in the collective belief system operating within Canadian cultural, social, political, and economic institutions.

Democratic racism arises when racist beliefs and behaviours remain deeply embedded in 'democratic' societies. Obfuscations and justifications are deployed to demonstrate continuing faith in egalitarian ideals, even while many individuals, groups, and institutions continue to engage in systemic racist practices that serve to undermine those ideals. Democratic racism is an ideology in which two conflicting sets of values are made congruent to each other. Commitments to democratic principles such as justice, equality, and fairness *conflict* with but also *coexist* with negative feelings about minority groups and discrimination against them (see Henry et al., 2000; Goldberg, 1993).

One of the consequences of this conflict is a lack of support for policies and practices that might improve the relatively low status of some people of colour. These policies and practices tend to require changes in the existing social, economic, and political order – usually by state intervention. This intervention, however, is perceived as in conflict with and a threat to liberal democracy. Thus, democratic racism holds that the spread of racism should only be dealt with – if it is dealt with at all – in such a way that basic economic structures and societal relations are left essentially unchanged (Gilroy, 1987). Efforts to combat racism that require intervention to change the cultural, social, economic, and political order lack political support. More importantly, they lack legitimacy, according to the egalitarian principles of liberal democracy.

Our recent research on racism in systems of cultural production and representation (Tator et al. 1998) suggests that the 'new' forms of racism are discursive and that democratic racism is demonstrated most clearly through thethrough the discourses of dominance. To examine this form of the 'new' racism, we require sensitive analytic tools to identify how racialized and racist meanings are woven into media representations and reproduced through them (Cottle, 2000).

**Discourse and Discursive Formations**

As a result of Michel Foucault's seminal work, *Power/Knowledge* (1980), the notion of 'discourse' has become central to postmodernist perspectives on culture and society. Foucault's theory of discourse focuses on the functions of particular discursive techniques. He is interested mainly in patterns of domination and in organized rituals of power. His primary concern is not to discover truth (i.e., powerful knowledge), but to understand how truth is formed. In his view, statements about the social, political, or moral world are rarely simply true or false, and the language used to describe alleged facts often interferes with the process of categorically defining what is true or false: 'The question of whether discourse is true or false is less important than whether it is effective in practice. When it is effective – organizing and regulating relations of power – it is called a "regime of truth"' (1980: 131). Foucault sees all knowledge, including historical knowledge, through the prism of discursive formations and techniques. In *The History of Sexuality* (1978) he examines the technique of the confession and suggests that it can be seen as the prototype for an entire range of similar discursive events. Tolson (1996), influenced by Foucault's theory of the power of discourse, suggests that the media can be understood as a series of institutional spaces that mobilize and reproduce discursive practices that constitute their own objects within their own specific fields of vision.

But the term 'discourse' is slippery, elusive, and difficult to define. Like cultural studies, it can sometimes include anything and everything to do with expressive human behaviour. At other times, it refers to the specific practices and expressions of people and their institutions. As Fiske (1994) notes, it has been used to refer both to a theoretical position and to the specific practices of a discourse.

Discourse is most closely associated with language and with the written or oral text. At this level, it challenges the concept of 'language' as an abstract system and relocates the whole process of making and using meanings from the abstracted structural system into particular historical, social, and political conditions (Fiske, 1994). Discourse is the way in which language is used socially to convey broad historical meanings. It is language identified by the social conditions of its use, by who is using it and under what conditions. Language can never be 'neutral,' because it bridges our personal and social worlds (van Dijk, 1988). It can never be 'objective' or detached' because it draws on myth and fantasy (Hall, 1973). It can never be totally free from the sociocultural influences and economic interests in which it was produced and disseminated. Ideology is a system of representations that includes semantics, accounts, narratives, images, icons, concepts, and myths.

Discourse thus carries social meanings, which usually are politicized in the sense that they carry with them concepts of power that reflect the interests of the power elite. Opinion leaders, including politicians, senior-level bureaucrats, lawyers and judges, editors and journalists, academics, and decision makers in the private sector, play a critical role in shaping issues and in identifying the boundaries of 'legitimate' discourse. These people can marginalize their opponents by defining them as 'radicals,' 'special interest groups,' or 'spokespeople who do not represent anyone but themselves.'

Social, cultural, economic and political elites[4] help define the boundaries of 'common sense' discourse by defining their preferred positions as 'self-evident' truths, and by dismissing other perspectives and positions as irrelevant, inappropriate, or without substance (van Dijk, 1991;

1998b). It has been argued (Herman and Chomsky, 1994; van Dijk, 1991) that elites have virtually exclusive access to and control over the mass media: 'Wherever it really counts ... the crucial decisions about inclusion and exclusion are made by the elites. It is therefore essentially the elites who pre-formulate many of the everyday ideological beliefs that have become widespread in racist societies' (van Djik, 1998). The mass media constitute a tool for reinforcing the dominant culture's ideologies and for promoting its political and economic interests.

A dominant discourse is distinguished by its power to interpret major social, political, and economic issues and events. Karim Karim (1993) observes: 'Dominant discourse maintains its superiority by being dynamic, continually co-opting and transmuting the words, images and symbols of other discursive modes that threaten its propaganda efforts. In this way it corresponds to the maneuverings of elites by whom it is produced and whose position it reinforces' (197).

The following, then, is the definition of discourse that informs our theoretical approach to this study: A discourse is a way of referring to or constructing knowledge about a particular topic of practice: a cluster or formation of ideas, images, and practices that provide ways of talking about forms of knowledge and conduct associated with a particular topic, social activity, or institutional site in society. A *discursive formulation* defines what is and is not appropriate in our formulation of, and our practices in relation to, a particular subject or site of social activity; what knowledge is considered useful, relevant and true in that context; and what sorts of persons or subjects embody its characteristics. *Discursive* has become the general term used to refer to any approach in which meaning, representation, and culture are considered to be constitutive.

As Goldberg (1993: 295) notes, the field of discourse involves 'discursive formation,' which is the totality of ordered relations and correlations of subjects to each other and to objects; of economic production and reproduction; of cultural symbols and signification; of laws and moral rules; and of social, political, economic, or legal inclusion or exclusion.

Because social reality changes so quickly in this postmodern world, which is characterized by massive globalization, any particular discourse is also influenced by these changes. Discourses therefore are always changing. Dominant discourse is not a single process, nor is it monolithic, static, or unitary; rather, it represents a plurality of discourses that constitute a *field of possible meanings*. Several dimensions or components of discourse can be identified (Goldberg, 1993). These include:

- A topic or area of social experience to which making sense is applied – for example, the social experience of race and racism in a postmodernist society such as Canada ...
- A social position from which this sense is made and whose interests it promotes – for example, who defines racial discourse, the position of power these people and their institutions hold, and how a racial discourse promotes the interests of those in positions of privilege who define it.
- A repertoire of words, images, and practices by which meanings are circulated and power is applied – for example exclusionary employment and promotion practices and media representations of people of colour.

Media representations are discursive formations that are part of our everyday culture, including the material fabric of institutional culture. Their discourses have enormous power not only to represent social groups but also to identify, regulate, and even construct social groups – to establish who is 'we' and who is 'other' in the 'imagined community' of the nation-state. At the level of public discourse, this creates an ideological climate that seems invisible and natural to those who are immersed in it, but that contains unchallenged assumptions about what the world is and how it ought to be. Images of and ideas about marginalized groups circulated and disseminated by the mass media and other systems of cultural production and representation play a critical role in controlling the access of those marginalized groups to cultural, social, economic, and political power. As Miles (1989) has noted, classifications of social groups, assumptions about natural divisions between people, assignments of attributes, and theories of the origins and meanings of group difference are all central to racist discourse.

**Systems of Representation Construct Meaning**

As we will demonstrate throughout the case studies in this book, the images beamed out by Canada's media (newspapers, television and radio, films, music, videos, literary works, the stage, and other vehicles of cultural production such as educational curricula) are not the images that African Canadians, Asian Canadians, or First Nations people would present of themselves. Those belonging to the dominant culture can feel secure in the wide spectrum of representations they see of themselves in these media. Minority communities do not have the luxury of such a broad spectrum of images and ideas. Members of minority groups are often intensely sensitive to negative images; this is directly linked to their feelings of marginalization and exclusion and their sense of 'otherness' within all these cultural and representational systems (Shohat and Stam, 1994).

It has been argued that socially empowered groups are not as gravely concerned as minorities about distortions and stereotypes. They don't have to be. A corrupt Anglo-Canadian politician is not perceived as stigmatizing an entire Anglo community; financial scandals are not seen as a negative reflection on White power; the lack of success of a White child in the educational system is not assessed in the context of the cultural deficits of the entire White community; and a crime committed by an individual of British or Italian origin does not generate any discussion about deportation to the United Kingdom or Italy. However, every negative image of an individual belonging to an underrepresented group quickly becomes charged with symbolic meaning (Shohat and Stam, 1994; Hall, 1997).

Hall (1997) draws an important distinction between the semiotic and discursive approaches to understanding these fields of meaning. Semiotics is the study of sign systems and how they produce social meaning (see Saussure; 1916; Barthes, 1977). Hall contends that the most significant difference between these two approaches to meaning is that the semiotic approach is concerned with how representation – that is, how language – *produces* meaning; the focus is on the 'poetics' of language. In contrast, the discursive approach is 'more concerned with the *effects and consequences* of representation in relation to its "politics."' The question of meaning is central to all aspects of culture – that is, to 'the construction of identity and the marking of difference, in production and consumption, as well as in the regulation of social conduct' (Hall, 1997: 4). Systems of representation are the cultural circuits through which meanings are transmitted. These systems function as symbols that represent the meanings that individuals, groups, and institutions wish to communicate. As will be seen in the case studies, the media, law enforcement agencies, and politicians, among others, produce, reproduce, and transmit racialized discourses that support their view of the world and the positions of minority communities in that space.

The consequences of these forms of representation – or discourses – are very significant, for they activate powerful feelings and sometimes call 'our very identities into question ... We struggle over them because they matter ... They define what is "normal," who belongs – and therefore, who is excluded. They are deeply inscribed in relations of power' (1997: 10).

The study of meaning has also called attention to the role of the audience. The convergence of Foucauldian theory, which emphasizes networks of power relations in society rather than a single dominant power source, and the increasingly pluralistic view of society promulgated by cultural studies theorists such as Hall and his colleagues at the CCCS, has led to other important changes in media studies (Hall, 1997). One of the most significant is that the audience is no longer conceptualized as a homogeneous, uncritical, passive receiver of messages. The audience is now understood as an active participant in defining the meaning of messages. The transmission of meaning is now seen as a complex interaction between on the one hand, the various levels of meaning inherent in a 'text,' and on the other, the audience, which has its own unique social, cultural, and economic position. The audience brings its own interpretation to the text, which may not necessarily coincide with what was intended. One of the landmark studies in this regard was that of Morley (1992), who studied the reactions of different groups to a documentary TV program and found that the responses of audience members varied with their discourses and with the institutions in which they were situated. It also revealed that within the same class level, audience responses varied as a function of subcultural affiliation.

The audience's role in receiving and understanding media messages is of particular interest for us because of the profound impact of racial stereotypes. Thinking stereotypically is part of the well-documented phenomenon of cognitive categorization, which basically involves people taking shortcuts when processing information. Media analysts have noted that people require discipline and active, self-critical awareness in order to counteract their schematic tendencies and stereotypic thinking. Most people – audience members – have neither the motivation nor the skills to challenge aspects of their own deeply engrained thought processes. This is especially evident when it comes to emotionally charged subjects such as race (Entman and Rojecki, 2000; Gandy, 1998).

The increasing pluralism of many societies, so evident in the global and transnational world of today, challenges the view that there is only one audience in a given society. Everywhere in the world, 'peoplescapes' are becoming more and more diverse, where once they were homogeneous. People from 'outside' cultures and ethnicities bring new values, ideologies, and norms to a society, as well as different readings and responses to media messages. In contemporary societies, race, ethnicity, gender, sexual orientation, and other factors play an important role; as a result, it is now recognized that the media 'audience' is heterogeneous not only in terms of its understandings but also in terms of its values. In other words, the 'audience' is diversified and pluralistic, and its members receive media messages in different ways depending on many differentiating factors. In the extreme, this has led to the idea of 'semiotic democracy,' or the notion that readers from many different subcultures construct their own meanings (Fiske, 1994). Researchers such as Fiske have extended this idea to its breaking point by arguing that the audience and its reactions have primacy over the meaning of the text. That being said, audience primacy cannot be complete; it is constrained by the very nature of pluralistic societies, in which there is inevitably an unequal distribution of power. Many groups within pluralistic societies are underprivileged in the sense that they do not have access to the many levels of meaning possible in a text. Some are constrained by limited education, others by lack of proficiency in the dominant culture's language. It is probably better to say that a dynamic relationship exists between text meanings and the 'mosaic' of readers.

One recent study of media effects considered people's attitudes toward and knowledge about AIDS (Miller and Kitzinger, 1998). The researchers found that although people gathered much of their information about AIDS from media sources, they also brought their own attitudes and experiences to the topic. Audiences interpret what they see in the media in terms of their past experiences, and in terms of attitudes they have already developed. Their positioning in terms of gender, age, class, and other variables affects how they understand events. In this particular study, some respondents were quick to accept the media view that AIDS originated in Africa because it confirmed their racist beliefs about Africa and African peoples. White people construct, report on, and accept 'African AIDS' in ways that feed on and into a racist agenda. Media coverage of 'African Aids was clearly influencing [white] public perceptions; and doing so because such reporting was plausible, acceptable and even useful within existing sets of images and beliefs' (176).

From this brief review of contemporary media research, it would appear that the impact of text messages on active, participating people who are already critical, active viewers and listeners, not passive and receptive objects manipulated by the media (Budd et al., 1990) weakens our argument that the media have the power to reinforce racist discourse. To this we would reply, first of all, that many generalizations about the media are drawn from studies of television rather than the print media, and that for many people the print media have greater salience. Moreover, the first step in media research – as is clear from the findings of the above study – must be to deconstruct given texts to show that they are not as innocent and unbiased as they first appear; they are in fact subject to more than one meaning, and their polysemic layers need to be uncovered.

### Different Approaches to the Study of Media

There are many possible approaches to studying racism in the media. Generally speaking, there are three categories of research in this field:

- Structural studies, which concentrate on media organizations and systems.
- Behavioural studies, which focus on the reactions, perceptions, and effects of the media on audiences.
- Cultural studies, which involve analysing meanings and language (McQuail, 1994).

Structural analysis includes the work of political economy theorists, who tend to view media organizations in terms of their ownership and management. They see the media as part of the corporate elite and as serving the interests of the dominant hegemonic class. In other words, a dominant ideology exists, and the main function of media organizations is to disseminate that ideology. The famous Frankfurt school, which has a strong Marxian orientation, falls at least partly into this category.

Marxians subscribe to a class domination theory of society, and view the media as part of the ideological arena in which class struggles are fought. They assume that at any one time there is only one dominant ideology defining the values and norms of society, and that the media are the main instrument through which this ideology is transmitted to its audience, the population. Media practitioners are under the control of owners and managers. This simplistic view of both societal ideology and the straight linear transmission of media messages to a passive and receptive audience has been challenged by advances in the field – advances stimulated mainly by the emergence of cultural studies and by the seminal theorizing of Foucault (1980).

Much research has been done under the category of behavioural analysis. One key to this approach is the concept of the 'audience.' In some of this research, the mass audience is understood to be passive consumers of media messages. Early research in the United States focused on the effects of media messages on an audience, rather than on the message itself; the audience was still conceptualized as largely one homogeneous mass. Thus, much behavioural analysis involved empirical studies of audience 'reactions' to ideological messages sent by the dominant elite.

A dominant model in this earlier period, the 'limited effects' model, tried to demonstrate that media effects are constrained in various ways:

- Mass communication is more likely to reinforce the existing attitudes, beliefs, and assumptions of its audience than it is to change the audience's opinion.
- People tend to see and hear communications that are favourable or congenial to their predisposition.
- People respond to persuasive communication in line with their predispositions, and change or resist change accordingly.

For example, with respect to violence and crime, it has been shown that portrayals of violence generally do damage, can be imitated, teach people about criminal behaviour and can cause people to commit crimes. On the other hand, media reportage can serve to act as a safety value for individual repressed aggressive desires. (McQuail, 1994)

These findings suggest that the media have limited effects; other research indicates they have several powerful effects. For example, Schramm and Porter have noted several powerful media effects:

- The media can bestow status on people, organizations, and policies. Thus, if a person or policy really matters to the functioning of society, it will be featured in the media.
- The media can impose the social values and norms of society by exposing the divergence from these norms on the part of people and their activity. This is especially important in our analysis of the racialization of crime, where the supposed deviation of people of colour who commit crimes is often featured by the media. This reinforces the prejudices that many people already hold about them. It also produces panicky reactions from the public, who fear that their society is

becoming crime ridden. Their panic in turn spurs policymakers to devlop more law-and-order policies.

- The media can, by disseminating large amounts of information, create an inactive frame of mind in the viewer/reader. Instead of doing something about an event, viewers may be 'narcotized' into not acting.

Much of the current research on pluralism can be related to these propositions, which uphold the idea that media effects are limited or constrained by gender, class, ethnicity, race, and other subcultural variables.

Another current model used to demonstrate the power of the media is the 'persuasive press inference' model (Gunther and Christen, 1999). This involves the belief that the media can influence not only thought, values, and ideology, but also 'an individual's perceptions of what other people are thinking' (Gunther, 1998) The opinions of others are important to individuals – for example, undecided voters can be swayed by polls that reveal how others are voting. Thus, the media not only directly influence opinion but it also have a more subtle or indirect effect on cognitive processes.

Another important dimension of structural analysis relates to the media's agenda-setting function. People assume that when the news media report something, it must be important; this confers on the media the power to set the public agenda and raise issues that might otherwise be ignored. This brings us to an important question. News managers have at their disposal a wide variety of sources from which to draw news, including the daily police reports sent to most media, naturally occurring events and disasters, community actions, government actions, and the like. How do media managers decide which events are newsworthy enough to report? And why are some issues ignored? What values underlie the choices that media managers make? This aspect of the media is especially important to the perspective we are taking in this study.

For example, in our case study of the racialization of crime, we demonstrate empirically that the media overreport the alleged criminal activities of people of colour relative to those of Whites. Moreover, crime stories are often accompanied by many photos, and their texts contain stereotypes and unproven assumptions about people of colour. Since most people have limited contacts with people of colour, their attitudes toward them are influenced by news reports. Similarly, people's notions about crime, and the moral panics that overzealous crime reporting can easily inspire, strengthen the perception that society is crime ridden. This in turn influences governments to develop 'tough on crime' policies and laws.

Yet it is not entirely correct to think that the media have a stranglehold on the public agenda. There are many examples of the reverse. For example, a government can release a negative report – say, of an ombudsperson critizing a government expenditure – on a day when many other news items are claiming headline space. Or a government or political party or politician can '*leak*' a story to the media for partisan purposes.

The media have a 'market audience,' who are in effect the consumers of media products. Many tools have been developed to measure the number of viewers and readers of media instruments. Audience size is an important indicator of program success and influences the media's ability to sell advertisements. Advertising revenue is often crucial to the success of a media organization.

Another model of media research is the 'uses and gratification' model. Here, the media are seen mainly as a source of gratification. The audience seeks and receives information and entertainment. That the media serve an entertainment need is obvious in commercial television programming, which is mainly concerned with entertaining the largest possible numbers of viewers. The media are also crucial as a source of information, especially in the perspective adopted in the present work. We argue, for example, that in an increasingly pluralistic society, most people get their information about others from the media. Most White people have only limited contact with people of colour in their daily lives. The media are the source for information and attitudes about communities that are perceived as outside the 'imagined community' of the state. According to the uses and gratification model, the media also have a social interactive function. When they can identify with people and events, readers or viewers feel connected to the society of which they are part. According to this view, the media actually help people identify with the norms, values, and appropriate behaviours of their society. The media provide their audiences with a sense of belonging. Related to this is the idea that the media reinforce individuals' personal identities by providing them with a sense of belonging.

Cultural analysis focuses on the language and levels of meaning encountered in media messages. Much of the newer research has a cultural studies orientation and so falls into this category (Curran and

Gurevitch, 1996). This form of analysis raises the following questions: How do things come to mean what they do? How is meaning created? How are signs perceived and understood? Much of this sort of analysis was stimulated by the study of semiotics – that is, the study of signs (Saussure, 1974). Research attention is also being paid to the polysemic or multiple-level meanings of text. A given text has no fixed meaning; rather, it is open to several levels of analysis. This makes the linguistic and semiotic deconstruction required to uncover the various levels of meaning in a text ever more important as a research technique.

In writing this book we have been strongly influenced by this third approach to the study of the media. We are especially indebted to theorists such as van Dijk (1991), Fairclough (1995), Wodak (1996), and Wetherell and Potter (1992), who have applied critical discourse analysis (CDA) in studying how racism is reproduced. CDA analyzes how dominance, inequality, and social power abuse are enacted by 'text' and 'talk' within systems of representation. We are also indebted to the contributions of scholars who have worked in the area of discourse and who have analyzed the relationship between gender inequality and the discursive practices of a society (Valdivia, 1995; West et al., 1997). Textual studies of media discourse show, for example, how women have come to be defined in relation to their marital and familial roles, and in contrast, how men are commonly defined in terms of their occupational roles. Gender textual analysis has provided a detailed picture of how, for example, the arrangement of nouns and verbs, the choice of active over passive voice, and the juxtaposition of competing discourses can create a context in which existing patterns of gender inequality seem natural.

The research on media is sometimes contradictory. Even so, there is general agreement on a number of issues. For our purposes, the most important of these is that the audience cannot be considered a homogeneous mass but is segmented by age, race, ethnicity, gender, and other variables. It follows that media messages are not received the same way by all elements of the audience. This means, for example, that mainstream readers may see nothing wrong with reportage or feature writing that uses stereotypes, identifying photos, and other ethnoracial characteristics to describe an event. However, members of the identified group will be offended by such reportage. Also, even if we accept the 'limited effects' model, the media do influence the attitudes and values of their audiences. This, combined with the well-documented idea that most people receive their information about ethnoracial groups from the media, leads us to conclude that the media do affect attitudes toward such groups (van Dijk, 1991).

**The Discourse of Democratic Racism**

How does democratic racism manifest itself in the daily lives, opinions, and feelings of people? What are the values, assumptions, and arguments of democratic racism? As Wellman (1977) has noted, the maintenance of a wide array of myths and misconceptions about racism has resulted in patterns of denial that have led to entirely inadequate responses to racism. These myths attempt to explain, rationalize, and resolve unsupportable contradictions and tensions in society. Myths arise at particular historical moments in response to perceived needs within society.

In its ideological and discursive forms, democratic racism is deeply embedded in popular culture and popular discourse. It is located within what has been called society's frames of reference (Hebdige, 1993). These frames of reference are a largely unacknowledged body of beliefs, assumptions, feelings, stories, and quasi-memories that underlie, sustain, and inform perceptions, thoughts, and actions. Democratic racism as racist discourse begins in the families that nurture people; in the communities that help socialize them; in the schools and universities that educate them; in the media that communicate ideas and images to them; and in the popular culture that entertains them. People learn this discourse at the very same sites where every other form of learning is provided.

According to Goldberg (1993), racist discourse involves a wide spectrum of expressions and representations, including a nation's recorded history; biological and scientific explanations of racial difference; economic, legal, and bureaucratic doctrines; cultural representations in the form of national narratives, images, and symbols; and so on. Racist discourse refers to the ways in which society gives voice to racism (Wetherell and Potter, 1992). Fiske (1994) notes: 'There is a discourse of racism that advances the interests of Whites and that has an identifiable repertoire of words, images and practices through which racial power is applied' (5).

The conflict between the ideology of democratic liberalism and the racist ideology present in the collective belief system of the dominant culture is reflected in the racist discourse that operates in schools, the media, the courts, law enforcement agencies, arts organizations, cultural institutions, human services, and government and politics. Schools, universities, newspapers, television stations, courtrooms, police headquarters, hospitals, and government offices, and Parliament itself, are all discursive spaces. Within these spaces, which are controlled mainly by the dominant White culture, there exists a constant moral tension: there is the lived reality and everyday experiences of people of colour, and juxtaposed against this are the perceptions and responses of those who have the power to redefine that reality, including journalists, editors, and broadcasters, educators, judges, police, cultural critics, writers, artists, arts managers, cultural funders, government officials, and politicians.

Many people resist antiracism and equity initiatives because they are unwilling to question their own belief and value systems, their own discursive practices, their own organizational and professional norms, and their own positions of power and privilege within workplaces and within society in general. As a result, they are unable to explore the relational aspects of cultural and racial differences and the power dynamics that are constructed around ideas about differences. To acknowledge that ethnoracial differences and racism make a difference in the lives of people is to concede that Euro-Canadian hegemony continues to organize the structures within which mainstream programs and services are delivered (Dei, 1996). In each of these discursive spaces (e.g., schools, museums, courtrooms, newsrooms), there is tension and resistance relating to how multicultural and antiracism ideologies and policies are 'imagined, internalized and acted upon' (Yon, 1995: 315).

Resistance may manifest itself as open and active opposition to racial barriers. But more commonly, it is articulated in more subtle forms of discourse. Discourses on race and racism converge with concerns about difference, Canadian identity, ethnicity, multiculturalism, and so on. Discourse provides the conceptual models for mapping the world around us; it incorporates both social relationships and power relations (Goldberg, 1993). Foucault (1980) uses the term *discourse* to refer to the ways in which language and other forms of communication serve as vehicles for social processes. However, dominant discourse is an elusive concept, since it hides within the mythical norms that define 'Canadianness' as being White, male, Christian, heterosexual, and English-speaking. Because the rhetoric of racism is illusive, racism finds it easy to hide itself.

Yon (2000) demonstrates this point in an important ethnographic study carried out with students and teachers at a Toronto high school.

In his research, he shows how discourse about identity and nation that never mentions the word race can also be read as racist discourse. Increasingly, in education, politics, and the media, the discourse of liberalism is juxtaposed with popular conservative ideology, and individuals slide ambivalently between the two. As Yon (1995) points out: 'Resistance and accommodation can be present in the same moment. Discourse often reveals ambivalence, contradiction and subtleties in relation to the issues of difference' (315).

For example, discussions about culture by teachers, journalists, and politicians are often framed in the context of being 'tolerant,' 'sensitive,' and sufficiently enlightened to appreciate and respect the diverse cultures of 'others.' Culture discourse tends to cover up the 'unpleasantness' of domination and inequity (Wetherell and Potter, 1992).

The discourses of dominance associated with 'democratic racism' include the myths, explanations, codes of meaning, and rationalizations that establish, sustain, and reinforce democratic racism.[5] This discourse is contextualized within humanistic, democratic liberal values. All of this illustrates Goldberg's (1993) view that the central values of liberal ideologies carry different meanings and connotations depending on the context. Tolerance, equality, and freedom of expression – central concepts in liberal discourse – have immensely flexible meanings. Mackey (1996) contends that these liberal principles often become 'the language and conceptual framework through which intolerance and exclusion are enabled, reinforced, defined and defended' (1996: 305).

Dominant discourses are able to mask their racialized ideas because they are so elusive (Fiske, 1994). Liberal principles and values expressed in liberal discourses include the primacy of individual rights over collective rights, freedom of expression, equal opportunity, tolerance, colour-blindness, and so on. But liberalism, as many scholars have observed, is full of paradoxes and contradictions, depending on one's social location and angle of vision (Hall, 1986; Goldberg, 1993). Parekh (1986) contends that 'liberalism is both egalitarian and inegalitarian.' It simultaneously supports the unity of humankind and the hierarchy of cultures. It is both tolerant and intolerant (82). From the perspective of marginalized and excluded groups, traditional liberal values have been found wanting. Within each of these liberal discourses are unchallenged assumptions and myths. Thus, one of our central purposes of this book is to deconstruct and decode the media's use of these discourses, which reinforce racism in Canadian society.

# 2

# Review of the Canadian Literature on Racism in the Print Media

In this chapter we review and summarize the body of Canadian literature on racism in the media from the early 1980s to 2000 (see Henry et al., 2000, for a more detailed review of the literature on racism in the media that incorporates the electronic media and advertising).[1] Included in the present review are studies by scholars and community-based organizations and the findings of government inquiries (for studies related to the racialization of crime turn to the case study on this subject). This overview also includes published writings and public presentations by people of colour who have worked in the media or are currently doing so.

There are three main themes in this body of research. First, the misrepresentation, invisibility, and marginalization of people of colour and First Nations peoples by the media communicates the message that members of these diverse communities are not full participants in Canadian society. They exist outside the boundaries of the 'imagined community' of Canada. Second, even though they espouse liberal democratic values –, fairness, equality, freedom of expression, objectivity, neutrality, and so on – the mainstream media are helping preserve cultural hegemony. Third, the tremendous concentration of media ownership among the White male corporate elite, most of whom hold conservative or neoconservative values, represents a serious threat to a pluralistic and democratic state.

## Invisibility of People of Colour

People of colour are practically absent from all areas of the print and electronic media. A brief submitted to a parliamentary subcommittee on equality rights (Canadian Ethnocultural Council, 1985) stated that people of colour are invisible in the Canadian media: 'The relative absence of minority men and women in the Canadian media is remarkable' (92). As an example of this, the Canadian Ethnocultural Council noted that hardly any racial minorities were working as anchors, reporters, experts, or actors, and that they were rarely found behind the scenes in production or administrative roles. According to the report, their limited participation in the communications industry was the result of both overt bias and systemic discrimination. Examples of systemic discrimination cited included the reliance on referrals from White people when hiring producers, writers, and editors, the lack of comprehensive outreach programs for people of colour, and the lack of recognition for qualifications and experience gained outside Canada.

The invisibility of people of colour in the print media is reflected in the hiring practices of media organizations. A study of recruitment procedures and promotion channels for women and minorities was conducted for forty-one English-language newspapers in Ontario (Mayers, 1986). Across the entire sample, people of colour, people with a disability, and Aboriginal people were rarely encountered as newsroom employees. Of the 1,731 full-time newsroom employees in the sample, thirty were from the above groups. Word-of-mouth recruitment was excluding a wide range of suitable applicants. At all the newspapers, promotions tended to be from within. The *Toronto Star* was the only paper with a policy for removing barriers to the employment and advancement of women and minorities.[2] Almost a decade later (1997), Cecil Foster wrote of his own experience as the only Black writer in the newsroom at the *Globe and Mail* for ten years: 'When I left 100% of the Black staff went out.'

A parliamentary task force looking at racism in Canadian society (*Equality Now*, 1984) heard dozens of briefs from people of colour declaring that racism in the media exists; for proof, they pointed to their invisibility in terms of both their images and their representation in media organizations. Groups from across Canada spoke with a single voice about the need for people of colour to have access to the print and electronic media, to media boards and commissions, and to oversight bodies such as press councils, as well as their right to participate in their on an equitable basis. Lynda Armstrong, a Black performer, commented: 'The White-only mentality of the Canadian establishment is weird when you consider that this is one of the most racially diverse societies on earth ... What we get in Canadian media is a fantasy' (*Equality Now*, 1984: 91).

One of the main factors in this invisibility is cultural racism and the belief in the concept of the 'rightness of Whiteness.' Whiteness is considered the universal norm and allows one to think and speak as if Whiteness described and defined the world. The president of a major brewery, when asked why there were no non-Whites in his company's commercials, answered: 'White sells' (*Equality Now*, 1984: 91). This attitude characterizes the collective belief system of Canadians and influences the norms and practices of the media.

### Misrepresentation and Stereotyping of Ethnoracial Minorities

The media in general produce negative images of people of colour. This is nothing new. A book on racism in Ontario's criminal justice system reveals that for at least a century, the media have played an important role in racializing crime. Mosher (1998) found that in the early days, Canadian newspapers routinely described the race of offenders, which 'served to identify Asians and Blacks as alien ... and justified to a certain extent their differential treatment by the criminal justice system' (126). He cites headlines such as these:

- 'Chinese gambled; These 18 Chinks were Roped in ...' (*Toronto Daily Star*, 29 March 1909)
- 'Warm Pipe Scorches Chink Opium User' (*Toronto Daily Star*, 3 April 1916)
- 'No more Chicken Dinners or Watermelon Feeds for ...' (*Hamilton Spectator*, 26 August 1909)
- 'The Black Burglar' (*Globe*, 20 November 1900)
- 'Negro Thieves given Stiff Sentences' (*Windsor Evening Record*, 20 October 1912)

Mosher also notes that court reporters often focused on the racial identity of accused people and witnesses. For example, one article described 'two hundred pounds of Julius Wagstaffe, a jet-black import from North Carolina ...'

In some news stories, the speech of Black defendants was rendered in dialect and their comments were ridiculed and trivialized. Clearly, there was 'extensive evidence of the stereotyping of Asians and Blacks and the racialization of crime in the media, especially between 1892 and 1930' (134).

The first attempt to identify and document racism in the print media in Canada was made in 1977 by Rosenfeld and Spina, who examined the *Toronto Sun*'s coverage of issues relating to immigration and racial and ethnic communities. They found considerable evidence of racial bias and discrimination. Their analysis revealed that the *Toronto Sun* presented readers with a prejudiced view of the world.

In 1982 the Canadian Arab Federation commissioned a study on the image of Arabs in political cartoons (Mouammar, 1986). Cartoons published between 1972 and 1982 were gathered from the three major Toronto dailies. Mouammar found that Arabs were repeatedly portrayed as bloodthirsty terrorists who were blackmailing the West. They were depicted in the cartoons as ignorant, cruel, and backward. One cartoon after another in the ten-year sample portrayed Arabs in a negative and stereotypical manner, using images suggesting that they were tyrannical, untrustworthy, amoral, irrational, and the architects of international terrorism. The researcher pointed to the danger of this kind of racism by suggesting that the foundations for the Holocaust had been laid by German caricaturists, who regularly depicted Jews in a similar fashion (Mouammar, 1986: 13).

Ginzberg's (1985) content analysis of the *Toronto Sun* was precipitated by the concern and frustration escalating among a number of racial minority groups in Toronto, who perceived that the *Sun* was consistently portraying people of colour and Aboriginal people in a negative manner. Also, there was a perception that the *Sun* had repeatedly distorted issues in which these communities were involved – issues such as race relations, immigration, discrimination in employment and education, apartheid, and affirmative action. Minority groups had for many years been expressing their concerns to the *Sun*'s management about its biased, inaccurate, and unbalanced portrayals of racial minorities. In 1984 the Native Action Committee on the Media developed an information package about the *Sun*'s racist coverage of Aboriginal peoples. The committee analysed the *Sun*'s content and concluded that its coverage was fostering hatred and misunderstanding toward Aboriginal peoples among the 'majority society.' The *Sun* made no attempt to respond to these concerns.

Ginzberg (1985) studied over 200 editorials and columns covering the period 1978 to 1985. This analysis was based on the work of Gordon Allport (1954), which emphasized that prejudice is not a single thought or behaviour, but rather a pattern or system of interdependent behaviours. When one behaviour is present, others are also likely to be present. Allport suggested that the component parts of prejudice include, first of all, negative stereotyping, defined as an exaggerated, overgeneralized belief, unsubstantiated opinion, or uncritical judgment about a group of people. Stereotyping justifies a certain type of conduct toward the stereotyped group. Through repetition, stereotypes become embedded in people's attitudes, reflected in their behaviour, and woven into the culture of the majority group. They can also deprive members of stereotyped groups of their sense of self-worth.

Stereotypes were encountered repeatedly in the *Sun*. People of Indo-Pakistani origin were depicted as violent, weak, passive, submissive, and barbaric. Gandhi was called a 'cunning and charismatic witch doctor' (McKenzie Porter, 17 December 1982, cited in Ginzberg, 1985). Democracy was described as 'beyond the aptitude of the majority of Asians' (Porter, 23 April 1984, ibid.). Furthermore, Arabs were violent, uncivilized, and primitive: 'A tendency to violence in the settlement of disputes characterizes the typical Muslim male' (Porter, 17 December 1982, ibid.). Aboriginal peoples were portrayed as immoral, drunken, useless, and primitive. Blacks were depicted as immoral, savage, uncivilized, and superstitious.

Ginzberg also found that the *Sun*'s columnists and editorial writers consistently tried to rationalize or deny their prejudice. For example, 'Gandhi did not seek peace but power'; 'Apartheid represents a successful plan to save South African cities from the squalor that affects Bombay, Delhi and Calcutta through the huge, uncontrolled flux of the rural poor' (Peter Worthington, 16 December 1982, ibid.).

Yet another component of prejudice woven into the words and images used by *Sun* writers was a belief in biological racism. The paper's writers often suggested strongly that the White race is genetically superior to non-White races:

- 'One cannot come out and say that these awful riots are caused by Black people who seem to be subhuman in their total lack of civility.' (Barbara Amiel, 2 October 1985, cited in Ginzberg, 1985)
- 'The Blacks of North America have diverged widely from their distant relatives in Africa. In their music and dancing and in their athletic prowess some specific genetic distinctions shine through the environmental influences.' (Mackenzie Porter, 15 July 1978, ibid.)
- 'Too many Afro-Asians abroad, even some of those with august rank of diplomat, possess only a veneer of civilization. (Porter, 23 April 1984, ibid.)

Ginzberg found many examples of demagogy, which is yet another component of prejudice. Over and over, the *Sun*'s editors and columnists made statements that were likely to incite fear and hatred. The most blatant example of demagogy was found in 'Our Nuremberg,' in which the editorialist claimed that Toronto was gradually evolving its own set of Nuremberg race laws. Words like '*Gestapo*,' 'fascist-like,' 'police state,' 'jackbooters,' and 'human-rights storm troopers' were trotted out to incite fear of human rights policies and race relations initiatives among the *Sun*'s readers.

The study concluded that the *Toronto Sun* was indeed abusing the fundamental freedoms and responsibilities that society extends to the press. The potential impact of a publication that has a daily circulation of over 300,000 readers – and on Sundays more than 460,000 – is enormous.

A smaller-scale study of the *Globe and Mail*'s coverage of immigration was conducted in 1985–86 (Ducharme, 1986). Of the seventy articles written about this issue between 1980 and 1985, twelve were considered biased or slanted. About 86 per cent of the articles focused on the numbers of immigrants and refugees entering Canada. News stories about immigration levels and quotas appeared approximately once a month over the five-year period, with varying figures and contradictory estimates. Ducharme noted misuse of language and a reliance on clichés and stereotypes: 'floods of refugees'; the need to 'stem the tide of illegal aliens'; the 'luring' of entrepreneurs into Canada; immigrants and refugees who 'wreck' and 'gatecrash' the system; the 'surge' in the number of immigrants; 'job stealers'; and so on.

Ducharme pointed out how both the headlines and the language chosen often distorted, confused, or hid reality. The emphasis was on the sensational details of immigration policy, rather than on comprehensive understanding and analysis.

In promoting and sustaining the values of the dominant society, the media often draw a line between the 'First World' and the 'Third World,' the 'West' and the 'non-West,' the 'North' and the 'South.' This line of demarcation is created by the constant production of images that distinguish between the attributes, capacities, and strengths of the West (largely positive) and those of the countries of the East or the Third World (largely negative). The First World is rational, progressive, efficient, moral, modern, scientifically and technologically ordered, and on the side of the good and the right. The Third World is linked with racialized premises; it is defined as traditional, underdeveloped, overpopulated, irrational, disordered, and uncivilized (Razack, 1998).

An example of how the media negatively stereotype people of colour is the coverage of the Sikh community by Vancouver's media. Press coverage of issues of concern to this community is sensationalized, and Sikhs are commonly depicted as militants, as terrorists, and as disposed to violence. For example, in the *Vancouver Province*, headlines of articles covering Sikh issues included 'Guns Alarm Cops' (27 March 1985), 'Close Watch on City Sikhs' (20 October 1985), and 'Sikh Militancy Grows' (7 November 1985). The articles conjured images of conflict, civil unrest, violent confrontation, terrorism, and destruction of property. The repetition of these images and stereotypes reinforces prejudice against *all* South Asians, not just Sikhs (Khaki and Prasad, 1988).

The Social Planning Council of Winnipeg (1996) undertook a study to test how racial minorities and First Nations peoples were portrayed in stories in the *Winnipeg Sun* and *Winnipeg Free Press*, that city's two main newspapers. Twelve articles published during a six-month period were selected, six from each paper. These articles were paired on the basis of similar content and then compared. They were then rated by an 'expert group' of six individuals and five journalism students. The study found the following:

• There was a lack of appreciation for diversity.
• The promotion of harmonious race relations was almost completely absent.
• A significant number of the articles had the potential to promote stereotyping and racist attitudes.
• The stories seldom presented a balanced view of the incident or event.

Miller and Prince (1994) conducted an audit of a random week's edition of six major dailies – the *Vancouver Sun*, the *Calgary Herald*, the *Winnipeg Free Press*, the *Toronto Sun*, and the *Gazette of Montreal* – to assess the amount and types of coverage of people of colour. They found that stereotyping and negative coverage of people of colour were common in terms of both language and images. Local stories were 49 per cent negative. Over half dealt with either athletes or entertainers. The study concluded that if people of colour are in the news, 'they are probably in trouble of some sort, and few make any contribution to business or have noteworthy lifestyles.'

In 1995, Goldfarb Consultants were contracted by the Canadian Daily Newspaper Association to explore whether daily newspapers had a readership problem among racial minorities. The objective of the research was to help newspaper publishers, editors, writers, and reporters better understand how effectively daily newspapers were serving the needs, interests, and concerns of visible minorities. Six focus groups were conducted with Chinese, South Asian, Black, Muslim, and mixed visible minorities and with White Canadians. The findings demonstrated the extent to which the attitudes of White people toward daily newspapers are dramatically different from those of visible minorities. Overall, regarding several aspects of the treatment of visible minorities by daily newspapers, White respondents considered that things were relatively positive. Yet, visible minorities identified several concerns about newspaper coverage. Almost half observed that newspapers were treating visible minorities like foreigners; almost half reported that daily newspapers were not portraying visible minorities fairly; the large majority said they were upset at the media for linking race and religion to crime reporting. The majority said that the papers were practising discrimination in their crime reporting and weren't covering their communities in a balanced way. They expressed concern that their communities and cultures were invisible in mainstream papers, and a large majority of them complained about the lack of coverage of world news, especially from their native countries and regions.

Fleras and Elliot (1996) contend that the media, through stereotyping processes, represent people of colour and Aboriginal peoples as monolithic groups who create social problems, even though their communities are actually quite diverse. The cumulative effect of constant stereotyping and misrepresentation is to create a polarization between 'them' and 'us.' As a result of repeated negative messages, racial minorities become the 'others.' They are portrayed as violent, irrational, and emotionally unstable, and as lacking basic decency, and as having a diminished respect for human life. The authors argue that the 'moral panic' generated by the media's hyping of conflict situations often leads to situations in which police, the military, and other public authorities perceive they have no recourse but to intervene to quell minority unrest and impose order. As an example, Fleras and Elliot cite the Oka conflict in Quebec (see Roth et al., 1995; Skea, 1993/4).[3]

Fleras and Kunz have examined the increasingly contested relationship between the mainstream media and ethnoracial minorities in Canada through the lenses of visual and verbal representation. In *Media and Minorities* (2001) they explore how constructions of ethnicity, race, and aboriginality are interpreted by the media and then become woven into public discourses. They uncover the rationale behind the media's misrepresentation of minorities, and examine the degree to which the media formulate ideologies of domination that affect the public's understanding of multiculturalism and diversity. They also identify the ways in which minorities have empowered themselves to challenge media misrepresentation. They incorporate examples from various sectors of the media, including newscasting, commercial programming, advertising, and film.

Skea (1993–4) examined the biases directed at First Nations peoples in Canadian newspapers by conducting a thematic analysis of all articles and editorials written about the Oka conflict over one week in fifteen major daily newspapers. He found that most of the articles and editorials offered a decidedly negative portrayal of Native peoples. In his study he also drew attention to the relationship between the federal and Quebec governments, and noted that journalists and editors uncritically accepted the federal government's position that this was a 'law and order' issue. Thus, the primary discursive strategy employed by both the newspapers and the government was to advocate paramilitary operations to end the blockade at Oka. Skea found that the Oka crisis was covered very differently by newspapers in Saskatchewan and Manitoba, and suggested that the newspapers in the provinces with the largest First Nations populations provided narratives that were more sympathetic to the Native people at Oka. This could be attributed to the fact that for sources these newspapers tended to rely more on Mohawks, who provided a very different interpretation and account of the problems they faced. Finally, Skea raised serious doubts about 'freedom of the press,' and about the 'objectivity' of mainstream newspapers as it related to their coverage of First Nations struggles.

Roth and colleagues (1995) provide a detailed and compelling content analysis of the mainstream media's coverage of the 'Oka conflict.' They offer a series of reflections on the Canadian media from both 'insider' and 'outsider' perspectives. In explaining their methodology, they note that the events at Oka were so complex that they could not be analysed adequately using conventional communications discourse. The issues of gender, culture, and race, which were central to this conflict, could not be analysed in an 'objective' or 'neutral' manner. A traditional content analysis would not fully reveal how the mainstream coverage mediated their experiences and reports about the 'crisis.' So these authors took an ethnographic approach. Two of the authors were Mohawk women who lived through the siege. The third, a non-Native woman, was involved in the community's radio training program before the conflict began, and kept in direct communication with the Mohawks throughout the conflict. The analysis is written as a series of parallel voices, moving between the three authors. They contend that in the long history of racist discourse in the media with respect to First Nations peoples, media stereotyping of First Nations people was never more blatant than during the siege at Oka. The media used fragments of information – often misinformation – to construct a highly negative picture of the Mohawks. Some of the headlines that appeared in the print media exemplify the racialized discourse that placed all Mohawks 'within a system of categories of violence' (1995: 77).

- 'The Mohawk Warriors: Heroes or Thugs?' (*Toronto Star*, 2 November 1990)
- 'Mafia Warriors' (Political cartoon in the *Gazette*, 30 April 1990)
- 'The Making of a Warrior' (*Saturday Night*, April 1991)
- 'The Fury of Oka: After the Showdown, Indian Leaders Promise a Violent Autumn' (*Maclean's*, 19 September 1990)
- 'Canada Cannot Tolerate Violence as a Political Tool' (The *Globe and Mail*, 18 August 1990)
- 'Police Find 30 Guns in Kanehsatake' (*Gazette*, 28 September 1990)
- 'Mohawk Militancy from Wounded Knee to an Adirondock Native Commune ... to Oka, an Idea Is Spreading' (*Ottawa Citizen*, 15 September 1990)

Writing five years after the Oka conflict, the authors observe that one of the lessons learned from the manner in which the mainstream media mishandled the Mohawk/government conflict is that journalists need to rethink their methods for accessing background information and sources within cultural and racial traditions about which they have received little professional training. The authors also advocate that journalists and broadcasters work more closely with First Nations peoples and other marginalized groups 'who have lacked access to public mediated forums in which to express, in their own words, their own accounts of the world' (78).

In another example of the widespread and pervasive racialization of minorities by the Canadian mainstream media, the Canadian Islamic Congress (CIC) published the results of its third annual anti-Islam media monitoring survey (see www.cicnow.com/docs/media-report/2000/anti-islam.html). This annual survey for 1999–2000 was conducted by the Media Watch Group of the CIC. Its purpose was to evaluate coverage and to provide examples of offending materials. The study documented anti-Islamic references for the period August 1999 to August 2000. Seven newspapers were monitored and assessed, including the *Toronto Star*, the *Globe and Mail*, the *National Post*, the *Toronto Sun*, the *Ottawa Citizen*, Montreal's *Gazette*, and *La Presse*. The study also included *Maclean's* and the Canadian edition of *Reader's Digest*. The CBC English-language news was also monitored. The researchers established a numerical grading system with ten levels to measure the extent of bias expressed by the newspapers. For the grading evaluation, the *Toronto Sun* was not included, as it had far less coverage of international news than the other newspapers. In all three years of the study, the *National Post* offered the most biased coverage of the Islamic community. The report noted that this paper made no attempts to improve even after its editors met with the CIC. According to the study, the *Post*'s anti-Islam grade was 230 per cent higher than that of the average newspaper. The report also recognized the *Toronto Star* and the *Globe and Mail* for demonstrating improvement over previous years. The *Star* moved up from being the worst offender in 1998 to the least in 2000. The *Globe and Mail* moved up from second-worst offender to second-least. *La Presse* showed less anti-Islam bias than its English counterpart, the *Gazette*.

**Critical Discourse Analysis Research**

Karim Karim has conducted a number of studies analyzing the power of discourse in symbolic constructions deconstructions, and reconstructions. In his 1993 study on the struggles between diverse discourses on ethnocultural terminology that reflect differing conceptions of Canadian society, he provided an important framework for understanding how dominant discourses exercise their hegemony and how these discourses interact with alternative or resistant discourses. He observes that the dominant discourse serves as a matrix for society's discussion of particular issues; however, the complexities of that discourse reflect the changing nature of structures of power, and are shaped by the constantly evolving and potentially contradictory combinations of assumptions and world views of socioeconomic and cultural elites.

Karim has also studied how Arabs and Muslims are portrayed in the media. In a 1997 article, using the tools of critical discourse analysis, he examined the primary stereotype or *topos* through which a particular culture's core images and beliefs can be generated. He examined how

Eurocentric constructions of the Muslim as other have provided 'a seemingly endless series of biased depictions of Muslim for centuries' (153). Although Karim does not deal specifically with the Canadian media, his analysis provides an important framework for those wishing to use critical discourse analysis to deconstruct the discursive strategies that create and sustain structures of power and inequity. Karim expands on the above analysis in *Islamic Peril: Media and Global Violence* (2000). In this book he examines in greater depth the heavily biased treatment accorded to a growing number of Muslims in Western countries, and contends that the hostility toward and oppression of Muslims in these countries resembles the 'Red Scare,' when people who did not conform to the dominant ideology were harassed, imprisoned, and driven to despair or even suicide. He links the increasing humiliation of innocent Muslims by Northern states to their negative treatment by the media.

Mirchandani and Tastsoglou (2000) use critical discourse analysis in a somewhat different way in their analysis of the social construction of 'tolerance' in the Canadian print media. The authors combine discourse analysis methods with content analysis. They examine eleven Canadian newspapers and identify how in each, a minimalist approach to the concept of 'tolerance' of minority groups serves as an ideological discourse and rhetorical strategy to avoid dealing with the issue of unequal relations and racism in Canadian society. Their analysis suggests that social relations of power are embedded in the practices, news values, and professional standards of journalistic 'objectivity.' They also identify how the news media express White hegemonic ideological points of view and establish the boundaries of public discourse so that they conform to the interests of hegemonic groups.

Riggins is using critical discourse analysis to examine how subtle social stereotypes of East Asian Canadians and Euro-Canadians are generated and disseminated through the print media. Riggins is also interviewing a sample of newspaper readers and journalists. The goal of this research is to examine the role of Canada's press in constructing images of 'self' and 'others' as they relate to Asian minorities in Canada.

In a book of readings he edited (1997), Riggins analyses the language and politics of exclusion and 'otherness,' and identifies some of the discursive strategies which ensure that differences between people are recognized and utilized. He condends that the rhetoric of 'othering' in the media and elsewhere dehumanizes and diminishes groups, and makes it easier for victimizers to exert control while minimizing the complicating emotions of guilt and shame.

## Commodification and Its Influence on Newsmaking

Fleras (1995; Fleras and Kunz, 2001) has explored the impact of the com-modification of the media from a number of perspectives. He contends that the mass media do more than codify and shape perceptions of real-ity; they constitute a constructed social reality of diverse forces – of inter-nal and external constraints. This constructed reality imposes restrictions on what the media may or may not do. He links the profit-seeking logic of media organizations to their need to seek and secure as many viewers, readers, and listeners as possible. That means 'entertaining' them. In sum, the mass media are business ventures whose bottom line is profit (i.e., accountability to shareholders). The media are corporatist in nature, and this places an organizational clamp on the kind of news they produce – often at the cost of conventional social values.

In *The Big Black Book* (1997), Maude Barlow and James Winter take a hard look at 'the most powerful couple in print journalism in Canada today' (208), Conrad Black and Barbara Amiel (Black). Amiel is one of the most widely read journalists in the country, with a column in *Maclean's* reaching half a million families every month, as well as col-umns in (potentially) 72 out of 105 Canadian newspapers, including the 60 papers in the Southham-Sterling-Hollinger chain, the 11-paper Sun chain, and the *Financial Post*. Her potential newspaper audience is around 3 million families in Canada. Until the fall of 2000, her hus-band, Conrad Black, controlled through his corporate holdings and CP subscribers all but four newspapers in this country. The influence of these two people extends also to the electronic media: Canadian Press's Broadcast News wire is picked up by 140 radio stations, 28 television sta-tions, and 36 cable outlets in just Ontario. Across the country they con-trol 425 radio stations, 76 television stations, and 142 cable outlets.

Barlow and Winter contend that Black and Amiel are not simply pre-senting their views in a marketplace of competing ideas; through their control of Canada's print media they have the power to influence the political and social landscape in ways that distort the freedom of press and present a danger to the future of democracy.

Black and Amiel hold strongly negative attitudes toward minorities. Amiel argues that the modern state cannot support either biculturalism or multiculturalism: 'This is a shame, but the truth. A sanitized, bloodless form of ethnic cleansing is the best we can hope for' (20 November 1995). She feels that instead of trying to eliminate the natural tendency toward discrimination by implementing policies that would embrace different cultures, a modern liberal state should be based on the principle of 'homogeneity of language and culture.' Ridiculing Canada for trying to address its multicultural reality through government policies, she compares its attempts to do so to Hitler's Germany: 'Nowhere in the world since the Third Reich has any country been quite as obsessed with color, ethnicity and religion as Canada' (27 May 1991). Conrad Black agrees with her, and trivializes the cultural impact of racism:

> Every regional, sexual, physical, ethnic, demographic, and circumstantial shortcoming has enjoyed an endowed martyrdom ... The hectoring, Orwellian presence of the state and its volunteer auxiliaries, hounds not only the cigarette smoker and the impatient motorist but the devotee of the ethnic joke, the amateur of traditional folklore, such as those wishing to see the authentic musical *Show Boat* and almost anyone with a lingering nostalgia for the efficacy of the free market ... According to my reckoning, about 400% of Canadians now qualify as officially recognized victims. (*Financial Post*, 6 November 1993)

At a launch party to celebrate the *Financial Post*'s new status as a daily in Canada, Black promised to give new meaning 'to that nauseating expression, minority rights' (in Black's autobiography, 1993). Amiel is also deeply concerned about the decreasing numbers of Caucasians in Canadian society, and poses the question: 'How can we preserve these endangered groups?' She links family, the work ethic, and motherhood to Whites – the groups she identifies as the norm in Canadian and Western society – and abortion, hedonism, and the weakening of the family with the 'replacement stock' (*Maclean's*, 28 October 1985).

Amiel has ranked immigrant groups according to how ideologically compatible or assimilable to the dominant culture she perceives them to be. She does not believe that Canada should open its door to 'all those anxious, pushy Orientals with outstretched palms and camp-smarts, try to worm their way into the West. They lack the stoic simplicity of African refugees who criss-cross that continent in eternal agony, seeking refuge from famine and civil war without bothering us for more than the odd blanket' (*Maclean's*, 20 November 1989).

James Winter (1997) has studied the impact of the tremendous concentration of newspaper ownership in the hands of a 'handful of corporate elite' that includes Black, Paul Desmarais, Ken Thomson, and Ted Rogers. He contends that all of these individuals hold to profoundly conservative ideologies and that these beliefs are strongly influencing newspaper discourse as well as the daily operations of media organizations. He argues that the media corporate elite are delivering a distorted picture of the world – a picture that is becoming part of our naturalized and commonsense perspective and that is blocking the formation of alternative visions and discourses. One media truism on minorities is that Native peoples are basically well cared for on reserves and would be better off if they would do something for themselves instead of relying on government hand-outs. A second pervasive truism in the everyday discourses of the print media owned by these handful of corporate elite is that immigration laws are too lax and that we let people from minority cultures in who take advantage of our generous social programs. Winter's most important finding is that today's news media are legitimizing a fundamentally undemocratic system.[4]

**The Media as an Imperfect Social Mirror**

In a study of journalistic practices, Hackett and Zhao (1998), examined the concepts of 'objectivity' and 'neutrality,' which supposedly govern journalism in North America. The authors contend that journalists use these constructs to enhance their claims of professionalism; at the same time, advertisers and media corporations employ the 'regime of objectivity' as a means of maximizing market reach and credibility. The truth is that journalism is influenced by the subjectivities of individuals and of the organizations to which they belong: 'Even the most "objective" forms of journalism have systematic consequences and allegiances, in favour of commercialism, liberal democracy and much else.'

With respect to the globalized concentration and conglomerization of media power, Hackett and Zhao have basically the same concerns as Barlow and Winter. They raise serious questions about whether authoritative objectivity is possible at all in Conrad Black's newspapers or even the *Globe and Mail*, given the close allegiance of these news organizations to the stockbrokers and bankers of Bay Street. They contend that journalists and their readers need to analyse the deep biases inherent in news production. In their view, journalists must learn to take a more self-reflexive approach and to acknowledge more openly their intrinsic values and interests.

In *The Missing News* (2000), Hackett and Gruneau and a number of other scholars point out that news is a manufactured product.[5] It is both selected and constructed. The news media transform events into stories, and a story must have an audience (which interprets the story according to its values and experiences) and a storyteller (who selects facts, arranges their sequence, and chooses the language for describing them). Throughout their book Hackett and Gruneau argue that news is a representation of the world, not a passive reflection of some pre-given reality, and that these representations are filtered through a number of different lenses, including ethnocentrism and nationalism. These ideologies serve to filter out news that upsets our collective sense of who we are. Moreover, the news is about *events*, not trends or processes; and in identifying these events, the news is anchored in institutions and their spokespeople, not in unorganized, unaffiliated individuals. Routinely, news is about events, not conditions; about conflict, not consensus; and about facts which advance the story, not about those which explain it.

John Miller (1998), building on many of these same themes, analyses how Canada's daily newspapers are failing the Canadian public; he also identifies as one of the critical issues the take-over of Canadian daily newspapers by profit-oriented corporations. One of the many areas of failure that he identifies is the following: 'Newspapers behave as if they're serving themselves, not us. When the motives and agendas of newspapers are hidden from us, when they arrogantly refuse to explain their behaviour or listen to the other side, when their sense of independence seems to isolate them from their communities ... then we can conclude they are in the business of making money and not to serve the public' (19).

Following on his earlier analysis (1994 with Prince), Miller contends that newspapers are 'imperfect mirrors,' and that newsrooms have isolated themselves physically as well as demographically from the broader community about which they write. He argues that the press feels free to critique every other institution, but is also the institution that is least open to any criticism of its own standards and practices. Given the weakness and powerlessness of press councils, media organizations largely control the channels through which criticism of them could be articulated and heard: 'This arrogance has helped to break the bond that must exist between newspapers and readers' (37).

Newspapers may well be 'imperfect mirrors'; however, there is some evidence that journalists themselves are becoming more reflexive about their own discipline. An interesting series of papers in *Canadian Communications: Issues in Contemporary Media and Culture* (Szuchewycz and Sloniowski, 1999) reveals that they too are beginning to be concerned about their power, as well as critical of their own role in shaping public opinion around vital social issues.

# 3

# Representation in the Media: An Empirical Study

Critical to any discussion of racism in the media is the question of representation as it affects the experiences of minorities working in the media. Our analysis suggests that the media in Canada do not reflect the growing diversity of this country, either in their hiring practices or in their journalistic practices. Nowhere is this better demonstrated than in the employment arena; hardly any minority journalists are employed in the print and electronic media, and their representation does not reflect their numbers in society. With a few high-profile exceptions – CBC or affiliate anchors such as Ian Hanomansingh, Suhanna Marchand, Ben Chin, and Carla Robinson – Canadian journalism is dominated by White people.

In a series of articles in the *Toronto Star* exploring the media's relationship to issues of diversity and representation, Haroon Siddiqui (2001) called our attention to the 'growing gap between the media and our increasingly diverse, urban populations. Little of what we see in the media bears much resemblance to the cosmopolitan citizenry of Toronto, Montreal, and Vancouver ... as well as the smaller cities' (22 April 2001).

In his analysis of the Canadian media, Miller makes a similar point, contending that hiring and promotion practices and a bias-free work environment are crucial to diversity and equity in the media (1994, 1998).

The importance of racial and cultural diversity and equity is clearly articulated by Irshad Manji (1995), a former editor of a Canadian newspaper, who argues that journalists cannot claim to be on the front lines of free expression when the very composition of their workplaces restricts debate. She adds that this perspective is ignored by many of the power brokers in Canada's newsrooms, most of whom are White, middle-aged men. Manji has raised a number of important questions that have provided a helpful framework for our own empirical study: How do the gender and racial identities of those who work in media organizations affect how accurately those organizations represent issues in a racially and culturally diverse society? How can journalists purport to be on the front lines of freedom of expression when their workplaces restrict debate? How can any newspaper claim to be offering readers an accurate picture of the world when that picture is sketched, refined, and reprinted by one group with a limited set of experiences?

An important goal of employment equity or affirmative action is to 'level the playing field,' at least to the point where the numbers in workplaces reflect the numbers in the population. In the United States, these strategies have had only moderate success in increasing the numbers of minority journalists. In Canada, media organizations have not implemented employment equity policies and practices, especially in terms of ethnoracial minorities. Though there are now more women in the media, discriminatory barriers continue to be pervasive in media organizations. It has long been thought that workplace representation strongly influences the policy decisions and practices of institutions and the media are no exception.

**Quantitative Analysis**

Racial minorities are significantly underrepresented in Canada's news rooms. Racial minorities now account for 11.6 per cent of the Canadian population, yet a 1994 survey of forty-one newsrooms across the country revealed that only 2.6 per cent of the professional, employed journalists were people of colour (*Canadian Newspaper Association's (CNA) Diversity Committee*, published by the Editorial Division, CNA – April 1994). That same year, of 2,260 professional print journalists of these forty-one papers, only sixty-seven were minorities – an increase of only three from a similar survey conducted in 1989. Other results from this survey include the following:

- The forty-one papers surveyed employed 2,620 newsroom professionals (supervisors, reporters, copy editors, and photographers/artists). Of those, sixty-seven were non-White. Chinese Canadians and Blacks were the largest groups of minorities in the newsroom, with seventeen and sixteen employees respectively. There were only four Native Canadians.

- Fifty of the sixty-seven non-Whites (75 per cent) worked in newsrooms with circulations over 100,000.
- Sixteen of the forty-one papers surveyed (39 per cent) had all-White staffs.
- Minorities were more likely to be hired as reporters or photographers than as supervisors or copy editors. Only ten of the forty-one papers had non-White supervisors. Twenty of the twenty-four minority reporters and ten of the sixteen minority photographers worked for papers in the over-100,000 circulation group.
- Fifty-four per cent of papers said that improving the racial balance of their newsrooms would have to wait until the economy turned around and their hiring freezes ended. However, the forty-one papers hired a total of forty-seven new full-time employees during 1993, and only three were non-White (6 per cent). Minorities did better in securing part-time work or summer internships, filling eighteen of eighty-nine openings (20 per cent).
- Only eleven of the forty-one papers declared they had a 'very strong' commitment to hiring visible minorities. A similar number said their interest was 'not very strong.' When asked why, nine in the latter group said they hired only on merit.

In a series of interviews eight years after Miller's study, Federico Barahona (2001) interviewed editors, reporters, and professional association representatives across Canada, and found that diversity is not on the agenda of Canadian journalism. In the United States, national bodies such as the American Society of Newspaper Editors (ASNE) have made diversity in newsrooms a top concern; they have established benchmarks and have issued annual surveys on newspaper representation. There are no Canadian organizations that have done the same. The publisher of the *Winnipeg Free Press*, who also sits on the board of governors of the National Newspaper Awards (NAA), told Barahona: 'That's a bunch of white guys ... There are white women, too, but it's a bunch of white guys.'

Gerry Nott, deputy editor of the *Calgary Herald*, told Barahona that he wasn't sure whether newspapers should even be trying to diversify their newsrooms: 'I don't think the media should go out and socially engineer the demographics of its newsroom to reflect the demographics of its readership ... I think that the best candidate for a job should get the job.' One of the barriers identified by Hamlin Grange, president of the Canadian Association of Black Journalists (CABJ), and identified by Nott as well, is that often people of colour are not part of traditional professional networks. This can result in them not knowing about possible job openings.

According to Barahona's survey, the only group that is actively engaged in trying to increase diversity is the Professional Writers Association of Canada (PWAC), a national organization of approximately 500 freelance writers, which has been running a series of workshops on challenging racial barriers in journalism. PWAC has also started an on-line symposium where journalists of colour can discuss issues of representation.

Obviously, Canada's newspaper industry has not done enough to ensure minority representation. As Solomon (1998) notes, the media show 'no signs of fatigue' when battling for market share. However, 'when racial equity is at stake, weariness is too overwhelming.' Unfortunately, there have been no studies of electronic broadcasting similar to Barahona's, but it is safe to assume that the findings would be much the same. Even a glance at the major television networks in Toronto indicates that there are very few non-White faces. In some networks there is virtually no minority employment.

In the United States, a similar problem exists. According to monitoring surveys conducted by the American Society of Newspaper Editors, minorities made up only 11.3 per cent of the newsroom staffs of American daily newspapers in 1996. This compares to 4 per cent in 1978, the year the first survey was conducted. The most recent study shows that in 2000, more than half of American dailies had no minorities in their newsrooms. Overall, newsroom employment grew by 1,100 between 1999 and 2000, from 55,100 to 56,200. This was the largest increase since the 1996 survey. Over the same period the number of minorities in the newspaper workforce increased by 300, to 6,700. This represented the largest increase in minority newsroom staffing since the 1995 survey. The first such survey, in 1978, showed that only 4 per cent of newsroom staff were minorities.

The current survey reveals that though minority representation has expanded across the board, Black journalists as a percentage of the workforce of newsroom staffs has dipped slightly. Currently, minorities make up 28.4 per cent of the American population, and they will grow to an estimated 38.2 per cent by 2025 according to the U.S. Census Bureau. Clearly, minorities are severely underrepresented in American journalism.

In the United Kingdom a similar pattern of under-employment is encountered. Ainley (1998) studied the representation of people of colour on national newspapers in the U.K. and found that there were at most twenty in the total workforce of around 3,000 journalists. As an excuse most newspaper managers noted that Caribbean, African, and Asian journalists have no formal training. Yet, these same newspapers often hire White graduates with no formal journalism training or experience and provide on-the-job training for them. One of the key barriers is that British newspapers do not usually advertise vacancies, and instead rely on 'word of mouth' (the same practice is widely used in media organizations in Canada). Ainley contends that when journalism jobs are advertised in, for example, ethnic minority publications, there is a huge response by people of colour.

**The Interview Study**

We felt it would be appropriate to include some of the current voices and direct experiences of minority journalists in this book. Accordingly, we selected more than twenty people working in the print and electronic media for extensive interviews. All the respondents were in the Toronto area. We asked them about their backgrounds, their experiences (if any) with workplace racism, barriers to finding employment or securing promotion, and their general experiences working in media organizations. Since there are so few minority journalists, we selected the sample from the membership list of the Canadian Association of Black Journalists. Members of other ethnoracial groups were easily identified by the researchers, given their small numbers; often we simply asked the Black respondents for some names. The interviewer was a Black journalism student. There were twelve men and eight women. Seven worked in the print media, the others in local television. None worked on national programs or on the radio. One respondent was retired; four were not interviewed for this project but had written on the subject, and we quote their ideas in different sections of the analysis. Most of the respondents had been born abroad and came here as young children. All had majored in journalism at a postsecondary school. The respondents came from the Caribbean, India, Korea, and Hong Kong.

We were able to identify many more minority journalists working in television than in the print media, as there has been slightly more hiring in the electronic media than in newspaper organizations in recent years. This is also true in the United States, where just over 11 per cent of minority journalists are employed in the print media, compared to 18 per cent in television (Biagi and Kern-Foxworth, 1997: 142).

One of the main reasons for this disparity is that one of the two national newspapers in Canada, the *Globe and Mail,* has only one minority feature writer, whose column appears only weekly. As she was not available for interview, the *Globe and Mail* is completely absent in our study. Cecil Foster, a noted journalist and author, was for ten years the only Black person in the *Globe and Mail*'s newsroom. Since he left in 1989, there has not been another. He notes wryly, 'When I left, 100% of the Black staff went out' (Manji, 1995). In his autobiography (1996), Foster is highly critical of the print and electronic media in terms of their treatment of Black journalists and broadcasters.

## Structural and Organizational Barriers Experienced by Journalists

*The Colour of My Skin*

One of the main barriers described by our respondents was 'the colour of my skin.' Several journalists stated that their colour was a barrier to being sent to cover a story. One told how he was prevented from seeking an interview about the Bernardo trial because his colour 'might have turned people off.' Another thought he had been 'passed over for a story' because of his colour, and a third knew of a photographer who was passed over for promotion many times despite his widely acknowledged superior credentials and experience. The journalists we interviewed also commonly felt that journalists of colour must be better than their White counterparts to get a job and keep it. One young man commented: 'My work has to be three times better than the person next to me who might not have a degree but their skin colour is different.' A few mentioned that their qualifications were carefully scrutinized; a common question asked of them was, 'Where did you go to school?'

A highly experienced Black journalist and broadcaster has written about how racism affects journalism in the context of everyday 'shop talk.' He cites a number of examples. Shortly after he joined the staff of a newspaper, a note went up on the bulletin board mentioning that he had grown up in Toronto and had gone to journalism school in Colorado and on graduation had worked on the *Rocky Mountain News*. No mention was made in the note of his far more recent and senior work experience as managing editor of *Contrast*, the newspaper that serves Toronto's Black community. He observes: 'It sent a very strong message to me that experience on a Black newspaper did not count, and that the way I was going to fit in here is to be part of the fraternity.' He added that after a few frustrating years, he left the newspaper, as his career was going nowhere.

*The Lack of Qualified Applicants*

Another issue related to bias is the claim newspapers make that there aren't any qualified applicants who are minorities. One woman auditioned for an on-air job and was called back several times, only to be told that she would not be hired as 'this is not going to work.' The news director than told her, 'We get pounded a lot for not hiring minorities, but the fact of the matter is no one is qualified. People are always creating a stir that they don't have representation. The fact is we don't have a large pool to choose from.' This common excuse hides the fact that there are qualified people but a variety of barriers keep them away from the hiring and audition process. Also, managers who don't want to hire a person of colour in the first place often use a shortage of qualified applicants as an excuse.

*Minority Journalists as 'Sensitizing Agents' in Understanding and Dealing with Ethnoracial Issues and Media Bias*

One of the most interesting and most common themes the interviewees raised related to how their role as journalists intersected with their social identity as members of ethnoracial communities. Many of them saw themselves as 'sensitizing agents' in the newsroom. They often described themselves as cultural interpreters and facilitators when it came to issues of race or ethnicity. Some felt it was their responsibility to cautiously point out to their colleagues that their language or their approach to a story could lead, unwittingly, to misrepresentation. Some of the journalists believed they had done much to sensitize their co-workers to their unintentional biases. A number of respondents talked about how many journalists link race and crime in their stories, and how the Black community is often vilified by the media for the criminal acts committed by a few individuals. A few respondents pointed to how racial bias was woven into the media coverage of the Just Desserts shooting (see case study). Some also discussed a story involving the shooting of a bank teller in Brampton and how an entire community got 'blamed and shamed' for the murder. Little was known about the suspects except the colour of their skin; even so, the media reported that the police believed they spoke with Jamaican accents. This led one reporter to surmise that the suspects stole green minivans as getaway vehicles because green is one of the colours in the Jamaican flag.

One outspoken TV reporter said he often told his colleagues that a description of a suspect such as 'male, black, and five feet tall' could fit any one of a thousand people in the city. He believes that as a result of his efforts, they were less likely to use vague racial descriptors. Some interviewees referred to the reporters' practice of pulling descriptions directly from police reports. Journalists of colour in our sample often told their co-workers not to rely on such standard police descriptions, since they targeted almost everyone in the community.

One of the most experienced, skilled, and successful journalists in the media, who rose to become an editor on one of Toronto's newspapers, has done much to illuminate how racism operates in media culture, both through his writing and through many presentations at media conferences. He has identified a number of attributes of media organizations that influence their coverage of minority issues and events, and he makes a number of important points. First, 'although media are on the frontiers of news, journalists are rarely on the cusp of social change.' Second, despite claims to the contrary, 'the media are the establishment.' Third, 'the media's black and white, no greys in between, view of the world hurts minorities.' And finally, 'although race relations is clearly one of the most important issues of our times, most media do not cover it, or cover it "on the run," looking for the easy hit.'

Another highly experienced journalist and former editor in the mainstream press spoke about how journalists must play an important role in monitoring and combating racism in the media. She cited the need for journalists to challenge more effectively the people they interview – people whose 'facts' they rely on for building their stories. She commented: 'What is required is a sonar of scepticism. The antennae of journalists must go into overdrive': 'The commonsense of whiteness affects what is seen as fact and what is interpreted as perception or ideological ... Being part of the White mainstream means that what you say is more objective, neutral, unbiased, uninfluenced by emotional or ideological content. Within the prism of whiteness what is said is accepted as common sense.'

Some of our respondents observed that they have found sympathetic editors who are willing to listen to their ideas about events and issues – not necessarily crime related – that can turn into positive and supportive stories about communities of colour. One interviewee noted that he had done a story about a Black church that had burned down, and his newspaper had accepted it even though it was not a hot news item.

A few respondents observed that they were sometimes cast in the role of experts themselves. One described how her boss 'asks me "are we saying this correctly"? Or just to verify things when they come up in the newsrooms.' She believed that her mere presence in the newsroom had made an impact. Another confirmed this view: 'Just because I am there I can point to different things to news directors and editors and say if something is wrong with a story.' One respondent offered, 'I've actually had editors come to me and ask me about certain issues.' A print media specialist confirmed this: 'My background sensitizes me to certain things,' and therefore she was able to answer her colleagues' questions. 'I've had a reporter ask me the difference between reggae and calypso,' she told us, 'or if she could use the word holocaust to describe the middle passage.' Her information was in fact used by her colleague. Yet another confirmed her role as an expert: 'Because I am a Black woman out there in the field there are issues that I take more sensitively. I change a lot of stories on copy when I have a chance to.'

Besides being 'sensitizers,' 'interpreters,' and 'experts,' racial minority journalists also see themselves as recruiters of other members of their communities. Managers often say that the pool of qualified minority journalists is small; noting this, those already in the job pass information into their communities – especially to journalists they know in those communities. A well-known, more senior journalist of colour says, 'I see my role as bringing more people of colour into the newsroom. I am an ambassador of such actions ... I sort of formed my own recruiting agency here.' Several other reporters made the same point: 'When a job posting comes up, I take it to my friends and inform them about these jobs.'

*Raises, Promotions, and Contract Employment*

Several journalists talked about raises and promotions, observing that these aspects of the job are so subtle that discrimination can be covert. One senior reporter talked about a photographer, a person of colour, who was not promoted because he was not 'aggressive' enough. Yet his job did not especially require aggressive behaviour. Another noted that a friend of hers moved to another province but returned a short time later. During her absence a White woman had been hired, and she was unable to get her job back. There was some discussion that the real reason was that the friend was a strong and assertive Black woman who had made her White colleagues uncomfortable.

Journalists are often hired on contract. A contract position may or may not turn into a permanent job. In several media organizations, a preponderance of journalists of colour were on contracts. In one organization, one minority person was permanent and five others were on contract, and of these latter, two had been on several periods of contract. Almost all of the interviewees had been hired on contract, and most of them were now permanent staff. The problem with this system is that while reporters are on contract, they are not in a position to challenge their editors on issues, nor are they as free to pursue stories of their own. This form of employment seems to be endemic in media organizations; that being said, it discourages journalists of colour from speaking out, challenging the system, or 'making any waves on our own.'

With regard to representative employment practices, one interviewee, a Korean Canadian, made an especially telling observation: 'For as long as I am here, it is highly unlikely that they will hire another Asian person on camera. They'll consider two Asian reporters as too many.' There is an ironic twist here: every minority person hired makes it harder for the next minority person to be hired.

*Story Assignment*

The interviewees often discussed how stories were assigned. There was some dissension in the sample on this issue. Some journalists felt that they did not want to cover only stories in 'their' communities. One young woman said that when she was hired, she made it 'clear that I don't only want to cover the Black community.' Another said, 'I have never been pegged about writing stories about the Asian community – even though I have access to the Chinese community, you should not only cover it [but also others]. If you are White they allow you to cover any community.' She and a few others believe that giving journalists of colour mainly their own communities to cover is in itself an act of racialization. They feel that such policies marginalize them, with the result that their status in the organization is lower than that enjoyed by their White colleagues. On the other hand, some feel that their unique position gives them an edge over White journalists. One Canadian Chinese reporter told us, 'I understood the culture and I told the story differently than let's say a White reporter would have.' Another print journalist commented: 'I can do Caribana and being non-White there are a lot more stories out there that I can cover, like the Rodney King riots and ... Caribbean community issues.' Similarly, a South Asian woman declared: 'I know more about one billion Indian people ... This week I was given a story to do on the Tibetan refugees and I speak that language.' The respondents, were proud of their ability to cover these communities better than mainstream journalists. One interviewee had an especially interesting story to tell about story assignments:

> There was a time when *Show Boat* (the musical) came to town and a lot of Black educators were up in arms. I was working in Hamilton at the time and we decided to cover this event and I said I want the story. When I mentioned this at a news meeting, one reporter jumped up and said, 'Just because you are Black you think it's your story, just think you are better equipped to cover this.' It was a good story, and I wanted it, and they were thinking that it would be biased if I covered Black stories. It is a feeling that because I am Black I won't cover these stories the 'right way.'

A number of issues emerged in this situation. On the one hand, her colleagues thought she ought not to be getting this story because it was an especially good one. On the other hand, there was an element of subjectivity involved in this debate. It was believed that the Black reporter could not cover it the 'right way' because she could not be objective about it. Paradoxically, it was argued that the White reporter was in a better position to be an objective observer on an issue relating to the Black community

A television reporter discussed this same issue. She recounted that a viewer had written to a station to say that 'they had no right to cover anti-Semitic issues.' The assignment editor defended himself, arguing that he had sent a Black reporter to cover the story because 'we thought he might know the issues more.' In this instance, the assumption was made that a Black reporter would be more sensitive to issues around anti-Semitism, possibly because of the common history of victimization. This does seem to be a stretch – there is little reason to believe that Blacks know more than other people about anti-Semitism. The editor seemed to believe that minorities are more sensitive to each other's concerns.

Another journalist commented that on a practical level, it was individual reporters, editors, and directors who put a certain spin on a given story. He cited a colleague's experience at a Calgary newspaper. That journalist wanted to do a story about Koreans who were being turned away from bars in downtown Calgary. The news director would not let her do the story, but gave no reason. As an excuse for discriminating against Asians in this way, the bars owners stated that Asians were heavily involved in gang violence, and the news director validated this argument.

*Role of Gender*

Some of the journalists also talked about the role of gender. It is alleged that there are more Asian women on air – at least in Ontario – because Asian women conform to a sexual stereotype of passive conformity. Asian men, on the other hand, are stereotyped as shifty, unbelievable, authoritarian, and aggressive. The electronic media therefore prefer to hire Asian women, who are seen as more believable as well as more demure and conforming. In the Black community of journalists, it is also widely believed that lighter-skinned Blacks with White features have a distinct advantage over dark-skinned, African-featured Blacks. As one Black journalist noted wryly, 'They feel the real-looking Africans are going to eat them when they are on screen.' Another, in commenting on the dearth of Black men on screen, said, 'I want to see more Black males in the newsrooms ... I don't know why it is, but some people still have a problem with a strong Black man.' Like their Asian counterparts, Black women are perceived as less threatening than Black men.

*Treating Racism as Humour*

Only one reporter mentioned this theme. However, racial humour is common in newsrooms (see the case study on Avery Haines). Very often, racism is shrugged off as humour – 'it was only a joke' – after some offensive comment has been made.

*Resistance to Using Experts Who Are People of Colour*

In stories that involve people of colour, and especially criminal activity, the experts cited are almost always Whites. Often they are also people in positions of authority such as police officers and lawyers. Rarely are the experts members of the community in question. One journalist noted, 'This person wouldn't have credibility on a particular issue, and I ask why? Their colour or race hinders them, but the producers and reporters won't tell you this is the reason.' (This is also true in the justice system, where White experts have more credibility than those of colour.)

*The Changes Needed*

The journalists saw the greatest need for change mainly at the level of management. The need to 'hire more management of colour' was mentioned often during these interviews. Many of the respondents felt that producers, directors, station managers, publishers, station owners, and the like need to be more representative of our culturally and racially pluralistic society. Several of the journalists contended that making the front-line workforce more diverse is important, but that the system will not change without more diverse management. One woman said, 'I would love to see an Asian woman being a news director of a newsroom one day or a Black man as CEO of a network.' In media organizations, just as in all others, decisions are made at the level of management. And as one journalist noted, media management is still basically 'white bread' and 'wasp.'

## Conclusions

There is some consensus among minority journalists in both the print and electronic media that racial bias is woven into the culture of media organizations in terms of norms, professional values, and everyday discourse. Some of the interviewees – especially the younger ones who had only recently been hired – expressed concern about speaking out too forcefully on issues on racism. Even so, it is clear from their comments that many are strongly committed to representing their communities more accurately. It is also clear from the interviews that many are committed to helping their mainstream colleagues respond more skilfully and appropriately to issues of diversity.

In the next section of this book we will explore the subject of media diversity and equity through a case study approach. The first two case studies provide an interesting contrast to the views and concerns expressed by journalists of colour in this chapter. In the first case study, on Avery Haines, and second one, on the *Globe and Mail*'s coverage of employment equity, we focus mainly on the voices of the White media and explore some of the prevailing assumptions, frames of reference, and the coded language of White journalists and editors in relation to the discourse of bias and discrimination in the media.

# PART II
# CASE STUDIES AND CRITICAL
# DISCOURSE ANALYSIS

# 4

# The Methodology of Case Studies and Critical Discourse Analysis

We have chosen a case study approach for this book because it is a good way to present a concrete and detailed account of how some of the media reproduce racism. In taking this approach, we hope to encourage our readers to use the tools and resources reflected in these case studies to engage in similar kinds of study and reflection (see concluding chapter). As van Dijk (1998) notes, such a study requires the development of a systematic account of the various levels, structures, and strategies of text and talk as well as a diagnostic set of instruments for understanding how racism is reproduced in everyday discourse.

For this study we have employed both quantitative and qualitative techniques. We created several databases for each case study by downloading relevant articles from the Canadian News Disc. We then read and categorized the articles, which included news reports, editorials, and op-ed pieces. We selected the case studies on the basis of how much media coverage was available to review, and also on the basis of how significant the issues were in terms of inequality and power relations in Canadian society. We focused on identifying media discourses of central importance to ethnoracial minorities. The issues at the heart of the case studies strongly reflect the tensions between how minority communities frame the events related to race and ethnoracial and national identity, and how the largely White mainstream media interpret these events.

In the case studies we take two parallel approaches to critical discourse analysis. The first of these is influenced by Wetherell and Potter's (1992) methodology, which is essentially macro-level and global and focuses on the broad rhetorical strategies, central themes and topics, and argumentative statements that the media use to racialize minorities. The second approach involves drawing on the van Dijkian (1991) categories of analysis and on Fairclough and Wodak's classifications (1997).[1] We analyse the articles by looking at the semantic and micro-level meanings of words, by examining the organization of the text – its structure and vocabulary, its sentences and sentence connections – and by dissecting rhetorical statements to find their core ideas and images. We examine carefully the relationship between global and micro-level text analysis. Each case study shows how some of the media constructed and analysed a particular discursive event and how they can create, solidify, change, and reproduce power relations.

**Critical Discourse Analysis**

Critical discourse analysis of language and text provides a tool for deconstructing the ideologies of the mass media and other elite groups, and for identifying and defining social, economic, and historical power relations between dominant and subordinate groups. CDA is a multidisciplinary approach to the study of language use and communication in the context of cultural production.[2] It is a type of research that mainly studies how social power, dominance, and inequality are produced, reproduced, and resisted by text and talk in the social and political arenas of society. CDA does more than analyse the social origins of linguistic forms; it also considers those sets of social relations ordered by a particular discourse, and identifies forms and practices and ways of behaving according to an identifiable discourse. Thus, in addition to texts, there are values, norms, attitudes, and behavioural practices associated with a specific discourse. CDA is an approach to studying language use and communication, and is grounded in sociocultural texts rather than in some abstract linguistic system. This form of discourse analysis sets out to show how the cognitive, social, historical, cultural, and political contexts of language use and communication affect the content, meanings, and structures of text or discourse (van Dijk, 1998).

Dellinger (1995) observes that a focus on both the structure and the social context of media text can offer a strategic approach that allows the media and analyst/critic to expose the take-for-granted nature of ideological messages. When combined with newer methods of discourse analysis, this can in turn create a broader common ground for analysis. Following this framework, Robert Kaplan (1990) writes: 'The text, whether written or oral, is a multidimensional structure,' and 'any text is layered, like a sheet of thick plywood consisting of many thin sheets lying at different angles to each other.' These sheets refer to syntax and lexicon, grammar and semantics. Yet, it is not enough to understand the grammar and lexicon of a text. Rather, Kaplan notes, one must recognize the 'rhetoric intent, the coherence and the world view that the author and the receptor bring to the text.' The comprehension of meaning involves more than a reading of the text; it also involves a complex interaction between the author's intent and the respondent's intent.

Fairclough (1992: 11) notes that there are three dimensions to CDA:

1. description of text,
2. interpretation of the interaction processes and their relationship to text,
3. explanation of how the interaction process relates to the social action.

Kress (1990) contends that CDA has a political agenda that distinguishes it from other kinds of discourse analysis and text linguistics. Many critical discourse analysts – including the authors of this text – are motivated in their work by the desire to produce counter or oppositional discourses that provide alternative ways of interpreting, understanding, and interacting with the world.

Discourse serves to make sense of the social reality of lived experience. Specific conditions are made sense of within the social relations that structure them. To make sense of the world is to exert power over it, and to circulate that sense socially is to exert power over those who then use that sense as a way of coping with their daily lives. At times, discourse becomes visible or audible, as in a text, a speech, or a conversation. But it also works silently, inside the cognitive make-up of individuals as they attempt to interpret their rapidly changing worlds. Fiske (1994) makes the important point that discourse may not produce reality, but it does produce the instrumental sense of the real that a society or system uses in daily life. The continuity between event and discourse produces a 'discourse event' or 'media event,' not a discourse about the event. In the following discussion we provide our readers with an understanding of some key concepts and tools that are commonly used in CDA.

## The Choice of Topics

Discourse begins with the choice of topics – the subject of the text – the discursive event. As van Dijk (1998) notes, there is an almost infinite number of subjects the media can select from, but only a few are actually chosen, and those repeatedly. An analysis of the topics is essential since they significantly affect how people interpret and understand events reported on by the media. Some of the most common topics addressed in this study include the following:

1. New (illegal) immigrants.
2. Political and public response to policies about immigration.
3. Social problems (e.g., drain on public resources) related to the arrival or integration of immigrants and refugees.
4. Social problems related to immigrants but generalized to apply to people of colour who may have been born in this country (based on the belief that members of these groups come from 'different,' 'deviant' cultures).
5. Polls and other monitoring mechanisms that assess the response of the population (e.g., polls and surveys that measure the degree of bias toward immigrants).
6. How immigrants/minorities are a threat to public safety, security, health, national unity and identity, harmony, civility, and stability.
7. Demands for preferential treatment, policies, and programs (immigration and employment equity and cultural programs and events).
8. Multiculturalism and antiracism as policy and practice.

In each of these instances, even potentially neutral topics come to acquire negative dimensions. Van Dijk argues that these topics 'manifest complex networks of professional, social and cultural ideologies' (1991: 71). The choice of subject expresses and reproduces the concerns, priorities, and agendas of the dominant White culture. It follows that a topical analysis of discourse is an important first step, that being said, a detailed semantic examination is also necessary to undercover the meaning of the discourse.

**The Structure of Newsmaking**

Choice of topic is not the only factor affecting news content and transmission. Language, the layout, the use of graphics, the type and length of articles, and the ordering of information within the article, as well as the particular sources cited, all communicate significant information to the newsreader. However, when we are analysing *specific linguistic practices* or *superstructures of news making*, it is important for us to note the twin processes of *selection* and *combination* that precede writing. Before a word hits the page, journalists and editors select what readers will get to read; and by combining the information that they do include in a certain manner, they also influence how it will be interpreted. This means that what gets left out of the story – that is, the information that is considered either irrelevant to the narrative or not important enough to print – can provide interesting insights into how a news outlet is telling or 'constructing' the story. In each of the case studies, we will point out what the news outlets have omitted from the narrative; we will also show how what has been selected for inclusion and how the selected information has been combined facilitate a certain 'reading' of the story.

Journalists often select information and construct their stories by linking news events to broader social narratives. In this way, a crime story like the Just Desserts case eventually gets linked to pre-existing social discourses on crime. A particular crime is likened to some crimes and differentiated from others, and in this way is linked to a more generalized 'law and order' discourse – namely, that Canada's urban centres are being inundated by an American-style crime wave. Our close analysis of the texts will reveal how all of Toronto's newspapers have contributed to the moral panic that has developed around the relationship between crime and immigration. This moral panic led to the passage of the 'Just Desserts bill' (see chapter 9).

Some of our case studies focus mainly on the specific linguistic practices used to communicate meaning; however, we will also show how other techniques of news making structure meaning both within newspapers in general and within texts in particular.

In the case studies that follow we apply CDA to various aspects of news transmission. For example, we analyse *headlines*, which are part of the text of an article. A headline imparts to the reader an overall idea of the story that follows.

Headlines are the first part of an article that is read – sometimes the only part. Their main function is to summarize the story's most important information. That is, they express its main 'topic,' and in doing so activate the relevant social knowledge that the reader will require to understand and contextualize the story. *Editorials* are also included in our analyses 'since they are probably the widest circulated opinion discourses of society, whether or not all readers of the newspaper read them daily' (van Dijk, 1996b). Because 'editorial opinion is generally institutional and not personal ... editorials count as the opinion of the newspaper and not just a single columnist or reporter' (ibid). The 'institutionalized opinions' expressed in the editorials of the most influential papers are followed by members of Parliament, corporate managers, and other elite members of society. In the 'Just Desserts' case, the opinions that were expressed in the editorials and columns of Toronto's newspapers influenced cabinet ministers and MPs in the debates surrounding Bill C-44. Similarly, the *Globe and Mail*'s coverage of employment equity strongly affected how Ontario's premier developed anti-equity discourse.

Editorials are mainly opinion pieces rather than sources of new information, so they are categorized differently from news reports. Some editorials amount to *summaries* of events that the paper has covered; others are *evaluations* of the people and issues involved in those events; and still others provide *conclusions* – that is, recommendations, advice, or warnings. As we will show, editorials often build on the arguments of an event to justify the editors' recommendations or advice.

In many of the articles we examine, *quotations* are commonly used as a linguistic strategy. Quotations serve a number of functions. First, they can be important in and of themselves – for instance, a president's declaration of war is an important news event. They also enliven the news. Furthermore, quotations from important news actors can lend credibility and act as important *sources of evidentiality* in news reports. Finally, quotations are a means of inserting subjective opinions into news items 'without breaking the ideological rule that requires the separation of fact from fiction' (van Dijk, 1991: 152). Thus, when reporters and columnists want to favour a particular point of view in an article, they can do so by quoting a source that reflects it, even while legitimately claiming that they are merely reporting a factual account of 'what has been said.' The use of 'officials,' police, and other authorities as sources rather than leaders and members of targeted communities is a common practice used to marginalize these communities. This will be especially obvious in the case study on the Tamil community.

In news analysis, it is important to identify precisely the sources of news information. Elites are the likeliest to have access to news outlets (van Dijk, 1991: 153), so their opinions are more likely than other people's to be reflected in news reports. Our numerical findings reflect this; so does van Dijk's 1991 analysis of news reports. According to van Dijk, news discourse represents mainly a 'white' elite point of view: 'Minority group speakers or sources are often found less credible because they are seen as partisan, whereas white authorities, such as the police or the government, are simply seen as ethnically "neutral," even in the definition and evaluation of ethnic events' (154). It is, of course, no more possible to locate a single 'White' point of view than it is a unified 'Black' point of view; even so, our discursive analysis will show how reporters rely on White representations of the social world when presenting the news.

**The Use of Argumentation**

Journalists do more than present the facts of a given event; they present those facts from a certain perspective. This means we can study the argumentative logic inherent in that perspective and the subsequent breaches of that logic in news reports. Argumentation fallacies are arguments that, though they do support the argumentative position, either do *not* support the conclusion or do *not* enable the argumentative interaction. Some of the argumentative strategies we identify in the case studies are *playing on the sentiments of readers, making false analogies, overgeneralizing, constructing 'straw men,'* and *claiming that everyone thinks it is right.* Other forms of argumentation include *topoi,* that is, the supposed 'commonsense' explanations of social issues. Fronting or *topicalization* involves the writer presenting a point in the first sentence of the article and thereby setting its tone. There are many other factors and devices that influence an article's meaning, including alliteration, vagueness, repeated phrases, lexical style, the use of hyperbole, negative descriptions of the actors involved in a story, assumptions and preassumptions, leaving a story incomplete, and resorting to metaphors.[3]

# 5

# The Avery Haines Controversy

Avery Haines worked for eleven years at the radio station CFRB before joining CTV NewsNet. After working at the station for two months and while still on probation, she was giving an introduction to a taped report on aid to farmers when she flubbed a line. Knowing that that she could do the take again on another tape, she said to an off-camera staffer: 'I kind of like the stuttering thing. It's like equal opportunity, right? We got a stuttering newscaster. We've got the Black, we've got the Asian, and we've got the woman. I could be a lesbian-folk-dancing-Black-woman stutterer.' Presumably, someone in the studio then made a comment, and Haines added: 'In a wheelchair ... with a gimping, rubber leg. Yeah, really. I'd have a successful career, let me tell you.'

An error in the control room led to the airing of the first tape, which replayed the above comments, rather than the 'clean' version. Immediately after, CTV phone lines began flashing with calls from irate viewers. Haines apologized twice for her 'insulting and derogatory comments.' Henry Kowalski, the station's senior vice-president of news, believed that the incident was very serious and could not be ignored. He considered the remarks disrespectful and unprofessional, and a few days later Avery Haines was fired. Three weeks later, CityTV signed her on as a reporter and anchor. A long-time Toronto producer commented: 'My hat's off to those guys, they cash in on the notoriety of hiring this woman who'd turned into a quasi-celebrity even though she made comments that offended Blacks, Asians, lesbians and the disabled on air' (Gayle MacDonald, 'Fired CTV Anchor Given New Home on CityTV,' *Globe and Mail*, 28 January 2000).

Several organizations protested Haines's comments vigorously. Dayne Ogilvie, past president of the National Lesbian and Gay Journalists Association, observed: 'It may have been a joke but where did the joke come from?' Many organizations complained that Haines's comments reflected the widespread bigotry against minorities in Canada. Laurie Beachell, national coordinator of the Council of Canadians with Disabilities, observed that the real danger in what Haines said was that it could send the harmful message that affirmative action and employment equity programs give special treatment to the disabled or to visible minorities (Dick Chapman, 'Anchor's Slurs "Hurtful,"' *Toronto Sun*, 17 January 2000). The president of the Canadian Abilities Foundation and publisher of *Abilities* magazine said that the main point driven home by Haines's slurs was that the choice of words used in the news media is crucial.

Jackqui Debique, former president of the Canadian Association of Black Journalists, in response to the incident, commented: 'It is perhaps the obvious absence of diversity that made Ms Haines feel so comfortable in making her comments.' Moy Tam, executive director of the Canadian Race Relations Foundation, observed: 'I found it disturbing that Avery Haines's remarks are only attracting attention because she was caught in the act.' Many people, including Tam, asked whether any form of disciplinary action would have been taken had Haines comments not been publicly aired (Alan Barnes, 'TV Anchor Fired for Offensive Comments,' *Toronto Star*, 18 January 2000).

**Quantitative Analysis of Media Coverage of the Controversy**

Table 1 provides a sampling of media coverage of the Avery Haines controversy. The table records forty-four articles, news items, and editorials on the subject in the print media. The actual total is probably higher, as we did not do a complete tracking (magazines and weeklies, for example, were not included).

**Discourse Analysis of the Media Articles on Avery Haines**

The Haines case study is somewhat different from the others we present in this book. It is not about targeting a community, which the *National Post* did when it investigated the supposed terrorist links of the Tamil community in Canada, and which the press in general routinely does when it covers Jamaicans or Vietnamese and their alleged criminal activities. Nor does this case study deal with the stereotyping of particular communities, which the *Globe and Mail* is guilty of in its coverage of the Native community. It is also different from the *Globe and Mail*'s concerted attacks on employment equity. The Haines case is about the

TABLE 5.1
Print and electronic media coverage of the Haines story

| Paper/Station | Journalist | Date |
|---|---|---|
| *Toronto Sun* | MacDonald | 16 January |
| | Chapman | 17 January |
| | Findlay | 18 January |
| | Goldstein | 18 January |
| | Dunford | 19 January |
| | Coren | 20 January |
| | Jonas | 20 January |
| | Braun | 23 January |
| | Brown | 23 January |
| | Steward | 23 January |
| | Williamson | 23 January |
| | King | 27 January |
| | Brioux | 8 February |
| | Bickley | 9 February |
| | Slotek | 10 February |
| | News | 22 February |
| | Brioux | 17 March |
| | Brioux | 16 April |
| Total | 18 | |
| *National Post* | News item | 17 January |
| | Blatchford | 18 January |
| | Coyne | 19 January |
| | Haines | 19 January |
| | Brown | 19 January |
| | Editorial | 19 January |
| | Foot | 21 January |
| | Wells | 19 February reference only |
| | | 16 February reference only |
| | Eckler | 29 April |
| Total | 10 | |
| *Globe and Mail* | MacDonald | 18 January |
| | Wente | 20 January |
| | Editorial | 20 January |
| | Column | 22 January (no author – 'Odds on Avery') |
| | Gill | 22 January |
| Total | 5 | |

TABLE 5.1—(*Concluded*)
Print and electronic media coverage of the Haines story

| Pape /Station | Journalist | Date |
| --- | --- | --- |
| *Toronto Star* | Barnes | 18 January |
| | Coyle | 20 January |
| | Timson | 20 January |
| | Zerbias | 23 January |
| | Siddiqui | 23 January |
| | Grange | 28 January |
| | Cameron | 16 February |
| Total | 7 | |
| Other print media | *Hamilton Spectator* | 19 January |
| | *Daily News* | 18 January |
| | *Ottawa Citizen* | 18 January |
| | *Ming PoA* | 18 January |
| Total | 4 | |
| Electronic media | | |
| CKHJ | | 17 January |
| CFRB | | 18 January |
| CHOR | | 18 January |
| CBM | | 18 January |
| CKLW | | 18 January |
| CFPL | | 19 January |
| QR77 | | 17 January |
| TVO | | 18 January |
| CBC 99.1 | | 18 January (Andy Barrie) |
| CBC 99.1 | | 18 January (Avril Benoit) |
| ABC | | American coverage of the Avery Haines Controversy: *The View* with Barbara Walters |
| Total | 12 | |

media itself, and how they close ranks when one of their own has made inappropriate remarks. The analysis we present here is therefore not a micro-level, linguistically based discourse analysis, but rather a descriptive accounting of what her colleagues had to say about the event. Because Haines was one of their own, an enormous number of articles and commentaries were printed about this subject. So, in effect, this is a case study of the media responding to an attack on itself. What makes this analysis especially interesting is the line of argumentation – the central discourses – her colleagues took in her defence. What do the media say about themselves when under attack? Our approach to this incident is to identify the rhetorical strategies and argumentative discourses that the media presented in defending a colleague. These formed the essential part of the dominant discourse related to the controversy. The first of these strategies, and the most pervasive and powerful, was denial.

*The Discourse of Denial: This Is Not Prejudicial or Discriminatory Behaviour*

In a democratic and liberal society where racism is seen as aberrant and as the beliefs and behaviours of isolated and dysfunctional extremists, denials of racism are pervasive in public discourse, including the discourse of journalists, editors, broadcasters, and news directors. These denials are often articulated in the context of doubt as to whether acts of discrimination actually occurred. Denial is usually followed by claims made by 'liberals' that people of colour and other minority groups are hypersensitive about prejudice and discrimination and often see bias where there is none. The assumption here is that because Canada is a society that upholds the values and ideals of a liberal democracy, it cannot be racist, nor can its major institutions be racist, and certainly not the media, which play such a vital role in preserving democratic principles. Central to this discourse is the need for positive self-presentation ('I am not a racist'). These denials are, of course, based on a very limited understanding of how racism manifests itself in contemporary society. Most people, including journalists, still understand racism in its overt and 'redneck' expressions. From this perspective, racists are those who use strongly pejorative words and labels, who physically attack people of colour and their property, and who have aligned themselves with extremist political movements. Everyday racism and racist discourses of a more sophisticated, elusive, and linguistically 'coded' type are poorly understood. Yet it is these forms that are the most pervasive in societies like ours. Below are a number of examples of the discourse of denial:

- 'There is not a racist bone in my body or a sexist bone in my body.' (Lorrie Goldstein, 'In Her Own Words,' *Toronto Sun*, 18 January 2000)
- 'It is interesting to note that nothing Ms Haines said was actually racist; or sexist; or even anti-Lesbian.' (editorial, 'Firing Squad.' *National Post*, 19 January 2000)
- 'There was nothing insulting or derogatory about what she said.' (Christie Blatchford, 'This Is CTV. You Will Not Be Funny,' *National Post*, 18 January 2000)

- 'Just fired CTV anchor Avery Haines made a couple of big mistakes in her fall from grace. Making racist comments wasn't one of them.' (Andrew Dreschel, 'Fired CTV Anchor Committed No Crime,' *Hamilton Spectator*, 19 January 2000)
- 'A sign of widespread bigotry, pronounced Canadians with Disabilities. The Black Journalists' Association protested, as did the National Lesbian and Gay Journalists Association. About the only group not heard from was the stuttering lobby.' (Margaret Wente, 'Open Mike with Avery Haines,' *Globe and Mail*, 20 January 2000)
- 'Neither Mr Kowalski nor anyone else has yet identified what, precisely, was so objectionable in her comments.' (Andrew Coyne, 'To Air Is Human,' *National Post*, 19 January 2000)
- 'I think it was a mistake [to apologize], because there was nothing insulting or derogatory about what she said.' (Christie Blatchford, 'This Is CTV. You Will Not Be Funny,' *National Post*, 18 January 2000)
- 'The often risqué banter of the workplace would lead to firings every day if it were irretrievably broadcast on television or published in print ... Ms Haines is almost all of us now and then.' (editorial, 'Lesbian Folk-Dancing,' *Globe and Mail*, 19 January 2000)
- 'Now what was all this? An expression of racism? Against lesbians, folk-dancers, the disabled? Wouldn't that have sounded something like – damn those black, lesbian, disabled folk-dancers?' (Bill Cameron, 'What Was Avery Haines' Real Sin?' *Toronto Star*, 16 February 2000)
- 'One of the most active groups in challenging discrimination in this country is the Canadian Jewish Congress and it is significant that it has issued not a word about the incident.' (Michael Coren, 'Apology Should Have Ended It,' *Toronto Sun* 20 January 2000)

*The Discourse of Reverse Discrimination: Avery Haines Is the Real Victim*

A common rhetorical strategy is to employ semantic and role reversal so that the perpetrators of the prejudiced commentary or act are portrayed as the innocent victims of a new form of oppression and exclusion. It is then argued that minorities are engaging in 'reverse discrimination.' Haines' defenders contended that she was being victimized by her employers, who were being hypersensitive to issues of diversity and who were espousing the doctrine of political correctness to the point of demanding an employee's dismissal:

- 'Avery said she has been flooded with calls of support from CTV staffers, family and others adding, 'Everyone is horrified and everyone is surprised that I've been fired.' (Lorrie Goldstein, 'In Her Own Words,' *Toronto Sun*, 18 January 2000)

- 'Not only was he [Henry Kowalski] committing a monstrous injustice against Ms Haines, who had done nothing to deserve such treatment ... You can be fired without evidence that you have done any harm, to your employer or anyone else.' (Andrew Coyne, 'To Air Is Human,' *National Post*, 19 January 2000)
- 'Ms Haines is a victim of a common mass delusion: In our irony-saturated age, most people have the sense to dismiss controversial comments made in jest.' (editorial. 'Firing Squad,' *National Post*, 18 January 2000)
- 'CTV senior Vice President of News committed a monstrous injustice against Ms Haines who had done nothing to serve such treatment ... Ms Haines has been wronged, ruined to spare those higher up some momentary discomfort ... Censorship is always disturbing. But scapegoating is simply contemptible.' (Andrew Coyne, 'To Air Is Human,' *National Post*, Jan 19, 2000)
- 'As harsh as it sounds I have to say [her career] is over.' (Robert Fisher, anchor for First National News on Global, in Desmond Brown, 'Broadcast Journalists Air Their Views on Firing of News Anchor,' *National Post*, 19 January 2000)
- 'The rookie anchor apologized for her humour before being fired by CTV. Had she asked me, I'd have told her to save her breath. One might as well be hanged for a sheep as a lamb. More importantly she said nothing that was untrue, or that TV executives I've known ... hadn't said in private ... One might think reverse discrimination is obligatory in Canada, only speaking about it is forbidden. Actually speaking about it is also obligatory, except one must do it euphemistically and sententiously, as the CRTC does in its recent marching orders to the CBC 'to more adequately reflect the multicultural and multiracial nature of Canada' and 'help to counteract negative stereotypes. The CRTC doesn't mind stereotypes as long as they're positive.' (George Jonas, 'When the Punishment Doesn't Fit the Crime,' *Toronto Sun*, 20 January 2000)

*The Discourse of Rationalization, Justification, Minimalization, and Mitigation: 'It Was Only a Commonplace Joke Heard Everyday; It Was the Techies' Fault'*

The third rhetorical strategy evidenced in this case study is minimalization, mitigation, and excuse. It is difficult to avoid blame or personal responsibility for acts of bias and discrimination. In this light, a powerful strategy often resorted to by the media is to deflect the negative action by resorting to justification, rationalization, minimalization, and mitigation. In the case of Avery Haines, there were two main rhetorical motifs employing this discursive strategy. The first was the claim that her comments were meant only as a joke.[1] The second was the claim that the fault did not lie with Haines herself, but rather with the technicians who allowed the tape to go to air.

- 'I thought my on-air 'oops' was akin to slipping on a banana peel, an embarassing joke.' (Avery Haines, 'Marv Albert Has a Job. I don't.' *National Post*, 19 January 2000)
- 'Worse stuff is said behind the scenes at any newsroom in the name of cynicism and bad taste humour ... Why is it that we treat people who commit gaffes worse than we treat muggers?' (Jim Slotek, 'Gaffing the Anchor: The Hook a Bit Harsh for Avery Haines,' *Toronto Sun*, 19 January 2000)
- 'Most of us have heard far harsher 'jokes' in their own workplace. Is irreverent black humour a surprise in media workplaces? Doesn't snappy sarcasm and insult fuel every pop culture reflection of the news biz?' (Gary Dunford, 'Newsnet's Humourless,' *Toronto Sun*, 19 January 2000)
- 'Her remarks added up to nothing but tastelessness, which shouldn't disqualify her to work anywhere, as well as attend most dinner parties.' (Judith Timson, 'Getting Sacked Can Be a Lesson in Life,' *Toronto Star*, 20 January 2000)
- 'And as many times as I read Haines' little joke, and that's what it was, really, a little joke, as little as a joke could be, a private, almost microscopic joke ...' (Bill Cameron, 'What Was Avery Haines' Real Sin?' *Toronto Star*, 16 February 2000)
- 'Given the gallows humour that goes on in the newsroom all the time, there but for the grace of God go I and anyone else who's done it.' (Lorrie Goldstein, *Toronto Sun*, 19 January 2000)
- 'Take the firing of CTV NewsNet Avery Haines. On Saturday morning, during a taping, Haines flubbed her intro and cracked some innocuous stress-relieving jokes ... On Monday she was fired. Please. It's time for CTV to lighten up.' (Vinay Menon,' What's All This Juice and Joy?' *Toronto Star*, 20 January 2000)

- 'There's all kinds of newsroom humour, and we'd all be in trouble if we were held to account for it. (Slotek, 'City Gets a New Pulse,' *Toronto Sun*, 10 February 2000)
- The tape editor that went to air with that stuff should be thrown out as well. (Desmond Brown, 'Broadcast journalists Air Their Views on Firing of News Anchor,' *National Post*, 19 January 2000)
- 'If anyone deserves to be disciplined, it is the tape editor who mistakenly played the wrong tape of the two Ms Haines had recorded.' (editorial 'Firing Squad' *National Post*, 19 January 2000)
- 'Why didn't CTV fire the moron who punched the wrong button, you ask? Go figure. Maybe he or she was an affirmative action employee.' (George Jonas, 'When the Punishment Doesn't Fit the Crime,' *Toronto Sun*, 20 January 2000)

*The Discourse of Otherness and Bipolarization: Political Correctness, Identity Politics, and the Tyranny of Special Interest Groups versus Avery Haines, the Good, Compassionate, Fair-minded Individual*

The media use a number of discursive strategies to distinguish between 'we' and 'they' groups (i.e., in-groups and out-groups). These are often framed in the context of examining the values and norms of the dominant population vis-à-vis minority groups. In the quotes cited below, there is an emphasis on positive self-presentation, and on information that is positive in relation to Haines and, by extension, all others who are part of the in-group. 'We' represents the voices of the media – reasonable, professional, fair-minded citizens of Canada – who include Avery Haines. 'They' refers to communities that have overstepped the bounds of civil society in order to pursue their own agendas, and thereby ignored 'our' most cherished values.

Political correctness is a rhetorical strategy employed to stifle or silence debate on a wide variety of issues, including the need to bring non-dominant voices and perspectives into public discourse. As rhetoric, it polarizes positions with respect to issues of representation, multiculturalism, and equity. Attempts to remove racist or sexist language from everyday discourse are met with derision by the media and other 'cultural authorities':

- 'I think we in Canada have seen just how insidious is this politically correct phase we in North America are going through ... Our language, our ability to make ourselves understood to our fellow man, has been hijacked by extremists who, in the interests of their own causes, have convinced us that we do not know our own minds. Convinced us that we are all, deep down bigots ... we have been bamboozled by the professional left-wing rights lobbyists ... The race card has been played so many times, we now play it ourselves. The very mention of the words [black, lesbian gay, disabled–even wheelchair] set the antennae to quivering in all of us and sparked the zealots into action.' (Hartley Steward, 'Bamboozled by the Politically Correct,' *Toronto Sun*, 23 January 2000)

- 'It's not so much about me any more. It's about people feeling they can't say anything.' (Haines, in Margaret Wente, 'Open Mike with Avery Haines,' *Globe and Mail*, 20 January 2000)
- 'It's clear that what she said does not represent a set of beliefs or philosophy ... She was making a joke about political correctness.' (Pamela Wallin quoted in Brown, 'Broadcast Journalists Air Their Views on Firing of News Anchor.' *National Post*, 19 January 2000)
- 'If you really want to hear how we used to talk about these issues before politically correct speech became a way of life, listen to the John Oakley Show on CFRB. More importantly, listen to the response from the people who phone in ... He is prepared to discuss the particulars of any race or religion in a free-wheeling fashion, even employing humour, bless him ... Oakley might be hosting the last bastion of free speech in America.' (Hartley Steward, 'Bamboozled by the Politically Correct,' *Toronto Sun*, 23 January 2000)
- 'What is not open to question is that Haines immediately delivered a heartfelt apology and is deeply sorry and upset by what she said. Thus the matter should have been considered closed. There might have been some extremists who screamed for blood, but history has taught us that lynch mobs should be put in their place as quickly as possible ... Ask people as diverse, for example, as a member of the Reform party, a pro-life activist, or a Muslim if they have been called names in the media and you will receive an overwhelming yes. Our concern should not be over a few seconds of embarrassment for a newsreader but a presently acceptable liberal fundamentalism that is genuinely sinister.' (Michael Coren, 'Apology Should Have Ended It,' *Toronto Sun*, 20 January 2000)
- 'I know her to be a good person.' (Bill Carroll, CFRB's news director and Haines' former radio boss)
- 'I know those comments don't reflect her views.' (in Alan Findlay, 'Loose Lips Sink NewsNet Anchor,' *Toronto Sun*, 18 January 2000)

- 'I read the story and thought of all the people ... She's the newsroom spokesman for the downtrodden. She's not a racist or a bigot in any way. Knowing her as I know her, I can see the irony in the joke she was making. The audience, of course, didn't have the benefit of that.' (Gayle MacDonald, in Bill Carroll, 'CTV Anchor Fired for Making Offensive Remarks,' *Globe and Mail*, 18 January 2000)
- 'Of all the causes it is dangerous to mock these days, identity politics ranks at the top. The status of the victim has never been higher, and membership in victimhood is now due to everyone except white males.' (editorial, 'Lesbian Folk-Dancing,' *Globe and Mail*, 19 January 2000)
- 'The Sun rounded up the usual suspects (the Council of Canadians with Disabilities, the National Lesbian and Gay Journalists' Association, the Canadian Abilities Foundation), whose spokesmen variously pronounced the offending remarks as tasteless, flippant and that lowest of blows, even inappropriate. It would have been news if they had done otherwise, since they are essentially lobbyists.' (Christie Blatchford, 'This is CTV. You Will Not Be Funny,' *National Post*, 18 January 2000)
- 'We will justify the fear that free speech cannot survive in a diverse and multicultural society because there are too many interest groups looking to be insulted.' (editorial, 'Firing Squad,' *National Post*, 19 January 2000
- 'Why is Canada, the fairest, most tolerant and nicest place on Earth, a seething hotbed of political correctness run amok?' (Margaret Wente, 'Open Mike with Avery Haines,' *Globe and Mail*, 20 January 2000)
- 'Haines has joined that station a month after leaving CTV NewsNet for making politically incorrect jokes on the air.' ('Avery the Sequel on City.' *Toronto Sun*, 22 February 2000)

*The Discourse of Coercion and Oppressive Public Policies: Employment Equity Legislation Is an Unnecessary and Discriminatory Intervention*

Very often, on defending Haines, the media resorted to *topoi* (i.e., commonsense explanations). These constituted much of the subtext of the media discourse related to Haines' actions. Specifically, it was suggested that employment equity has a negative impact on media organizations (see the case study on employment equity). Many of the following comments reflect a backlash against equity policies – a backlash driven largely by White, able-bodied males. This, even though such policies have produced very little change in most workplaces for people of colour, people with disabilities, and Aboriginal peoples – three of the groups specifically covered by the federal government's Employment Equity Act (Employment Equity Act Annual Report, 1999). (Regarding the fourth group – women – there has been some improvement.)

- 'I was making fun at myself. I was poking fun at employment equity. I wasn't slamming any group.' (Avery Haines, in Gayle Macdonald, 'CTV Anchor Fired for Making Offensive Remarks,' the *Globe and Mail*, 18 January 2000)
- 'She was fired two days later. Why? Because her comments touched on a controversial subject: preferential hiring.' (editorial, 'Firing Squad,' the *National Post*, 10 January 2000)
- 'Thinking her ad lib would never make it to air, she poked fun at herself in a way that also lampooned the excesses of employment equity.' (Andrew Coyne, 'To Air Is Human' the *National Post*, 19 January 2000)
- 'If you purged all the newsrooms of everyone who's ever said anything rude about affirmative action, they'd be empty. Most other workplaces as well. And everyone knows it.' (Margaret Wente, 'Open Mike with Avery Haines,' the *Globe and Mail*, 20 January 2000)
- 'All things being approximately equal, minority or disadvantaged job candidates get the edge. I believe that may be CTV's policy ... As a female, she may have had the benefit of the policy; she certainly hadn't been harmed by it. But she was poking fun ... at a corporate and government policy without a license. That's what she's guilty of.' (Bill Cameron, 'What Was Avery Haines' Real Sin,' *Toronto Star*, 16 February 2000)
- 'Now it seems that Haines has become the [unwilling] poster girl for those who resent government-imposed employment equity rules ... for those who might have been passed over for a promotion because a woman/black/Asian/lesbian/paraplegic got the job instead. (Antonia Zerbisias, 'An Inadvertent Poster Girl,' *Toronto Star*, 23 January 2000)
- 'In the hierarchy of White male prejudices, group rights for women are now acceptable but not those for ethnics and the disabled.' (Haroon Siddiqui, 'Anti-Women, Anti-Minority Dinosaurs,' *Toronto Star*, 23 January 2000)

*The Discourse of Popular Support: Most People Don't Think What Avery Haines Did Was Wrong*

In this discourse, minorities are excluded from the construction of the 'Canadian self.' The media resort to polls and surveys, and to commentaries by 'important' cultural figures supporting prevailing dominant culture perspectives, to stifle the voices and views of minorities.

- 'The case of Avery Haines ... was featured yesterday on ABC's *The View,* where viewers were asked to call in their opinion on whether she should have lost her job. More than 80% of viewers said she shouldn't have been fired ... She has won the support of 99.9% of the people who had anything to say about this ... She is now a hero. She is now known and admired by influential persons, such as Barbara Walters.' (Liz Braun, 'She Should Look on the Bright Side,' *Toronto Sun,* 23 January 2000

- 'Most people, I think, said: "This doesn't offend me and I'm sure it isn't racist, homophobic, etc, but it sounds like it might be ..." The fact of the matter is most people aren't offended. Weren't offended. It only seems like most people because a minority – the language terrorists in this area – are kicking up such a racket, with the help of the media, they have won the day.' (Hartley Steward, 'Bamboozled by the Politically Correct,' *Toronto Sun,* 23 January 2000)

**Alternative Discourses**

The dozens of articles cited above demonstrate that most of the mainstream media constructed a dominant discourse with respect to the Haines controversy. There were very few alternative or oppositional discourses that critically analysed the media's account of the incident. Most journalists and editors either shared the views articulated above, or felt it would be too risky to challenge the deeply entrenched biases of their fellow journalists and editors – biases reflected in the language they used. However, there were a few exceptions to this: Jim Coyle, a columnist with the *Toronto Star;* Haroon Siddiqui, Editor Emeritus of the *Toronto Star'*s editorial page; and Hamlin Grange, a former journalist with the *Star,* who is now a CBC broadcaster and anchor.

In 'Callous Neglect of Words' Power Sank TV Anchor' (*Toronto Star,* 20 January 2000), Jim Coyle observed that one of the central arguments resorted to by the many journalists who defended Haines was that her words did not really mean anything significant, and that those who felt maligned should simply 'lighten up.' He responded that such a view reflects 'the cover that's been used for every slur that ever crossed human lips.' Haines's defenders also insisted that these statements did not reflect anything about the values that Haines holds or the kind of person she is. To this assumption, Coyle replied that though 'none of us can ever truly know about another's heart and mind, it's by our words and actions that people go ... And phrases like "gimping rubber legs" don't tend to cross the mind – much less the lips – of those who don't think of the handicapped in those demeaning terms.' Coyle finds it surprising that so many of Haines's colleagues 'opted to devalue the power and meaning of words – the very currency in which we trade.'

In 'Anti-Women, Anti-Minority Dinosaurs' (*Toronto Star*, 23 January 2000), Haroon Siddiqui argued that Haines's defenders were keen to canonize her 'as a martyr to political correctness.' He added: 'They chose to embrace all her feeble excuses to whitewash her inexcusable utterances against Asians, Blacks, stutterers and those in wheelchairs "with gimping, rubber legs" by saying that her joke was a simply a shot at herself.' Siddiqui challenged this notion, pointing out that self-deprecating humour 'is at one's own expense not others.' Although Haines claimed she was really only satirizing employment equity, she was, in Siddiqui's words, 'maligning minorities.'

In 'Journalists Don't Get It on Diversity' (*Toronto Star*, 28 January 2000), Hamlin Grange contended that Haines was naïve and ignorant of the harmful impact of her words on her colleagues working in the news media. According to Grange, her remarks were 'a reflection of the environment in which she and I work ... There is a derisive attitude in newsrooms toward diversity and employment equity.' He went on to state that any mention of the need for the media to be more diverse is met with either lip service or derision in the industry: 'Many in the media resent any observation that the media is primarily lily-white, at times insensitive, or out of touch with a vast number of Canadians who are not White.' He ended by noting that the media rarely put their own profession under scrutiny.

## Conclusions

Of the over forty articles that we analysed in this case study, almost thirty were highly supportive of Avery Haines and defended her actions and words. It is important to note that all of the oppositional discourses cited above were from the *Toronto Star*, and that all of the writers worked at the *Star* except for Grange, who once worked there. From the dominant discourse around the controversy, it seems clear that Haines as an individual is unwilling to engage in any form of critical self-reflection, and neither are the media in general. It can be argued that the media saw no problem with what Haines said because these kinds of discourses are normal in media organizations. Moreover, the dominant discourses employed by many journalists and editors served to stifle and silence alternative discourses. The media's first line of defence was to challenge and dismiss the claims made by minority organizations and communities that there was a serious problem with Haines's language. The media's refusal to even acknowledge – let alone validate – the voices of 'others' amounted to a clear demonstration that most of the media are locked into a collective mindset that is deeply threatened by the issues of inclusion, representation, and equity. All of this book's case studies underscore a key point about discourse – it is a terrain of struggle on which language is both a weapon and a defence. However, the contest between dominant and alternative discourses is not conducted on a level playing field; both power and resources are unequally distributed. People participate as socially constituted subjects whose discursive exchanges are shaped by power relations.

# 6

# *Globe and Mail* Editorials on Employment Equity

In this case study we analyse the *Globe and Mail*'s discourse on the subject of employment equity. Using two different forms of critical discourse analysis (CDA), we examine how that newspaper through its editorials sustains an anti-equity ideological position. The first form of CDA we apply utilizes a macro-level framework to explore the erroneous assumptions, myths, and misrepresentations that underpin the *Globe*'s editorials. This will help illuminate how 'text' and 'talk' (van Dijk, 1988) are used to promote, support, and communicate a particular ideology – in effect, to maintain the power held by White, able-bodied males. The *Globe* uses a form of argumentation that draws on democratic liberal values and principles. The second method of CDA focuses on the linguistic structures the *Globe*'s editors use in constructing their editorials. We examine the organization of the text, and show how through the choice of specific words, images, and sentence structures, a discourse is constructed. The timeframes we have selected are related to periods when the issue rose to the top of the public agenda.

Van Dijkian critical linguistic analysis (1998) strongly emphasizes editorial writing. It is important to analyse editorials because they are not merely idle statements of senior writers' opinions; often they express the broader ideological stance of the newspaper's owners and managers. They are evidence of the interlocking power structures of any given society; in fact, they are often addressed not only to the reading public but also to society's economic and power elites. Van Dijk (1991) categorizes editorials according to the following elements:

- *Definition.* The editorial defines a situation or event and summarizes what actually happened to create it.

- *Explanation.* The editorial explains the situation.
- *Evaluation or moral commentary.* The editorial discusses 'what will happen, what should happen or what should be done' about an event or situation.

At the time these editorials were written, the *Globe* was the only 'national' newspaper in the country. It was also the main media vehicle for Canada's conservative elements and political right wing. Its criticisms of employment equity legislation did much to undermine that legislation, and may well have helped ensure that it was rescinded in the province of Ontario. It is worth noting here that in the debate on Bill 8, 'The Job Quotas Repeal Act, 1995, that took place in the Ontario Legislature, a Conservative MPP stated: 'Let me also quote very briefly from a Globe and Mail article "Designed by well meaning people to encourage integration, employment equity in fact works against it, encouraging Canadians to huddle together in groups and feed the unhealthy obsession with race and gender that has seized Canadian society in the 1990's."' Later, the same MPP quoted the *Globe* again: 'Every Canadian should give it hearty good riddance' (Hansard, 30 October 1995, session 36.1)

### Background to the Enactment of Employment Equity Legislation

Concern over employment discrimination against people of colour (visible minorities), women, people with disabilities, and Aboriginal peoples led the federal government to establish a royal commission on equality in employment (Abella, 1984). Its task was to inquire into the employment practices of eleven designated Crown and government-owned corporations and to explore the most effective means of promoting equality for the four groups cited above. Its findings echoed earlier studies and public inquiries: bias and discrimination were endemic in the employment system. The commissioner, Judge Rosalie Abella, argued in the commission's report that strong measures were needed to remedy the impact of discriminatory attitudes and behaviours.'

She recommended employment equity legislation. The Employment Equity Act became law in 1986, and applies to Crown corporations and federally regulated employers with 100 or more employees.

The act was intended to achieve equality in the workplace and to correct the conditions of disadvantage in employment experienced by four designated groups: women, aboriginal peoples, people with disabilities, and members of visible minorities (Agocs et al., 1992). Employment equity legislation provided a framework to support a diverse workforce. Employment equity was supposed to identify workplace policies and practices that, though neutral in their intentions, were discriminatory in their effects or results. The goal of employment equity was fair treatment and equitable representation throughout the workplace.[1]

Equality in employment means that no one is denied opportunities for reasons that have nothing to do with inherent ability (Abella, 1984). The act required all federally regulated employers to file an annual report with the Canadian Employment and Immigration Commission. This report was to provide information for a full year on the representation of members of designated groups by occupational group and salary range, and on members of those groups who had been hired, promoted, or terminated. Employers were also required to prepare an annual employment equity plan with goals and timetables, and to retain this plan for at least three years. The Employment Equity Act was revised by Parliament in 1995; the legislation was strengthened, and the public service, the RCMP, and the military were brought under the purview of the act.

The language of the federal act was not itself racialized; however, responses to the legislation within and outside of government were racialized in a number of ways. Efforts to make the Canadian public service more representative of the Canadian public had failed. The 1996 annual report of the Canadian Human Rights Commission documented in stark numbers the huge gap between the government's commitment to a fully diversified public service and its dismal record in promoting minorities.[2] In examining some of the reasons for this failure, Senator Noel Kinsella – a one-time senior bureaucrat with Heritage Canada – noted that 'Institutions act as collective memory carrying forward values, principles and traditions' (in Samuel and Karam, 1996).

Faced with the finding that discrimination against designated groups was widespread, persistent, and systemic, Ontario in 1993 became the first province in Canada to introduce employment equity legislation. On 13 December 1995, the Harris government rescinded that legislation, employing the rhetorical strategies that the *Globe* had developed. The title of the act, 'Bill to Repeal Job Quotas' and the name given to the new legislation, 'Equal Opportunity Plan,' reflected a discursive shift from the discourse of the former NDP government. The Conservative government was rejecting the concept of systemic discrimination, in effect declaring that the Ontario Human Rights Code and Commission could deal with any individual cases of discrimination (Goldberg, 1996).

**Rhetorical Arguments Used by the Globe and Mail**

We analyse the first set of editorials by focusing on the central arguments the editors used to challenge the concept of employment equity and the legislation pertaining to it. Our analysis shows that the editors utilized a discourse that was based on the discourse of liberalism. However, these editorials utilized discursive elements that were based on a number of misrepresentations, unsubstantiated assertions, anecdotes, and erroneous assumptions. They disguised their attacks on employment equity as defences of traditional Canadian values. The central discourses, which were closely interlinked, were as follows:

*'Employment equity is reverse discrimination'*

In their editorial 'The Discrimination Clause' (8 March 1995: A18), the editors argued that the law 'effectively discriminates against some individuals on the basis of colour and gender.' Farther down it became clear that the editor's target was ... 'overt discrimination in hiring against white, able-bodied males.' In 'Why Merit Matters' (13 October 1995), the editors contended: 'The bill is clearly discriminatory. By requiring employers to favour members of designated groups, it effectively requires them to discriminate against members of the undesignated group: that is, able-bodied white men.'

*'Employment equity is hiring by quotas and ignores the merit principle'*

In 'Why Merit Matters' (13 October 1995), the editors argued that the legislation 'was unquestionably a quota law ... The main evil of the law is its implicit attack on the principle of merit.' The editors went on to argue that the merit principle has

> always been cherished most dearly by the disadvantaged who regard it as a ladder to better things. For generations, even centuries, disadvantaged people have pleaded to be released from the pigeonholes in which others place them and evaluated on their ability as individuals ...

> The supporters of employment equity *would* throw all this out the window ... Instead of disregarding the group identity of people in hiring and promotion, we will fixate on it. Instead of encouraging employers to hire the best person for the job, we will require them to tote up their workers like so many jelly beans.

On the editorial page, on 18 March 1995, in an opinion piece titled 'This Is No Way to Run a Railroad. Or a Newspaper. Or a Province,' the *Globe*'s editor-in-chief, William Thorsell, argued that 'ambitious social engineers in Ontario have taken us beyond the negative option of human rights law ... and into the affirmative option of hiring quotas.' He went on to contend that affirmative action *requires* discrimination in hiring based on sex, race, and ability.

The *Globe* editorial 'Real Employment Equity' (13 June 1995) supported the election promise of the Conservative government to rescind employment equity. It stated that the legislation 'set up a quota system for hiring in Ontario. It would have prevented some companies from hiring the most talented people. It would have required employers to discriminate against some individuals (especially able-bodied white males) to benefit others.' This editorial went on to argue that employment equity encourages 'Ontarians to think of each other – and resent each other – as racial and gender units.'

The theme of identity politics was revisited in the editorial 'Please Identify Yourself' (18 June 1996: A14), in which the editors contended: 'The decomposition of true liberalism into identity politics afflicts more than interest groups such as the National Action Committee on the Status of Women.' This same piece said of the rescinding of employment equity in Ontario: 'Ontario came within a hair's breadth of state employment quotas based on race and disability.'

This same editorial concluded by sharply criticizing the University of British Columbia's advertisement for a president for including a statement of concern about the underrepresentation of women, Aboriginal people, visible minorities, and people with disabilities. The *Globe* understood the statement 'the university welcomes all qualified applicants, especially members of these designated employment equity groups' to mean that 'UBC is prepared to discriminate in hiring on the basis of race, gender and disability in hiring its President.'

*'Employment equity challenges the fundamental tenets of liberalism such as individual rights and equal opportunity'*

On 18 March 1995, in a piece titled 'There Are Not Two Kinds of Equality in the World,' Thorsell wrote that there are two kinds of equality: equality of opportunity as enshrined in Section 15(1) of the Charter of Rights and Freedoms, and equality of outcomes as sanctioned by Section 15(2) of the Charter. The Charter sanctions affirmative action laws, programs, and activities as means of ameliorating the conditions of disadvantaged groups. He contended that 'the individual's right to equal protection and benefit of the law' in Subsection (2) is a right that 'defines our democracy.' He rejected the notion of substantive equality – that is, that the state must ensure that all social groups reap equal benefits from the law, even if different or special treatment is required to ensure such equality. He argued that equal opportunity allows all individuals to participate in all aspects of Canadian life. In his article of 18 March, he declared that we are in 'a moral and philosophical mess. The nullification of individual rights in favour of group preferences mocks the very foundation of our democracy.'

The ideological schemata underpinning Thorsell's perspective are based on the following implicit and erroneous assumptions:

1. The only 'qualified,' meritorious individuals for jobs or promotions are White, able-bodied males.
2. Discrimination may exist in isolated instances, but women and minorities do not suffer from systemic discrimination. Most employers are 'colour-blind,' and neutral in their attitudes toward hiring and promoting women, people with disabilities, and Aboriginal peoples.
3. In a liberal democracy, individual rights must take primacy over group rights. Any recognition of group rights leads directly to the unravelling of the democratic state.
4. Equal opportunity is presumed to exist, so employment equity is an unnecessary intrusion and intervention by the state. Fairness is best achieved by treating everyone the same.
5. Employment equity requires that White, able-bodied males be excluded from workplaces and results in an epidemic of reverse discrimination.
6. Any legislation or public policy that targets a particular group for 'preferential treatment' (other than White, able-bodied males) leads to victim-focused identities, conflict, and division.
7. Employment equity and other proactive, affirmative-based programs are a serious threat to a liberal democratic society.

## A Micro-Level Linguistic Analysis of the Discourse of Employment Equity

In the following section, we carry out a more detailed linguistic (micro-level) analysis of the *Globe*'s discourse on employment equity, examining the actual structure of news making through editorial writing.

*Editorial 1: 'Time for Debate on Employment Equity' (17 February 1995)*

This editorial's headline calls for a debate, but the editorial itself nowhere does. The use of the term 'debate' makes it sound as if the editorial writers want true dialoguing or debating to take place, rather than unilateral actions. The article does not really call for debate except in the last paragraph, where it asks political parties to take a stand on the issue of employment equity. In sum, it is asking Canadians not to debate employment equity but to fight it. 'Canadians like to think of themselves as more liberal and progressive than Americans, but in at least one area, the United States has been "ahead" for years ... Pollsters say Californians would approve the proposition by a big majority. No doubt Canadians would too, if asked a similar question.'

The *source* or *evidence* for this assertion is 'pollsters.' No other source for this or the following statements is offered. That Canadians would also follow this lead shows *presupposition without evidence*; there is no indication that Canadians would also approve the proposal. 'Though most would support removing barriers to equal employment in the workplace, the idea that governments ... is as repugnant to most Canadians as it is to Americans. Some opinion polls here have shown a three to one majority against affirmative action.' The phrase 'though most would support' is not backed by any evidence that most Canadians would support removing barriers. It is based on an *assumption* which refers back to the 'liberal and progressive' ethos of this society and which reinforces the view that Canadians are really progressive people and that this legislation is not in keeping with such progressiveness. Moreover, by citing the figure of a three-to-one majority against affirmative action, the editorial is playing a *numbers game* the intent of which is to impress readers with how many are against that policy.

This quote is also *vague* in that nowhere does it state the numerical basis for the three-to-one judgment. 'Last year, it brought in the country's most heavy handed employment equity law ... How are Canadians going to fight these laws?' The use of language such as 'heavy handed' is an example of hyperbole, or the use of exaggerated language. So is the idea that such laws need to be 'fought.' 'Not obviously through human rights commissions ... not through direct democracy either ... not even through the charter.' By calling into play other government agencies created through legislation, the editorial is *impugning* the human rights laws that already exist in Canada and dismissing them as incapable of 'fighting' against employment equity legislation. Furthermore, it is planting by *autosuggestion* the idea that the people have lost their voice because 'direct democracy' and its procedures will not work. It is suggesting that this legislation is so terrible that ordinary democratic procedures cannot stop it. 'Not through the Charter of Rights and Freedoms. Section 15(2) explicitly exempts from the normal equality provisions of the Charter 'any law, program or activity that has as its object of amelioration of the conditions of disadvantaged groups.'

In a strong *leap of logic*, the sentence goes on to state: 'Such programs are [clearly] discriminatory and do violate basic principles of equality.' It makes the *assumption* that the framers of the Charter were motivated to exclude ameliatory actions simply because they believed them to be discriminatory. There are likely many other reasons why these actions were excluded – for example, the difficulties in defining or interpreting the law – that are not acknowledged in this piece. Here, an important and complex piece of legislation such as the Charter is cited to legitimize the editorial's claim that existing legislation cannot be used to fight employment equity.

How are Canadians going to fight these laws? The editorial claims that the fight must use 'ordinary political processes' and calls on political parties to show how this legislation 'accords with Canadian values of fairness and equal opportunity.' By again referring to these Canadian values, the article is once more framing the employment equity legislation as negating or being against these basic and positive Canadian values.

The moral of this editorial is that employment equity needs to be placed again on the 'political agenda' and that every party should be 'forced' to take a stand. The *implication* is that not every party wants to take up this issue. The editorial is castigating the present government that introduced this legislation in the first place, it follows that the 'party' that needs to be 'forced' is the NDP. So this editorial is not only criticizing the legislation but the government as well.

*Editorial 2: 'Employment Inequity,' 1 September 1994*

The headline begins with *negativization* in that that the word 'inequity' is used rather than equity; the headline thus sets the tone for a negative appraisal of the issue. It immediately alerts the reader to how the editorial views the legislation, and without any delay offers its opinion about it.

One of the most common strategies used in presenting an editorial argument is *frontage* – that is, placing a key point, idea, or item at the very
beginning of an article. This point is the most important one to be made
in the piece and the one the writer wants to impress on the reader immediately. In this editorial, the point placed at the *front* or first position is
that employment equity is responsible for the unemployment of Ontarians who are not Native or people of colour – more specifically, people of
African origins. 'Unemployed Ontarians would be well advised to ferret
out that ancestor who claimed native roots or a history on an African
slave ship. Or they might even consider inventing such a relative.' The
words '*ferret out*' are suggestive of exaggeration or *hyperbole*, in that this
term reflects the action of an animal engaged in furious digging. The
suggestion is that as a result of employment equity legislation, unemployed Ontarians need to work furiously hard to make claims to an ancestor of colour in order to ensure they will be eligible for employment.

The reference here to Native roots and African slave ships *trivializes*
the history of both groups. But the most striking form of *argumentation*
being resorted to here relates to the word 'inventing.' The implication is
that unemployed Ontarians have been made so desperate by this iniqui-
tous legislation that they must falsify or 'invent' relatives of colour.
These are the depths to which such people must sink in order to find
employment in present-day Ontario.

In the very next paragraph the editorial hedges its bets: 'That, it
seems, is the doorway to a job.' Through the use of the words 'it seems,'
the writers are retreating somewhat from the strong position they took
in the opening paragraph. This linguistic technique, known as *hedging*
or *vagueness*, allows writers to distance themselves from responsibility for
their statements. Having caught the reader's attention to the point
being made, the editorial retreats slightly. In this way it can claim a
degree of objectivity.

The editorial then turns its sights on the minister. It states that the
legislation, 'which comes into effect today and promises, at least as far as
Citizenship Minister Elaine Ziemba is concerned, a new tomorrow.'
Here the minister's words are being subjected to a degree of mockery
and *ridicule*. The implication of this statement is that the promise of a
'new tomorrow' holds for the minister but not for anyone else. It continues: 'Ms. Ziemba says in a recitation of high principle that is so much a
part of her government.' 'High principle' is yet another example of
arguing by *opposites*. In fact, the editorial believes there is no high princi-

ple involved here, and is using those words deliberately to make the point that there is not.

The editorial continues. 'Employers have been given the word, explicitly or otherwise.' The words 'explicitly or otherwise' send a vague but also *threatening* message to the reader. This is because the term 'otherwise' is not further explained or defined. What are we to read into the term 'otherwise'? What will happen to an employer who ignores that word?

'Rather than deal with the hiring process, the government has chosen to monitor the results and has created a 63–member bureaucracy to deal with the masses of reports that businesses will have to feed into the system to make sure the universe is unfolding as it should.' This sentence is based on an untried and unproven *assumption* that the government is not interested in dealing with the hiring process. It could be argued that the whole point of employment equity legislation is to deal with exactly that! The editorial then notes that a bureaucracy has been created. In specifying the exact number of members, the editorial is using the *numbers game* to frame its argument. The reader is supposed to be aghast at this vast number of bureaucrats who will deal with the issue. It could be argued, however, that governments are in the business of creating and maintaining bureaucracies – so why make an issue of this? At heart, the argument is framed in terms of contrast: instead of dealing with the hiring process – which they rightly should – the government is creating more bureaucracies. Yet the argument is based on the *faulty premise* that employment equity does not deal with the hiring process.

'Masses of reports' is another example of playing the *numbers game*; furthermore, these words are an example of *exaggeration* and *hyperbole*, in that they imply there will be large numbers of reports. This is based on an unproven *premise*.

The trite expression 'the universe is unfolding as it should' is used to *trivialize* the issue. It *ridicules* the government for believing that its legislation is important enough to influence the universe; at the same time, it trivializes the legislation itself.

Later, 'there is still the occasional woman who chooses to describe herself as an unpaid homemaker. Such options will wreck havoc for the bureaucrats who crunch numbers at Queen's Park.' Use of the term 'occasional woman,' when the editorial writer knows there are far larger numbers of women who are homemakers, is an example of *minimalization*. This strategy is used here mainly to criticize the methods that bureaucrats will be using to measure the results of the equity act, and suggests that the legislation is flawed because those results cannot be measured properly. Moreover, this one supposed *fact* is used to besmirch the entire process. The next sentence goes even further by resorting to strong *hyperbolic* language, such as 'wreck havoc,' to describe the work of the 'number crunchers' (another example of *trivialization*).

'The NDP government is nothing if not reasonable, and it does not expect all this to fall into place overnight.' This is argumentation by *reverse,* in that the meaning is exactly the opposite of what has been written. The editorial writers really believe that the NDP government is unreasonable, and they frame this point not only by reversing it but also by using the double-negative. A double-negative often requires the reader to read slowly or several times to fully comprehend its meaning. It is used here to imply that the government is not reasonable, but that the writers are too charitable, objective, or fair to say so.

Finally, 'Of course, this utopian ideal carries a price tag, and the Ontario taxpayer will be billed $9.3 million in 1994–95 for the exercise. The cost of compliance for businesses is anyone's guess.' Here the legislation is *ridiculed* by being described as 'utopian.' The *assumption* is that it cannot be effective; after all, utopias, being ideals, are unattainable by definition. The real moral or conclusion of this editorial that a great deal of money is going to be spent in an attempt to attain an unrealizable objective. By citing the amount of $9.3 million, the writers are again employing a *numbers game*: readers are to be shocked by the size of the amount. Furthermore, the cost is to be born by Ontario taxpayers. The language here resorts to *personalization* techniques to bring the issue home. It is made to sound as if each and every Ontario taxpayer will be billed in order to reach the budgeted figure. It is hoped that such an appeal to each individual Ontarian's purse will make the reader more readily agree with the editorial's criticism of the legislation. Finally, it seems rather *superfluous* to point out to the sophisticated readers of the *Globe and Mail* that the costs of implementing the employment equity legislation are to be borne by the taxpayer, considering that all government programming is paid for by the public purse! The only reason to include such an obvious point – especially at the very end of the editorial – is to further convince the reader by *personalizing* the issue.

*Editorial 3: 'Employment Equity's True Colours,' 12 November 1993*

By using the word 'true' in the headline, the writers are establishing the *assumption* that there has been something hidden in the past.

'In politics, a gaffe is when you tell the truth.' This lead sentence places in the forefront the point that the government is not telling the truth. This is an example of *topoi*, a special form of argumentation that involves resorting to commonplace or commonsense notions to explain events. The idea that politicians are dissemblers is widely held. What makes this fronted argument especially noteworthy is that the government being impugned has been formed by the NDP, a party that the generally conservative *Globe and Mail* is highly critical of.

'On Tuesday ... made a whale of a gaffe ... slicing the great beast open, allowing its putrescent vapours to fill the air.' In this extract, several techniques are used. The size of the gaffe is being compared to that of the world's largest animal – an example of *metaphor*. The language throughout this line – 'great beast,' 'putrescent vapours' – is highly *exaggerated* and *hyperbolic*. The reader is meant to be repulsed by the magnitude of the government's actions.

'There is an opening ... a position paying $74,000–$111,000 a year.' By including the salary, the editorial again uses the *numbers game*. The hidden message is that this government is paying out substantial sums of money. Yet in all likelihood, the sum is drawn from the civil service schedule of salaries and is in line with what senior managers are generally paid.

'Nice work if you can get it.' This short expression coming immediately after the job description is rather snide in tone. The bulk of the criticism in this editorial focuses on the job posting being restricted to members of the employment equity groups, so it is really unnecessary for the main argument. It is used, it seems, mainly to take another pot shot at the NDP government and its legislation.

'English speaking white males, thank you for not applying.' By describing those who need not apply, the editorial is *playing to the sentiments of the readers*. The article has already *assumed* that 'many of those reading this newspaper' could not apply for the position. With this line, the editorial is identifying many of its readers who are in the mainstream majority group. In this way it is reinforcing and legitimating any biases these readers already have. The final phrase thanking them is an example of *sarcasm* being used to hammer home a point.

'Honesty is one thing that has been missing from the debate on employment equity, with the truth obscured by layer upon layer of carefully scripted pseudo- science, bafflegab and out and out lies.' The descriptive words used in this passage – pseudo-science, bafflegab, out and out lies – are examples of *hyperbole*. The entire sentence is an example of the technique of *parallelism*, in that it unites three different word/

phrase combinations and culminates in the *repeated* 'out and out' to strengthen the point of dishonesty.

'Behind the rhetorical Potemkin Village that Queen's Park has built around employment equity.' Here the techniques of *metaphor* and strongly negative *imagery* are being used. 'Potemkin village' is a historical allusion associated with secrecy, hiding, spying, and hypocrisy. It reflects the writers' awareness that the *Globe*'s elite and educated readers will know what is being referred to, and will *compare* the government's secrecy around employment equity with a particular period of Russian history characterized by negative features such as extreme secrecy.

'Such 'positive measures' are now government policy.' By putting quotation marks around the words 'positive measures,' the editorial is suggesting just the *reverse*. Actually, it believes these measures are negative.

'... goes on to explain that blatant discrimination – whoops, 'positive measures' Here, the writers are clearly expressing their opinion that the measures constitute blatant discrimination. However, by injecting the childlike words 'whoops, positive measures' into the argument, they are *trivializing* the meaning of 'positive measures.' A similar form of argumentation is involved in the following sentence, which begins, 'Funny, that's not what the government has been telling the public.' Usually a sentence in an editorial in such a newspaper would not begin with the word 'funny,' but this one does, for the sake of *trivializing* the issue.

'The truth about Bill 79, ... can hardly be seen for all the saccharine coating.' Continuing with the theme of disguise that the term 'saccharine coating' suggests, the editorial now states with a degree of *assertiveness* that it knows the real truth behind this legislation. It then goes on to provide some carefully chosen excerpts from the bill. This is an example of the strategy of *incompleteness*. Not all aspects of the legislation are cited, but only those with which the editorial disagrees most strenuously.

'The goings-on in the Ontario Public Service make it clear that employment equity is about quotas, pure and simple. Yet the government insists that the great virtue of its legislation is that it contains no quotas, only 'goals' and 'timetables.' There's no difference, of course, but the government assumes its citizens will never figure that out.' The expression 'pure and simple' reflects the strategy of *simplifying* or even *oversimplifying* ideas that are rather more complex. By making this blanket assertion, the editorial is simplifying a very complex argument. It continues in this assertive manner, stating 'there's no difference' without providing any *evidence* or *proof* that there is no difference. It then underlines the point by adding the words 'of course.' In so doing it is also resorting to *topoi* – that is, it is suggesting that the fact of 'no difference' is patently clear and obvious to all except the government, which has stated that there is a difference. Finally, it argues that the government is deliberately misleading the public, who are too stupid to realize it. In this way the editorial is insulting not only the government but the people as well.

'As the OPS shenanigans show ... in the interest of getting the 'right' numbers ... this is what ... calls 'equal treatment and fairness.' This is what the NDP calls 'social justice.' This paragraph begins by using the *pejorative* word 'shenanigans' to describe the government's actions. It continues by placing quotation marks around all the words drawn from either the legislation or the words of the minister. This is again an example of *reverse* or *opposite meanings*: the editorial does not believe that the legislation will create 'right' numbers, or that it is an example of 'equal treatment,' or that it will bring about 'social justice.'

'And so his lunacy on stilts marches on, mindless of the warped society it is dedicated to creating.' The phrase 'lunacy on stilts' is a clear example of hyperbole. So is the term 'warped society.' In both instances, an extreme form of language is being employed to make the point.

'The only way to stop it is [sic] for the NDP government to make a few more gaffes. The only way to stop it is for a few more people to speak the truth.' In this final paragraph, the editorial reaches its concluding moral. It reverts back to the theme of the NDP government's dishonesty, stating it should make more gaffes because only through its inadvertent mistakes will the real truth – which it wants to keep hidden – come out. The technique of *substitution* is used so that the word 'gaffe' really means 'truth.' The same words – 'the only way' – are used to begin the last two sentences of the editorial. This is *parallelism* at work.

**Conclusions**

In this case study we have a clear example of how editorials are used to communicate with particular constituencies that form part of the reading audience. Moreover, the newspaper is even cited in parliamentary debate. Through these editorials, the *Globe and Mail* is addressing the social, economic, and political elite, which constitutes its main readership. The central narrative, and the myths, assumptions, and images that the editors draw on to construct this discourse resonate with those who do not need proactive programs and measures to preserve their power and privilege. The editorials reassure White, able-bodied males about what they are not: they are not unqualified recipients of unfair advantage; they are not demanding special interest groups; and they are not the recipients of costly government assistance programs. The *Globe* presents the privileges of maleness, Whiteness, and able-bodiedness as natural and normal. It also presents any attempt to change the status quo as a threat to the nation's most cherished liberal values.

The *Globe*'s editors frame almost all their arguments on the notion of liberal equality, which is premised on the claim that all people begin from the same starting point. From the liberal, meritocratic point of view, society merely provides the conditions under which individuals who are differently endowed can make their way. The individual is seen as autonomous, as essentially unconnected to others, and as dedicated to pursuing his or her own interests. If all begin with the same opportunity and have the same rights, then the outcome must be fair. Thus, according to the 'liberal' arguments employed by the *Globe*'s editors, neither collective (group) rights nor state intervention are required to ensure justice (see Wetherell and Potter, 1992; Goldberg, 1993).

This case study also illustrates how dominant or backlash discourse draws clear connections between marginalized groups in order to marginalize them even more. To make its case against employment equity, the *Globe*'s editors had to trivialize the multiple social disadvantages experienced by the disabled, racial minorities, women, lesbians, and so on. It had to draw on the discourse of liberalism and the reassuring ideals of individualism, equal opportunity, fairness, and merit to reinforce the message that what is at stake in this debate is not only the well-being of White, able-bodied males, but also the future of the democratic state. It resorted to the rhetorical strategies of hyperbole, exaggeration, mitigation, oversimplification, trivialization, and ridicule to tell its master narrative. However, as journalist, editor, and broadcaster Irshad Manji (1995) has suggested: 'With all the stories in the media that focus on employment equity, very little is said about employment practices within the media.' One could very well ask whether the *Globe*'s vehement opposition to employment equity lies in the fact that it has practised a form of preferential treatment for almost all of its history for the benefit of White (mainly male) journalists, editors, and managers.

## PART III
## IMMIGRATION DISCOURSE

The next chapters offer case studies on the issue of immigration. In chapter 5 we focus on *The National Post* because many ethnoracial communities see it as having a strong anti-immigrant bias. It is also one of the two national newspapers published in Canada. The first case study in chapter 5 looks specifically at a number of articles about immigration written by one columnist, Diane Francis. The second considers how the *Post* has racialized the Tamil community; this analysis includes news stories, columns, and editorials.

Van Dijk (1998) provides an ideological schema for everyday text and talk as it relates to the *subject* of immigration. By *subject* we mean either a single concept, such as education or crime, that reflects a large social or political domain; or, a complex issue about which the media offer a number of specific news reports, columns, and editorials. The media's coverage of the subject of immigration incorporates the following rhetorical motifs:

- Who belongs in this country?
- Who should be admitted to (or removed from) the country?
- What policies should be enacted to keep *them* out?
- What are the goals of immigration restrictions?
- What values and norms are applied in these activities?
- What are the relations between *us* and *them?*
- What is at risk for 'Us' (health, education, welfare system, social stability, etc.)?
- What resources do *we* have to deal with the problem (public policies, legislation, enforcement procedures)?
- What new actions are required to protect our space, our national identity/citizenship, and culture?

Most rhetorical arguments used in the case studies in chapter 7, 'The *National Post's* discourses on immigration, Refugees, and the Tamils,' chapter 8, 'News Discourses and the Problematization of Chinese Migrants,' and chapter 9, 'The Racialization of Crime,' define the power base and the interests of the in-group. Underlying the immigration discourse is this fundamental question: What do 'we' need to defend to maintain our (dominant) position? As van Dijk points out, similar values and assumptions can be used to organize the attitudes people have about immigrants or minorities in the workplace. The overall intent is exclusion or inferiorization. Racist ideologies help self-define the in-group as superior – as having, both individually and collectively, quali-ties and attributes not possessed by the 'others.' Thus, in this study of the immigration discourse we find that the function of racialized dis-course is to identify and describe 'threatening' out-groups against which bias and discrimination can be rationalized and excused.

# 7

# The *National Post*'s Discourse on Immigration, Refugees, and the Tamils

In this chapter we examine the coverage of immigration as published in the *National Post*. This newspaper was selected for intensive analysis because of its well-known anti-immigration perspective. We begins by offering some examples of how the *National Post* deals with immigration issues; then we focus on two case studies. The first case study examines a series of articles written by the *Post*'s featured columnist on immigration and refugee issues, Diane Francis. The second case study deals exclusively with the *Post*'s targeted coverage of Canada's Tamil community.

A search of the *Post* archives between December 1998 and the end of September 2000 revealed a total of sixty-one articles in which immigration was the main theme. Included in this total are editorials, columns, and a few feature articles written by guest writers.

The articles can be categorized as follows: thirty-two articles dealing with negative aspects of immigration (policies and practices); seven dealing with Chinese refugees; seven dealing with justice/crime issues; four dealing with politics; one dealing with business; three dealing with specific country cases; and three dealing with other topics. In addition, there were ten positive articles on immigration. In total, then, there are sixty-seven articles (although there were 61 articles, several fit more than one category and were counted more than once, increasing the category count to 67). The overwhelming majority of the articles, features, and editorials are opposed to current immigration policies and practices and critical of the values and norms of immigrants and refugees. Only 6.1 per cent can be classified as positive, and of the ten articles in this category, guest columnists rather than staff reporters wrote more than half.

The *Post* treated any issue that dealt with immigration, from whatever part of the world, as a discursive event/crisis. For example, on 28 September 2000 the paper published an article about an actor from Hong Kong who was denied entry into Canada because of his alleged connections to a triad gang. The only evidence cited for these connections came from the U.S. Sub-Committee on Asian Organized Crime. In another article, dated 30 September 2000, the country in question was Jordan and described how the RCMP had discovered a large and 'ingenious' immigration smuggling scheme involving fifty-seven 'would-be' Jordanian immigrants. In another article, dated 19 April 2000, China was again the subject of inquiry; the journalist was writing about the warning to China sent by Elinor Caplan, the immigration minister, about the risks of human smugglers. It noted that a public education campaign would be launched to dissuade people from smuggling. This was followed, on 26 September 2000, with another piece about smugglers raising their fees. This was interpreted as meaning that Ottawa's anti-smuggling program was proving effective. In another piece, it was suggested that Ottawa's policies were contributing to the traffic in sex slaves: 'Canada's open immigration policies are contributing to its emerging role in the international trafficking of sex slaves, according to women interviewed for a year-long federal government study on the issue' (15 April 2000).

Only ten *Post* articles on the subject of immigration could be viewed as positive in tone and approach. One of these was an opinion piece by a guest columnist, John Koopman, titled 'We Benefit from Immigrants' (26 April 1999). Koopman made the argument that immigrants benefit the economies of countries such as the United States, and concluded that as *The Economist* states, 'taken at face value the data suggests that deterring immigration ... would be a short-sighted strategy with long-run costs likely to exceed by far any immediate benefits.'

Though the *Post* holds to an anti-immigration discourse in almost all of its coverage, this discourse is articulated most clearly by one of its columnists, Diane Francis. She openly acknowledges that she is on anti-immigration 'crusade,' and it is she who has written most of the articles criticizing Canada's immigration and refugee policies. In the following section we analyse some of her articles using critical discourse analysis (CDA).

## Case Study 1: Diane Francis's Discourse on Immigration

In her 'crusade' against the country's immigration and refugee policies, Francis has embraced a great many rhetorical themes, all of which are based on the following assumptions and allegations:

- Most refugee claims are 'bogus.'
- Refugees are 'illegal' entrants to this country.
- Refugees 'defraud' out system by hiring lawyers, using court time, and so on.
- Refugees use up millions in tax dollars in pressing their claims through the system.
- Refugees commit crimes against Canadians.
- Refugees are a health hazard to Canadians; they bring illness and even death to Canadian citizens.
- Ottawa's refugee determination process is flawed, expensive, and unwieldy and allows too many bogus refugees into the country.
- Immigration ministers have been Liberals, who are too soft and who collude with the 'Immigration Industry.'
- There is an 'Immigration Industry' comprising people who want to bring refugees and immigrants into the country.
- Any government official or any member of the public who challenges the government policy is called a 'racist' or 'redneck.' This keeps 'soft-hearted' Canadians from complaining about immigration and refugee policies.
- It is erroneous and 'against the facts' to think that the country requires immigrants.
- Right-wing groups like the Canada First Immigration Reform Committee, headed by Paul Fromm, are cited with approval and as sources of information.
- 'Good' refugees include those from Kosovo (and presumably those from other White countries).

Though Francis has written on many aspects of immigration, one of her chief targets has been the Chinese boat people who began arriving in British Columbia in 1999 (see case study on the Chinese migrants). She often uses the Chinese boat people as a 'lead in' to her general criticism of immigration policies: 'Chinese boat people and stowaways illegally entering Canada have grabbed headlines but 2,000 bogus refugees per month are getting in without so much as in interview with an immigration officer, says a government source' (8 January 2000). Note the use of the *assumption* in this statement that all of the 2,000 are, in fact, bogus. In fact, their status as refugees is determined when their cases are heard. Francis here is also using the old journalistic strategy of citing unnamed government sources. In the same article she later cites the same unnamed source as follows: '"I don't think in all my experience that I have seen one person that we would normally think of as a true refugee," said the source disgustedly.' Francis then comments on this statement: 'So say the "R" word and you're in with all the goodies that Canadians enjoy. Once in, they use our tax dollars to hire Legal Aid lawyers to wear out the system but never their stay.' In this excerpt, *trivialization* is evident in the trite and trendy capitalization of the word 'refugee.' Moreover, the statement that refugee claimants use tax dollars to hire lawyers is a completely unsubstantiated and unwarranted *assumption*.

Francis goes on to claim that the 'wholesale defrauding of our refugee system' costs taxpayers $1.25 billion per year. Again, this dollar figure is not sourced, nor is any evidence for it cited. She continues by declaring that 'the cost of crimes committed against Canadians and our companies plus the injuries or deaths caused against Canadians ... is exponential and unlimited.' Although she does not make the connection explicitly, she seems to be implying that refugees commit crimes and cause injuries and deaths to Canadians. Again, she provides no *evidence* or *facts* of any kind for this claim, which seems to come out of nowhere. This is an example of what van Dijk calls *incoherence*. He notes that when 'meaningful sentences are combined with each other in a meaningful sequence, we say that this is "coherent"' (1991: 178). In the above example, Francis argues *incoherently* by putting two unrelated ideas together and making it sound as if they were related. In other words, the defrauding of the system by 'bogus' refugees leads to crimes and even to the deaths of Canadians. Yet nowhere is the connection between these two ideas discussed.

Francis ends her article by castigating the immigration minister. Here she resorts to *innuendo, irrelevance,* and *absurdity.* She describes Caplan's 'intransigence is unacceptable but hardly surprising. Her brother-in-law made a bundle as an immigration lawyer until he was handed a patronage appointment as a judge in 1998.' In other words, the immigration minister supposedly kept a malfunctioning refugee system going solely to enrich her brother-in-law and his law practice. Having enriched him sufficiently, she then helped ensure he was named to the bench. She is using this illogical and absurd argument to explain why Canada's refugee system does not work. In earlier articles the columnist criticized the system when it was under the jurisdiction of other ministers, and Caplan and her brother-in-law can hardly be responsible for how the system operated when it was in other hands. Yet in less than three months,

Francis used the discourse against the minister and her brother-in-law in four different articles.

In a later article, 'Ottawa Pursuing an Incompetent, Dangerous Policy: Canada Should Call Moratorium on Immigration' (4 January 2000), Francis opens with a strong statement: 'Times Square and the Seattle Space Needle did not blow up on New Year's Eve, no thanks to Canada's embarrassing, sieve-like and dangerous immigration and refugee system.' She then discusses how she 'broke the story' about Algerian terrorists living in Montreal who were going to 'blow up high-profile targets in the United States.' The article opens with strong *hyperbolic* language suggesting that these dangerous terrorists were about to destroy these landmarks. Again, she presents no evidence of this, and cites only unnamed European sources. She continues the use of *hyperbole* by describing one of the arrested terrorists as 'pure trash.'

Moreover, she describes Canada's system in equally *exaggerated* and *hyperbolic* terms: 'Canada's silly system, ... sleazy Canadian immigration lawyers or accomplices.' The article ends by describing the system as 'no longer a joke, [it is] life-threatening to Canadians and to the rest of the world.'

In one of her most serious and *misleading* statements, Francis talks about the government's policy for sponsored immigration: it has 'ended up by putting grandma and grandpa or nieces and nephews on our welfare rolls by the hundreds of thousands over the years. Never mind the needless burden on our health care system of bringing in 2,000,000 elderly in a decade allegedly "sponsored" by their loved ones.' Here, she cites no *source* to support her allegations. She is also playing the *numbers game* by tossing up figures that have no basis in fact. Furthermore, the *mocking* use of the kinship terms such as grandma and grandpa serves to trivialize the system.

This article again cites Caplan's denial that she has a conflict of interest in regard to her brother-in-law, who 'made a fortune as an immigration lawyer until becoming a judge a year ago.'

Francis attacked the minister even earlier than this, in an article dated 31 August 1999. In this one, her lead sentence talks about our 'flawed immigration and refugee system.' She cites Caplan's assistant as saying that the minister does not have a conflict of interest regarding her brother-in-law becoming a judge. Here, Francis again resorts to strong *hyperbole*: 'But what this all means is that the minister who should be trashing and revising our immigration and refugee policies is related to a man who was a ranking member of the Immigration Industry. This is what I call the lawyers and lobbyists and special interest functionnaires who make millions of dollars by blocking any and all sensible efforts to protect our border from undesirables and bogus refugee claims.'

In this extract Francis is using a variety of linguistic strategies. One is strong *argumentation*; another is *logically incoherent relationships*. The minister is incapable of doing her job because of her relationship to a former immigration lawyer who is part of the 'Immigration Industry.' All of this *presupposes* that such an 'industry' exists and that its purpose is indeed to 'block sensible efforts to protect our borders.' Our borders are thus exposed to danger because various people, including the minister's relative, are there to make money from 'bogus refugees.' This argument is illogical and irrational and is supposed to make the reader believe that such relationships exist. She continues by citing the ethnic origins of the people making bogus claims: 'Tamils, Indians, Pakistanis, Sri Lankans, Eritreans and Ethiopians.' One wonders if the citation of only people of colour is merely accidental.

Another series of articles deals with the alleged health problems of refugees and immigrants. In an article dated 31 August 1999, Francis begins with a *discourse of denial*, noting that neither she 'nor the vast majority of Canadians, mostly tolerant people,' who agree with her anti-immigration stance 'are coming from' a racist position. She then moves into her main argument – that Canada's immigration and refugee policies have 'allowed [in] an influx of criminals, terrorists, fake refugees, undesirables and now, I have discovered, many sick people because Ottawa is not doing its job properly.' The evidence for this is that Canada is supposed to have the highest number of cases of leprosy in the Western world as a result of poor screening. In three subsequent articles on immigration and health, Francis cites one source, a physician who claims that 'my dog has more protection at the border than I do.'

One especially powerful article by Francis related to immigration is titled 'Illegal Aliens Should Be Sent Back: Nothing "Racist" in Upholding the Law or Protecting Borders' (24 August 1999). She begins by reassuring the reader that there is nothing racist in her position. She notes that 90 per cent of Canadians want the boat people to be sent back but that Ottawa 'keeps stonewalling.' This 'underscores the country's biggest flaw. Canadian are pathologically polite and anyone who criticizes immigrants or refugees, or the policies and process in place, is labelled a "racist" by vested interests.' After stating that such a label is 'totally inaccurate,' she moves on to discuss how going public with such an unpopular view involves paying a price. She then cites the experience of a group calling itself the 'Canada First Immigration Reform Committee. This group has urged that the notwithstanding clause of the Constitution be used to overturn judicial decisions that make it 'impossible to secure Canada's borders.' According to Francis, the group's director, Paul Fromm, has been treated badly by the media, supposedly because of his views. Having denied at the beginning of the article that she is racist, Francis states that she supports this group, which is known for its right-wing and neofascist views, and whose director has been charged with incitement to hatred and with disseminating racist ideology and has been called before the Canadian Human Rights Commission.

Francis then offers seven assertions about why her position is not racist. She contends that it is not racist to question how many people should be allowed in, to deport criminals and their families, to want our government to uphold the laws of the land, and so on. She ends by stating: 'It's really that simple and has nothing to do with bigotry.' The repetition of the words 'it is not racist' is a device known as *parallelism*, which resorts to repeated negations to underscore an argument.

Francis also resorts to a *we/they* strategy of argumentation when she comments in a *ridiculing* manner that she could sponsor dozens of American relatives in order to give them access to the 'bargain rate health care here. That's just plain unfair to my fellow Canadians ... Yet when applied to a taxicab driver from Somalia or Guatemala, the policy is assumed correct. Truth is, people who think that what's good for the Somalian is not good for the American are the racists.' Here Francis is *implicitly* arguing that ethnoracial minorities are to be distinguished from 'real' Canadians like herself and, presumably, other White Canadians.

Elinor Caplan is not Francis's only target. In the first part of 1999, she went after the minister's predecessor, Lucienne Robillard. An especially strong piece dated 8 April 1999, 'How Much Does Immigration Cost? Lets Do a Net Benefits Study and Actually Find Out,' was written in the form of a letter to Robillard. It began with *hyperbolic* and *ridiculing* language: 'You and your immigrants ...' Francis went on to allege that the minister listened only to 'members of this country's Immigration Industry – lawyers and lobbyists and multicultural trough artists.' Note the use here of capitalization, which is a device of *legitimation*. The purpose of the strategy in this article was to mislead the reader into believing that such a group actually exists. Francis did not point out that she herself coined the term. Moreover, she declared, anyone who criticizes immigration and refugee polices is 'automatically labelled a redneck or racist by the Immigration Industry. And a generation of wimpy politicians has been too frightened to stand up to these people and demand answers.' Here Francis was using the mechanism *denial of racism*: 'wimpy' politicians were being politically correct in declining to challenge the Immigration Industry. She was also implicitly using the political correctness strategy in suggesting that debate on immigration issues was being stifled or silenced for fear of offending special interest groups.

Francis then showed her own biases with respect to the kinds of people Canada should be letting in. She expressed her preference for (White) refugees from Kosovo. Noting that Ottawa had pledged to take in 5,000, she then warned: 'We cannot afford more than that because Ottawa's let in too many illegitimate refugees and other unacceptable people.' She further displays here bias in favour of Europeans with the *repetition* of 'apart from Kosovo and legitimate refugees ...' She then moved on to her main point – that a net benefits study should be undertaken because 'Canadians have a right to know how many of these people have ended up on welfare rolls and for how long and where? How many have been getting unemployment or disability benefits. How many live in subsidized housing ... Getting pensions ... received expensive medical treatment ... convicted of criminal offences?' In this paragraph Francis was using at least three linguistic strategies to send a disapproving and stereotypic picture of refugees to the reader. First of all, her questions were making unwarranted *assumptions*, since she presented no evidence to show that refugees fall into these categories in disproportionate numbers. Second, she was using *repetition* in repeating the words 'how many' seven times in one paragraph. Repetition reinforces arguments. Third, she was using *negativization* in subjecting to question only the worst elements of the refugee community. The query could just as easily have been phrased positively: 'How many refugees are now gainfully employed, pay their taxes, and contribute to the economy?'

Francis then called for a study to determine how much the refugee system costs the government. This would include how much has been 'forked out' on ESL classes, resettlement programs, refugee claims, immigration infrastructures abroad,' and, finally, motel rooms for refugees and multicultural grants.' This paragraph used *ridiculing* language – 'forked out' – and closed with a subtle *interpolation* of ideas. She added 'multicultural grants' to the list of expenses 'forked out' by the government to aid refugees. In this way, she cleverly brought in a new thought: grants for multiculturalism are yet another expense of Canada's refugee program (unless they are provided to refugees from Kosovo). This, even though multiculturalism is the law in this country.

Francis answered her own 'how much' question without doing the study she herself was proposing. The *preassumption* was clearly stated in her next sentence: 'It's billions of dollars each at a time when Canadian health and education is in financial distress.' Going back to the idea of a study, she stated that the only 'study' was a 'royal commission-style road-show attended by ranking members of the Immigration Industry ... as usual they bleated about the system.' Again the language she used to describe this study relied heavily on *mockery* and *ridicule*. An element of *trivialization* was also evident, in that she described the royal commission as a roadshow.

The article ended with her strong opinion that 'the facts are that every unskilled immigrant or refugee ... takes a job away from some unemployed Canadian-born unskilled worker ... who lives in subsidized apartment ... is spending tax dollars that need never have been spent ... shouldn't have cost the courts and cops a fortune.' She presented these 'facts' without any evidence. Moreover, they flew in the face of a great number of legitimate research studies, which generally show that after a period of adjustment, most immigrants and refugees become substantial tax-paying and contributing members of society. Many, in fact, take jobs that Canadians do not want.

**Conclusions**

Diane Francis misrepresents some of the facts, presumably in an attempt to influence readers to share views about immigrants and refugees. But her 'crusade' has not gone unnoticed. Several oppositional discourses have been directed against her. The Centre of Excellence for Research on Immigrant Settlement, led by Dr Morton Beiser, organized a seminar that specifically addressed Francis's biased columns. Several health specialists were among the panelists, and they generally agreed that Francis has her facts wrong. Referring specifically to her statements about the health risks that immigrants present to Canadians, it was noted that she was wrong in stating that malaria is a sexually transmitted disease – in fact, it is transmitted by mosquitoes. Moreover, her claim that 25,000 refugees were allowed into the country without medical screening ignores the fact that within two months of their arrival all refugees must undergo a rigorous medical examination. Her comment that there are many 'Typhoid Mary's' loose in Canada is also in error: there are only '40 to 80 cases of this disease reported in Canada annually and the vast majority occur among Canadians who have traveled abroad' (Clarkson 2000: 6–9).

The Canadian Council of Refugees tracked the media's reporting about the arrival of the Chinese refugees. Most of the media were very negative (see the case study on Chinese migrants), and it was the *National Post* that contained the strongest anti-immigrant perspective. This organization wrote to Ken Whyte, the *Post*'s editor-in-chief, to protest about the 'disproportion of negative news stories and commentary concerning immigrants and refugees in Canada,' and singled out Diane Francis for her particularly aggressive anti-immigrant 'crusade.' The *National Post*'s lawyer sent back a letter stating: 'The menacing tone of your letter and its slanderous allegations cannot form the basis of any constructive discourse between your Association and the newspaper.' The paper was advised not to meet with the council, and repeated telephone calls and e-mails to the editor and Francis were simply ignored.

To date, these oppositional discourses have had little effect on either the general policy of the *National Post* or this particular columnist. Even so, it is important to note that an attempt to reach this media organization was made. In the long run such efforts may improve the quality of journalism in this country by demonstrating that the audience is not always a passive receiver of the biased perspectives of some writers.

**Case Study 2: The *National Post*'s Racialization of the Tamil Community**

In this section of the chapter on the racialization of immigrants by the *National Post*, we document the newspaper's targeting of the Tamil community in Canada – more specifically, its targeting of the Tamil Tigers.

*Background to This Community*

There are between 160,000 and 200,000 Tamil-speaking people in Canada. The vast majority have settled in and around the Greater Toronto Area. Most came because of the civil war in their home country, Sri Lanka, where the majority Sinhalese hold the reigns of power and have blocked attempts by the Tamil minority to establish an independent homeland in northern Sri Lanka. Depending on one's perspective, the Tamil Tigers are either freedom-fighters trying to establish a state for themselves, or insurgent terrorists whose goal is to destabilize the country. Most of the Tamils who have migrated to Canada are fleeing from the civil unrest in their country.

The Tamils have become somewhat controversial, mainly because of allegations that some of their organizations in Canada are fronts for the Tamil Tigers. They have been accused of raising money for this 'terrorist' organization and of involving themselves in a variety of criminal activities. These perceptions seem to be the basis for the campaign that the *Post* has waged against this community.

### The Campaign against the Tamil Community

Between 6 May to 20 July 2000, the *Post* published twenty-four articles linking Tamil organizations to terrorism. From 25 August to 31 October, it printed ten more articles, bringing the grand total to thirty-four (our tally is now thirty-five). The campaign was so intense that on four occasions, the *Post* published two articles on the subject on the same day.

### Analysis of Headlines of Tamil Articles

The first image that catches a reader's eye is the article's headline. According to van Dijk, headlines serve 'to summarize the most important information of the report. That is, they express the main "topic"' (1991: 50). Furthermore, he suggests, headlines set the cognitive tone – in effect, they tell the reader how to think about the subject of the article. Sometimes the headline is the only part of a news report that is read. The information contained in headlines also serves for readers as 'an overall organizing principle for the representation of the news event in memory.' After reading about an event (e.g., a riot) that is described in a particular way, the reader has been programmed to read subsequent reports in these terms. Headlines are written by newsroom specialists, who typically set out to express the most important part of the story. This can result in bias. Van Dijk summarizes the influence of headlines on ethnoracial affairs as follows: they 'summarize events that the white newspaper, reporter, or editor finds most relevant for the white readers, that is ... these headlines at the same time define and evaluate the ethnic situation, as the white Press sees it' (51). Van Dijk has developed several categories of analysis that can be applied to the examination of headlines. Some of these are described below.

### Words in Headlines

The actual words used in headlines communicate opinions and emotions. They are not mere descriptors since the writer has a choice of words. Regarding the Tamil community in Toronto, the word the *Post* used most often in its articles was 'terrorist.' That word appeared thirteen times in the thirty-five headlines. Examples:

- 'Martin to Dine with Terrorist Front' (6 May)
- 'Tamil Terror Allies Use Toronto Schools for Fundraisers' (30 May)
- 'Terrorism, the Truth and FACT' (17 June)
- 'CSIS Warns Canada Could Be Adding Terrorism' (5 July)
- 'Ottawa Confirms Terrorists Raise Funds in Canada' (8 July)
- 'Slain Terrorist Honoured at Event at School' (25 October)

The word 'terrorist' sends a clear message. Other, more neutral words to describe Tamil activities, such as 'activist,' 'dissenter,' or even the slightly stronger 'militant,' could have been selected. Instead the most extreme word, terrorist, consistently appears in the headlines. Stuart Hall (1991) has made a profound observation on this point. He cites Foucault, who noted: 'Statements about the social, political or moral world are rarely ever simply true or false ... because facts can be construed in different ways. The very language we use to describe the so called facts interferes in this process of finally deciding what is true and what false' (280). As an example of this process, Hall cites the events and language used in another context – one that bears a close resemblance to the reporting on the Tamil community that we analyze here. The Palestinians who are fighting to regain land on Israel's West Bank can be described either as 'freedom fighters' or as 'terrorists': 'It is a fact that they are fighting; but what does fighting mean? The facts alone cannot decide. Whether the Palestinians are terrorists or not, if we think they are, and act on that 'knowledge,' they in effect become terrorists because we treat them as such. The language [discourse] has real effects in practice: the description becomes "true"' (293). The readers of the *National Post* are in a sense being programmed to believe that the Tamil Tigers are terrorists. It is not even necessary to read the full reports: the headlines make the point. They may or may not be terrorists; another perspective – and certainly their own – is that they are 'freedom fighters.'

The headlines also resort quite often to emotion-laden terms such as 'insurgents' and 'killer.' Also, the term 'street gangs' comes up several times, since the activities of the alleged gangs are related to those of the Tamil Tigers.

The terms 'Tamil' and 'Tamil Tiger' are often encountered in *Post* headlines. They were used twenty-four times in the headlines of the stories we analyzed. This frequency allows the reader no doubt that most 'Tamils,' who are an ethnic group from Sri Lanka, are also 'Tigers.' The reader cannot help but associate all Tamils with membership in Tiger organizations, although only around 10,000 Tamils in Sri Lanka are thought to be members. The sources cited in the *Post* believe that there are 6,000 Tamil Tigers in Canada. Even if that number is accurate, it reflects only 10.5 per cent of Canada's Tamil population.[1] In any event, a very good case can be made that when the average reader hears or sees the ethnic descriptor 'Tamil,' he or she immediately thinks of 'terrorist Tamil Tigers.'

Thus, the headlines alone indicate that Canada's entire Tamil community has been associated negatively with an alleged 'terrorist' organization. In other words, an entire group has been tainted by the actions of a few. As we will see, one of the main problems in this kind of journalism is that it is one-sided. Nothing positive is ever written about this community.

*Articles: The FACT Dinner*

The articles themselves can be grouped into several categories. One category of stories concerns two federal cabinet ministers who attended a dinner organized by FACT, the Federation of Associations of Tamil Canadians, on 6 May 2000. There were seven articles devoted exclusively to this dinner, including three editorials, the same event would be mentioned in almost every subsequent article. The first article in this category announced that Paul Martin, the finance minister, and Maria Minna, the Minister for International Cooperation, would be attending the dinner, where they were expected to present greetings from Ottawa. This article was headlined, 'Martin to Dine with Terrorist "Front": Two Ministers to Attend Tamil Event Organized by Alleged Fundraiser for Rebels.' Its first paragraph stated that the ministers would attend even though the U.S. State Department had described FACT as a 'front' for terrorism.' The only evidence cited for this statement at this point was an American document. The story went on to say: 'Canadian law enforcement officials who have been working to counter the infiltration of the Tamil Tigers into Canada were shocked that politicians would agree to appear at the dinner. "I thought we didn't support terrorist causes," said one official.'

Strong hyperbolic language such as shocked was used to make the argument. Another 'source,' an unnamed official, was then cited to indicate that FACT indeed supports terrorism. The idea was thus firmly planted in the reader's mind. To strengthen the point, several para- graphs later the RCMP and CSIS were added to the sources claiming that the Liberation Tigers were indeed supported by fundraising activi- ties: 'front businesses and organized crime, including extortion, drug smuggling and immigration and passport fraud.' By this point in the article, the group organizing the dinner (FACT) had been identified as a front; it was also implied that the group was taking part in criminal activities. Clearly, the strategy of *association* – bringing two apparently unrelated ideas together – was being used to inform the reader that the ministers were attending an event organized by a criminal front group. The article continued to rely on authority to make its case, noting that Canada was drafting legislation to outlaw terrorist fundraising activities. It cited the decision of a Federal Court of Canada judge that an alleged Tamil Tiger member would be deported. The next level of authority cited was the Sri Lankan government, which was waging a war against the Tamil Tigers and seeking international aid. That country's High Commissioner in Ottawa was quoted as saying he was 'surprised' and 'saddened' by this ministers' behaviour.

Toward the end of the article, it was claimed that an unidentified man who called FACT's office was told – by another unidentified person, who presumably answered the phone – that the event was not a fundraising one. The article ended by reverting back to the U.S. State Department's report saying that the group was, among other things, procuring weap- ons and bomb-making equipment. Finally, it cited a Canadian govern- ment official who said that members of the FACT organization had joined the Liberal Party.

The main problem with this article is that its sources of evidentiality are so skewed. A U.S. State Department report, an RCMP Intelligence report, a Canadian federal judge's decision, and the Sri Lankan govern- ment and its High Commissioner are its sources. The Tamil organiza- tion is contacted, but neither party to this event is identified – both remain faceless and anonymous. Yet a powerful message is being sent that FACT is a front for criminals.

In the second article, from 11 May, 'Sri Lanka Protests Martin, Minna Speaking at Tamil Dinner: High Commissioner Asked to Explain,' the debate moved to the international level. It is began by noting: 'A diplo- matic row has erupted over the appearance ... at a dinner hosted by a Canadian Tamil organization that has been branded a front for a terror- ist group.' The government of Sri Lanka had 'summoned Ruth

Archibald, Canada's high commisioner to a meeting to protest the conduct of its ministers.' It then reiterated material from a CSIS report that called FACT an 'umbrella front organization,' and referred again to a FACT member whom the government was trying to deport. It noted that officials for the ministers had 'downplayed' their appearance at the dinner, calling FACT an umbrella for community groups and the event a celebration of the Sri Lankan New Year. It then cited another source: 'John Thompson, an executive director of the MacKenzie Institute, a think tank that studies national security issues, said that he was stunned the minister had attended a FACT event.' Following this was a statement reiterating that the Tamil Tigers had killed hundreds of civilians and politicians, using suicide bombs and other devices.

Again, this article relied entirely on high-level sources, including officials of the governments of Canada and Sri Lanka. It ended by citing the director of a well-known and very conservative right-of-centre 'think tank' as an expert, who declared himself 'stunned.' No other sources were cited, and the reader was again reminded that the Tigers were responsible for killing civilians.

On 12 May the *Post* published an editorial, 'Dancing with Tigers.' Its front sentence quoted Martin as saying, 'It was a celebration of dance,' and Minna as saying that a Tamil national event should be celebrated, as are other cultural events in this country. By its headline and 'fronted' sentence, the editorialists were engaging in the strategies of *ridicule, trivialization*, and *mockery*. They were ridiculing the minister's description of the event by suggesting he was dancing with members of a known terrorist group. They were trivializing Minna's office – the Ministry of International Co-operation – by saying, in parentheses, 'yes, there is one.' And, it was mocking the notion that the event celebrated the Tamil new year when it stated, 'Mr. Martin and Ms. Minna *think* the dinner commemorated ...' By using the word *think*, the editorial was challenging the knowledge and possibly the veracity of the two ministers. Furthermore, it described Minna as being 'nonchalant' when she said that perhaps one or two individuals might be involved in terrorist activities. The word 'nonchalant' suggests that the minister was not being serious about an important issue. The editorial continued restorting to hyperbole, stating that the ministers' 'insistence that FACT is a normal, run-of-the-mill group ... is alarming.' It went on to repeat in some detail material from the same sources as previously cited: the U.S. State Department and CSIS and RCMP reports. And it specifically added that the author of the CSIS report was an Australian expert on Southeast Asian security, who said the Tigers 'frequently operate through cultural and social cover/front offices.' It quoted from this source, restating the point that that these organizations engage in heroin trafficking, extortion, and passport fraud. The editorial noted that all these indictments of the Tamil Tigers and their front groups were not classified or confidential, and then indulged in ridicule again: 'except to cabinet ministers.' It continued mocking the ministers, asking why these Liberal ministers were sticking to their stories and suggesting that an answer could again be found in one of its main sources, the CSIS report, which it quoted: 'Many Western politicians believe that it is the ethnic or the minority vote that makes a difference in an election [and do not want to] impinge on their local electoral support base by seeming unsympathetic to grievances.' In other words, the ministers were being accused of seeking political and electoral advantage by designating this group as just another innocent ethnocultural organization. The editorial went even further than this, indicating the entire Liberal government by stating in its next paragraph another explanation: 'The Liberals are being unduly influenced ... Raymond Chan, the Secretary of State for Asia-Pacific, declared that FACT members had joined the Liberal Party and even flew a FACT representative to Ottawa to discuss Canada's role in brokering peace in Sri Lanka.'

In its final paragraph the editorial used the strategy of *disclaimer* dismissing its two anti-government explanations by inserting the phrase 'for whatever reason' in the opening sentence. Yet at the same time it went back to its original point of criticizing the ministers in strong, hyperbolic language: 'It is scandalous that, for whatever reason, Canadian Cabinet ministers are undermining the global fight against terrorists by blessing FACT with their presence, their morally neutral attitude and their excuses.'

The story of 31 May was headlined 'Martin Fumes over Terror Charges: Hosts of Dinner He Attended Linked to Tamil Tigers.' This piece was fronted by the idea that Martin was faced with continuing accusations 'that he showed poor judgment.' It described Martin as 'lashing out' at critics. Thus, the minister was pictured in hyperbolic language as both 'fuming' and 'lashing out.' The story then developed that his critic in Parliament was a Canadian Alliance MP, who was using the already cited reports as well as a photograph published by the *National Post*. The photo, showing Tiger supporters in camouflage and carrying assault rifles, had been taken at a rally at a Canadian school. The Alliance MP was quoted as asking whether this was 'the sort of things Cana-

dians should celebrate.'[2] The article cited the minister as continuing to
defend his appearances at the dinner, which was also attended by busi-
nesspeople and workers of all kinds. He strongly reminded the Alliance
that just because there was a civil war going on in Sri Lanka did not
mean 'these people are terrorists – that is not the Canadian way.' The
article now came to its next major point, citing a 'new report by a leading academic authority' at the Centre for the Study of Terrorism and
Political Violence in Scotland and the Institute for Counter-Terrorism
in Israel, who had disclosed that an estimated $33 million had been
raised in Canada to support the Tigers.

On the same day, the *Post* published another editorial on this subject,
'Tiger Tales.' In it, Martin was again taken to task, along with other Liberal MPs who attended the dinner. This editorial raised the question of
why he attended, in the face of 'documented' evidence that FACT is a
front for terrorists. The editorial noted that when an Alliance member
questioned him in the House, Martin implied that the questioner was
intolerant: '"That is not the Canadian way," he huffed to reporters.' In
describing Martin and his actions, the editorial often resorted to quirky
language such as 'huffing.' Other examples: 'strange tactics,' and the
minister did an 'odd thing' in defending the organization. At the same
time, there was mounting evidence 'of an alarming activity,' and the
paper had published an 'astonishing' photo. The language throughout
this editorial was hyperbolic and intended to imply that the minister
really did not know what he was doing. This was further confirmed
when the editorial recalled the Air India bombing and the arrest of a
suspected Algerian terrorist and asked rhetorically: 'Will it take a similar
incident for Mr Martin to take the Tamil Tigers seriously?' The editorial
reverted back to the theory that the minister attended the dinner in
order to court electoral support in this community, and ended by issu-
ing a warning: 'But it should draw the line before they venture for voters
into the CSIS's blacklist.'

The article of 31 May focused on further questions raised to Martin in
Parliament ('the third successive day of questioning'). In this article the
newspaper applauded itself by drawing attention to how it had documented 'how Tamil Tigers supporters are raising funds ... through
migrant smuggling, passport fraud, organized crime ... and rallies at
Toronto-area schools featuring men in camouflage uniforms carrying
mock assault rifles. They are also planning civil war celebrations this
month at three venues.' Using the strategy of reiteration, the story made
sure to mention all the allegedly negative activities this group had com-

mitted, leaving the reader firmly of the view that FACT is indeed a front for terrorist activities.

Almost four months later, the *Post* again reverted to the theme of Martin's attendance at the FACT dinner. A news article dated 28 September 2000, 'Tiger Terror Warning Ignored,' fronted with the statement that Canada's high commission in Sri Lanka had sent an advance warning to officials in the foreign affairs office about this event. The warning had been based on information from CSIS and the U.S. State Department that had already been used to source earlier articles. The article's first sentence gave the reader the impression that new information had come to light. Yet in the following paragraph the same old sources were cited. The rest of the piece was pretty much a rehash of what had been reported in May. One of the strongest points made in this article was that the *National Post* had 'revealed' in May the minister's plan to attend the dinner; not only that, but the *Post* articles were being picked up by the 'international media.' It quoted Ms Archibald, the Canadian high commissioner, asking for help because the *Post*'s weekend story might 'may get some play over the next few days.' Thus, the *Post*'s focus on the Tamils and FACT was made a centerpiece of this article. The newspaper was giving itself pride of place.

But this news article was not enough for the *Post*. An editorial it published the same day, 'Answer the Question,' began by stating that the Canadian Alliance had spent still more time in Parliament asking Martin about his attendance at the dinner, in the light of new information. As in the earlier editorial, Martin was described in strong language: he was 'stubborn,' questions should be raised about his 'judgment,' he had compounded his 'error,' 'things reached a low point,' he 'scolded,' he used 'inflammatory personal vitriol' he 'obfuscates,' he had indulged in 'specious evasions.' Hyperbolic language pervaded the piece, which painted the minister in very unflattering terms and strongly implied that he was indulging in more than poor judgment.

These editorials were making the point that the minister was courting electoral favour and thus behaving like a politician, and at the same time was ignoring a threat to the country's national security. However, the newspaper's attacks were also politically motivated. The editorials seemed to be subscribing to the Alliance's version of events, judging by how they quoted so often the position taken by this party. The *Post* was using the controversy incited by the Tamil dinner to launch a fight against the Liberal government as personified by one of its leading ministers. It was using this event for its own political agenda. This may be acceptable media practice; the problem is that in so doing, the paper was communicating to its readers a largely negative image of the Tamil community in Canada. In pursuing its political agenda, the *Post* was categorizing an entire community as 'terrorist' without at any time publishing any positive or supportive pieces about the community and its members.

*Street Gangs*

The *National Post* has also attempted to link Tamil youth gangs to the alleged criminal activities of Tamil community organizations. For example, in an article dated 18 May 2000, Tamil youth gangs were alleged to be expanding into activities such as home invasion, drug dealing, migrant smuggling, and arms trafficking. The same article drew parallels between Tamil youth gangs and Asian street gangs of an earlier period. It suggested that members of Tamil youth gangs had had military training, and that some of them had even escalated into 'sophisticated crime' such as casino and bank fraud. Immigration fraud, for which Tamil criminals are said to have an 'international reputation,' was cited as a main activity. According to the article, there had been more than forty Tamil gang shootings. Yet a report issued by the Canadian Tamil Youth Development Centre, unreported by the *Post*, made the point that Tamil youth gangs in the GTA were not connected to the Liberation Tamil Tiger Eelam (LTTE).

This article is extremely interesting because of the sources used. It was based on an RCMP intelligence report. As with so many articles about Tamil community groups and their activities, the main sources were official police or U.S. State Department reports. However, this RCMP report was not released by the police, but rather by the Canadian Alliance, which got it through the Access to Information Act. Thus, two other parties had joined the expanding project of targeting the Tamil community. The Alliance, having challenged Martin's attendance at the FACT dinner, then released this report, which was duly reported on by the *Post*. The story ended by rehashing the various official reports on this community and citing two Tamil organizations in Toronto as 'front' organizations for the Tamil Tigers.

All the highlights of the new report were repeated in summary form in another story on the same day. This is an excellent example of *over-completeness*, a common journalistic device that involves providing an unnecessarily detailed analysis of an event. Many of the *Post*'s articles on

Tamil activities were very detailed, citing several reports and recounting all the incidents that had been reported on earlier. In this example, *over-completeness* was achieved by actually publishing two versions of the same story.

In another piece, dated 29 June 2000, the *Post* reported that the shooting of a seventeen-year-old Tamil woman one year earlier was indeed 'linked to Tamil gangs.' It referred to the *Post*'s own role in making the connection between the shooting and gang activity by noting that just days after the event, 'the National Post reported that police were looking hard at this theory. For the past year, however, police would only say they had a "definite direction" in the case.' In other words, the *Post* was congratulating itself for explaining the crime by linking it to Tamil gangs even before the police had sufficient evidence to do so.

*Miscellaneous Themes*

Canada Post has launched a new service that entitles individuals to make postage stamps from private photos. Apparently it received a large order for stamps bearing a likeness of the leader of the Tamil Tigers, Vellupillai Prabhakaran – an order described as 'mysterious' by the *National Post.* According to another *Post* article, Toronto schools were being used to hold fundraising rallies in support of the Tamil Tigers. A 30 May article on the subject included a photo of Tamil soldiers in military gear carrying replica rifles who appeared at school rallies (this was later identified as a photo from a play, but the correction was never made by the paper).

In another story about a school incident, dated 25 October, the *Post* reported in the lead sentence that 'a martyred terrorist was honoured at an area high school this month, raising new concerns taxpayer-funded Canadian schools are being used to stage events that glorify violence.' The World Tamil Women's Organization and the World Tamil Movement organized this event. The latter is identified in a U.S. State Department report as a front organization for the Tigers.

In yet another piece, the *Post* reported that Ottawa had spent $25,000 on a meeting for which an 'alleged Tamil Tiger' had been flown in as a consultant. The article, which described the man as a 'high-ranking' leader of the Tamil Tiger terrorist group, fronted the idea that he had been flown in at 'taxpayers expense' to give foreign policy advice to the Canadian government. It criticized the government for its actions and noted that although it deplored terrorism, Liberal MPs had 'repeatedly' met with alleged supporters of this separatist group.

Another example of the *Post* going to extremes to report on any activity of Tamil groups is dated 5 October, when it was reported that a leader of a 'Toronto based ethnic Tamil organization' admitted that his group supports a 'terrorist force waging a campaign of violence in Sri Lanka.' The article went on to identify Tamil organizations, and to note that one of them had received a $2 million grant the previous year from the Canadian government for settlement and language programs: It also noted that a senior cabinet minister, Paul Martin, attended a community fundraiser organized by the Tamil community; and that the government accused the Canadian Alliance of being anti-Canadian when it attacked Liberal policies in the House. What is noteworthy about this report, however, is that it was taken from a documentary that appeared on Australian television! This indicates the lengths to which the *Post*'s investigative journalists will go to continue their attacks on the Tamil community.

Finally, there is the case of the International Conference on War-affected Children, which was held in Winnipeg by the Canadian government. A *Post* editorial announced that the conference would be hosted in Winnipeg in September, perhaps because Canada was the first signatory of a UN protocol against the use of children in armed conflict. In its second paragraph the editorial stated, 'If his attachment to the cause is genuine, we urge Mr. Axworthy to take a hard look at Sri Lanka.' Citing a 'widely confirmed report' issued by the University Teachers for Human Rights in Jaffna (Sri Lanka), which stated that the Liberation Tigers were 'forcibly conscripting children, some as young as nine years old,' and that its recruiting activity was being funded with money collected from 'Tamils living in Canada.' The confirmers of this report were not cited, and the report itself was open to question.[3]

The *Post* followed up on this editorial by reporting on the conference itself on 18 September 2000. Its headline communicated the idea that the report would again centre on the Tamil community: 'The Children and the Tigers: Canada Is a Haven for a Group That Trains Young Children to Be Killers.' The story indicated that 'dozens of workshops and meetings' on this subject were held, yet it reported on only one case – that of the 'terrorist organization – the Liberation Tigers of Tamil Eelam ... And when it comes to producing war-affected children, the LTTE has few equals.' Its next paragraph provided an example of a terrorized child. The entire article then moved on to criticize the Canadian Immigration and Refugee Board, whose policies were responsible for admitting known terrorists into the country. After citing the many ways that Tamil terrorists can beat the system, it ended with by noting that the Canadian government had made a number of 'half hearted moves to tighten the system.'

It is highly probable that many examples of children abused by war were cited and discussed at this conference. The *Post* highlighted only the Tamil organization's use of children. Again it was targeting this one community, even though there may well be other groups in Canada that also abuse children during war.

Taken together, these articles indicate that the *Post* will seize on any event to report on the Tamil community's organizations and activities. In effect, the *Post* has mounted a concerted campaign against the organizations of this community. On the evidence cited above, it can be argued that the *Post* takes advantage of every possible opportunity to portray events involving the Tamils in a negative light – even when those events take place in a foreign country.

*Oppositional Discourse: The Tamil Community's Response*

The Tamil community has responded to being targeted by the *National Post*. On 15 June 2000 a press conference was held Queen's Park by the Colleges and Universities Tamil Students Union. The union noted in its press release that the community was 'outraged and appalled,' and went on to state that the *Post* was mounting a 'calculated effort to marginalize and silence the Tamil Canadian community.' It noted that the 'calculated attack' was harming the community and accused the *Post* of being unfair and biased in its reporting. The community had tried to meet with the *Post*'s editorial board but had been rejected. This group was going to try to ensure that the *Post* would be accountable by creating a media watch committee, attempting to form a coalition with other groups, and holding a symposium to make journalists more sensitive to issues in the community. The press release ended by discussing the achievements of the community and its members and their pride in being Canadian.

On 14 June the community's newspaper, *Eelam Nation*, sent an appeal to the *Post*. This appeal stated that the *Nation* was amazed by the 'assertions that members of the Tamil community indulge in drug traffic, extortion, organized crime,' and challenged the newspaper to prove its assertions. The *Nation* recognized that there had been a 'few cases of passport fraud and migrant entry' but cited as reasons the need to flee from Sri Lanka. It admitted that Tamils in Canada do raise money but maintained that the funds were being used for those 'starving for essentials' as a result of war. It disputed the *Post*'s use of the term 'terrorism,' noting that the UN believes that war for liberation 'is acceptable' and that violence is part of war. The Tamil paper also made the point that Tamils are desirable immigrants because they are a 'cultured community ... highly intelligent and industrious, and with a high degree of literacy.'

In another detailed article, published in *Pundit* magazine, Harini Sivalingam maintained that the *Post* had 'deliberately targeted the Tamil community ... [and] provided a negative and stereotypical image.' Sivalingam went on to state that the *Post*'s articles had painted the entire Tamil community as criminal because of the actions of a 'minute fraction.' Also the *Post* was using the community as a 'political pawn' to further Conrad Black's own anti-Liberal agenda. Throughout, the author maintained that the *Post* was failing in its journalistic duty in that its unsubstantiated accusations were tarnishing the entire community. All of this highlighted the need to ensure that messages sent out were accurate and would not bring harm to any community or group. Finally, the community had taken the unusual action of launching a lawsuit against the newspaper and had engaged Clayton Ruby, a prominent lawyer, to conduct its case.

In essence, the articles published by the Tamil community in a variety of places amount to a discourse of community resistance. They are attempts to provide an alternative perspective to that of the mainstream *Post* and to challenge and resist the discourse of criminality and terrorism propounded by that newspaper.

The *National Post* responded to the community's attempts to mount a counterdiscourse by organizing a news conference. On 16 June the *Post* reported on the news conference, headlining its article, 'Tamils Threaten to Sue the Post.' The deputy editor of the paper, Martin Newland maintained the *Post* was 'standing by its stories.' Using one of the classic rhetorical strategies, *denial*, he said the stories 'could not be characterized as racist, or as attacks on Tamils in general' (the mainstream conservative media often deny they are racist). He then resorted to *admission* or *disclaimer.* 'We are not in the business of arbitrarily sectioning off part of the Canadian populace and painting them all as terrorists ... We recognize that the Canadian Tamil community as a whole represents a rich and important part of the tapestry of ethnic communities.' In light of the fact that the *Post* has not published one positive story about anything relevant to the Tamil-Canadian community, one must wonder how their importance in the tapestry of ethnic communities is, in fact, being recognized. If the print media do not specifically print articles or features or editorials that make this point, and instead rely on editors' statements made only *after* the community has organized a discourse of resistance and launched legal action, how is the reading public to know that they believe this community to be a 'rich and important' part of Canadian society? Newland continued in the same vein: 'We have no argument with the Tamil community, but we do believe that reporting on how Canadian dollars are diverted to help fight a civil war in Sri Lanka, in part using terrorist methods ... represents basic public-interest journalism.' In the first part of this quote, *denial* is again used. Newland then tries to define what 'public interest' journalism is. However, as this analysis has amply demonstrated, the *Post*'s many articles covered many more themes than the $2 million dollar grant given to one of the Tamil organizations for language and settlement help. The articles alleged criminal activities, terrorism, and violence, and accused community organizations of acting as fronts for the 'terrorist' liberation Tamil Tigers. In this statement, the deputy editor was using the tactic of *incompleteness* by identifying only one of the many themes covered in this series.

An assistant deputy editor of the *Post*, Douglas Kelly, responded to the Tamil community's concerns by writing a letter to the *Tamil Canadian*. He began his letter by saying, 'We are alarmed and concerned about the article you published on May 13 about the coverage by the National Post of the domestic politics of Sri Lanka.' The choice of words is quite significant – especially the use of 'alarm.' One must wonder why the community's alarm is greeted by the 'alarm' of the newspaper! He continued by defending the reporter, Stewart Bell, who had been sent on this foreign assignment, and who had 'followed all standard practices' in a foreign country, and who 'as a professional journalist (is) not affected by the agendas of the people he is reporting on.' He also called the article criticizing the *Post* story 'an unworthy attack on a good reporter.' Kelly here was using the very common strategy of insisting that a professional had followed all standard procedures. Furthermore, he was claiming that professionals are objective in their reportage. Much has been written on the issue of subjectivity in reporting, with respect not only to the values of individual journalists but also to the entire process of selecting what is newsworthy. Also, journalists must make many decisions in the process of communicating to the audience, almost all of which are subjective in nature (van Dijk, 1991; Hackett and Zhao, 1998; Fowler, 1996). The issue of selectivity is so well documented that it makes a mockery of Kelly's stating that the reporter was unaffected by the agendas of the people he was reporting on. His letter ended in a patronizing manner, with the suggestion (later repeated) that 'you may want to write a letter to the Editor for consideration for publication in the newspaper.'

The *Post* continued to defend its position in a strongly worded editorial of 17 June, 'Terrorism, the Truth and the FACT: Tamil Federation Must Explain Itself Rather Than Hurling Spurious Charges of Racism.' This headline was more than provocative; also used another favourite semantic device of the conservative press, the *double entendre*. The word 'fact' implies the truth but is also the acronym of the Federation of Associations of Canadian Tamils. In this way the idea of terrorism as truth and fact was irrevocably linked to the federation and its activities.

Maintaining that 'this newspaper stands by its stories,' the editorial again cited 'authoritative' official reports from CSIS, the U.S. State Department, and others. It noted that representatives of FACT disputed these findings, and then added, 'It is suggested, in short, that this newspaper is engaged in a racist effort to incite antagonism toward Canada's Tamil community.' Furthermore, it noted that FACT had charged the *Post* with 'trampling upon every Tamil-Canadian's right to free association, free assembly and free expression.' It called these charges 'reductionist' and 'hysterical.' Defending its own position again, the editorial took two long paragraphs to maintain that most Tamil Canadians possess the same qualities as do other ethnic groups – citing Portuguese, Jewish, Lebanese, Ukrainian, and Chinese Canadians as examples – who are all tax-paying, hard-working people worrying about health, education, and crime. Though it compared Tamil Canadians favourably with these other groups, the fact of the matter is that these other groups had not been targeted with more than thirty-five articles about their domestic and foreign practices. In this light, the comparison was actually a linguistic sleight of hand designed to fool the reader. FACT was accused of conjuring up a 'spectre' of the kind used all too often to silence 'all further inquiry or doubt': any person 'who asks questions is an anti-immigrant, close-minded bigot.' The use of 'asks questions' was an attempt to neutralize the full power of the series of articles, which did far more than merely raise questions. There was a deliberate attempt to *obfuscate* and *neutralize* the issues raised by the *Post*'s articles. Resorting to strong *denial*, the editorial maintained 'there is no racism – inherent, implied or "calculated" in the *Post*'s articles. It strongly defended its use of official documents and maintained that by using these documents, it was not 'casting aspersions on the entirety of an ethnic minority population. If it did, then we would have to believe that every Italian-American is a member of the Mafia, and that every Muslim in Canada covertly works on behalf of radical Islamic terrorist groups.' Again, sleight of hand was being used in this sentence: the *Post* was offering absolutely no proof that it did not hold those views about the other ethnic groups.

The editorial continued by criticizing FACT, citing police and CSIS reports again and describing the 'enforcer' activities of a Tamil gang operating in Toronto. Finally, it noted that the *Post* had received 'floods' of letters from Tamil Canadians who 'give thanks for exposing these links and illicit activities,' and cited 'poignant' quotes from some of these letters, including this one: 'Keep your spirit and expose what you believe is wrong.' The hyperbolic term 'floods' gave little indication of how many such letters were in fact received. And by citing letters from Tamils approving of the *Post*, the editorial was using the tactic of *implicitness*. It was implying to the reader that its perceptions and its targeting of FACT had to be correct and accurate, since even members of that very community supported their efforts. The editorial closesd in a self-righteous manner by suggesting that the 'legitimate law enforcement, judicial, financial and political structures of Canada itself' would be eroded and undermined if terrorist acts went unreported 'merely to avoid accusations of racism.'

**Conclusions**

Underlying these defences is The *National Post*'s refusal or perhaps inability to recognize that despite all its disclaimers, it does indict an entire community by directing a huge number of articles against them. This indictment may not have been intended, but it is the natural consequence of the many negative articles and editorials written on this subject. As in many areas of discrimination, intended or inadvertent, the effects or consequences of actions indicate that disadvantage has taken place. The reader, who has not met many – or any – Tamil-Canadians, is likely to be strongly influenced by the discursive messages contained in the media coverage of this community. Readers of the *Post* are exposed to excessive negative reports about the alleged terrorist sympathies of Tamils. Their organizations are identified as fronts for terrorist activities in their home country, and they are accused of many illegal activities.

Reporting like this can only result in the creation and dissemination of negative stereotypes about this community. Tamil Canadians are branded as 'them' – people who, unlike 'us,' condone terrorism and illegal activity.

Moreover, all of the *Post*'s stories relied on official, 'authoritative' sources such as the police, the RCMP, CSIS, and the U.S. State Department. The very nature of these sources made the newspaper 'stand by its stories,' since it clearly accepted that such documents were indeed authoritative, final, and definitive. It was especially significant that at no time was a member of the community – an official of FACT or of any other Tamil organization – interviewed. The only Sri Lankans ever mentioned were government officials, most of whom are of Sinhalese heritage. The community voice was entirely silenced in these stories. Furthermore, no other expert opinion was solicited – no experts, academic or otherwise were cited in these reports.

In addition, the *Post* was using the Tamil issue to further its own political ideology. The newspaper is known as a conservative, even right-wing newspaper, and its founder Conrad Black is known for his ultraconservative politics. So the paper takes every opportunity to criticize the Liberal government in Ottawa, and this probably accounted for the substantial number of articles criticizing a minister's presence at a Tamil dinner. Thus, the newspaper was using the issue around the Tamil community to pursue its own political agenda. The problem is that in so doing, it was damaging the entire community.

No positive stories about this community or any of its members were published alongside these stories. However, on 4 November 2000, the Canadian Tamil Youth Organization held a dinner to celebrate awards that had been given to deserving Tamil youth. This event was reported fully in another Toronto newspaper. The *Post* did not take this opportunity to cover a positive event in the Tamil community, even though it publishes a special 'Toronto' section on Saturdays.

# 8

# News Discourse and the Problematization of Chinese Migration to Canada[1]

*Sean Hier and Joshua Greenberg*

> There is no reason today to believe that the desire people in poor states have to migrate will diminish in the foreseeable future as long as economic conditions make life generally harsh. People understandably will search for a new home where they and their dependents have at least a chance to find economic prosperity, social tranquility and political stability.
>
> Dirks, 1998: 393

In this chapter we draw on the concept of moral panic to discuss the relationship between the growing presence of the Chinese in Canada, news discourse, and the problematization of nearly 600 migrants who arrived in Canada from July to September 1999. The following is based on the assumption that news coverage acts as a 'discursive space' in which social agents struggle to penetrate the narratives around which news is constructed. By studying coverage of the migrants, we can learn a great deal about how Canadians construct and reconstruct their collective national identity – in particular, how they designate who is and who is not a true 'Canadian.' We are especially interested in how news discourse about the migrants was constructed and reproduced, and how the migrants' arrival was 'problematized' and transformed into a discursive 'crisis' focused on national security. We contend that the news coverage of the migrants holds broader ideological resonances that extend beyond a unilateral concern about the Canadian immigration and refugee systems. We argue that the news reporting of these events well illustrates Canadians' collective anxieties stemming from social change, racial integration, and contested Euro-Canadian hegemony.

A heightened sense of insecurity concerning the relationships between immigration, citizenship, and national identity has developed in Canada. This is greatly due to uncertainties stemming from globalization and ideological realignments associated with the rise of neoliberalism.[2] These insecurities draw a great deal of strength from the anxieties generated by the increasing presence in Canada of an upwardly mobile Chinese community. These anxieties were given a strong boost when nearly 600 migrants from the Fujian (or Fukien) Province of China landed on Canada's west coast in 1999 – and when the English-language press covered their arrival heavily. This went carried particular ideological resonances that mobilized various factions in the country to confront the phenomenon of *illegal* migration by 'unwelcome' foreigners, which was perceived as a problem requiring decisive intervention.[3] A large part of the public and the news media came to view the immigration and refugee systems in general, and *illegal* migration in particular, as a threat to national identity and an index for the 'problem' of Canadian state security.

In this chapter we invoke the notion of a moral panic in an effort to assess the extent to which the mainstream newspapers constructed a *discursive* crisis[4] around the 'illegal entry' into Canada of several hundred Fujianese migrants. We look at how the press used four marginal events to articulate wider anxieties pertaining *inter alia* to globalization, social change, and the escalating presence of the Chinese in Canada. In doing so, we draw on a theoretical foundation (Althusser, 1971b; Edelman, 1977, 1988; Fowler, 1991; Hall, 1977, 1980; Hall et al., 1978; Hay, 1994, 1995, 1996; Laclau, 1977; t'Hart, 1993) that suggests media discourses have the capacity to recruit and mobilize newsreaders as *active* participants in the social construction of moral panic. We hope above all to demonstrate how the mainstream newspapers' coverage of the migrants encouraged Canadians to perceive their arrival as a crisis. By examining the reactions of the media and the public to the arrival of the migrants, we can better understand how sovereign states constitute and maintain themselves through a racialized discourse of citizenship and national identity.

**Conceptual Foundations: Moral Panic and the Media**

Any discussion of moral panic must properly commence with Stanley Cohen's groundbreaking study, *Folk Devils and Moral Panics: The Creation of the Mods and Rockers* (1972), one of two classic analyses of news texts and the mass media's participation in the social construction of reality.

Basically, moral panic refers to the tendency for a large part of a society to consolidate in response to a threat, which can be real or imagined. This threat is believed to be so dangerous to the social body and the 'moral order' that 'something must be done,' – that is, some regulatory process must be mobilized. 'Doing something' usually involves reconsidering or amending existing mechanisms of social control. Consider Cohen's original definition:

> Societies appear to be subject, every now and then, to periods of moral panic. A condition, episode, person or group of persons emerges to become defined as a threat to societal values and interests; its nature is presented in a stylized and stereotypical fashion by the mass media ... Sometimes the subject of the panic is quite novel and at other times it is something which has been in existence long enough, but suddenly appears in the limelight. Sometimes the panic passes over and is forgotten ... at other times it has more serious and long-lasting repercussions and might produce such changes as those in legal and social policy or even in the way society conceives itself. (1972: 79)

According to Cohen, every moral panic has its 'folk devil': the personification of evil, susceptible to instant recognition based on 'unambiguously unfavorable symbols' (41). This folk devil is stripped of all positive characteristics and endowed with pejorative evaluations. Importantly, however, the nucleus of any moral panic is not the object of its symbolic resonances – not the folk devil itself. Rather, the folk devil serves as the ideological embodiment of the moral panic. When transmitted through the media, folk devils are revealed to the general public in a narrow and stereotypical fashion; they are constructed as wrongdoers and deviants, as threats to the social fabric necessitating immediate custodial intervention.

Cohen's framework corresponds to what Goode and Ben-Yehuda (1994: 124–43) describe as the 'interest group' theory of moral panic. According to this model, moral panic is the unanticipated and unintended outcome of moral crusades undertaken by particular interest groups – professional associations, police, the media – in their efforts to draw public attention to a specific 'moral evil.' Goode and his colleague distinguish the 'interest group' model from the 'elite-engineered' model; the latter explains a moral panic as the conscious and deliberate outcome of a manufactured campaign designed to divert attention from a real social crisis. Hall and colleagues (1978), for example, contend that moral panic is a mechanism resorted to by the ruling class to mystify deeper crises in the capitalist system. Cohen maintained that moral panic originates mainly in the media; in contrast, Hall and colleagues content that although the media are the key disseminators of moral panic, the real point of origin is the processes of capital accumulation and the 'crisis of profitability.' In times of crisis, the ruling elite 'orchestrate hegemony' by manipulating the media, who reproduce structures and relations of domination. The implication is that the news is not a creation of the media per se; rather, the media reflect pre-existing relations of domination.

Goode and Ben-Yehuda propose a third theory, the 'grassroots' model. According to this one, moral panic originates not among the ruling elite, and not in the mainstream media, but rather with the general public. The visible expressions of anxiety observed in the press or in political debate can be explained as manifestations of a more widespread anxiety that cannot be expressed directly.[5] According to the grassroots model, moral panic provides a cathartic release for more fundamental, deep-seated reservoirs of social insecurity. It follows that neither politicians nor news manufacturers are capable of fabricating public anxiety where none exists.

The grassroots approach helps a great deal to explain the important but generally neglected links between immigration, national identity, and moral panic on the one hand, and the processes of racial exclusion on the other. As Anderson (1983) has argued, racialization is key to creating and reproducing 'imagined national communities.' Similarly, Gellner (1983) has proposed that without a strong sense of national identity, be it 'real' or 'perceived,' individuals feel lost. Thus, commonsense perceptions of the imagined national community constitute an important foundation for how citizenship is understood. In this era of accelerated transnational population movements, one of the most important considerations for granting citizenship centres on state security and perceived threats to national sovereignty. When refugees and economic migrants can select themselves (i.e., when we don't specifically invite them in), this undermines the ability of sovereign nations to decide who can and cannot rightfully gain entry to the state, and to decide how they will come and how many will come. As a result, 'a sense develops that the state's legitimate authority, resting on the doctrine of sovereignty, is being eroded and, with it, the state's security' (Dirks 1998: 382). Western capitalist democracies are tightening their borders to refugees and undocumented migrants; as a result, the category of 'refugee' is being

reconstructed in dominant state discourse as an object of fear and criminality (Whitaker, 1998).

## Setting the Discursive Context

As the world watched, Canada found itself having to deal with the arrival
of four separate ships carrying almost 600 largely undocumented
migrants (19 July 1999 to 11 September 1999). From the arrival of the
first boat, a tensions mounted in the country: Canada was committed to
extending humanitarian aid, yet it could not allow itself to appear too
lenient to would-be asylum seekers.[6] There was little *verifiable* information about the migrants' point(s) of departure, or why they had left, or
why they had chosen to land in Canada; this did not prevent the newspaper media from quickly and uncritically using these four events to construct a *discursive* crisis around the state of Canada's immigration and
refugee policies. In effect, the media were 'manufacturing an immigration crisis where none existed' (Clarkson, 2000).[7]

To better understand how the migrants came to generate collective
anxiety about Canadian immigration and refugee policies, and about
national security and collective identity more generally, it is instructive
to consider some of discursive strategies the media used to recruit readers for a moral panic.[8] Collin Hay (1995) set out to find a way to treat
news readers as more than passive vessels of dominant ideology, and to
that purpose arrived at 'three modes of address' that the media use to
transform random occurrences into ideologically invested, mediated
events. The first mode of address concerns *the event itself*: the arrival off
Canada's west coast of four boats carrying 599 migrants. One week after
reports that a 'ghost ship' had gone down off the Queen Charlotte
Islands, the Canadian media reported that the RCMP had intercepted a
driftnet fishing boat en route to Canada from China's Fujian Province
containing 123 Fujianese migrants. Over the next two months, reports
of three additional vessels transporting upwards of 500 migrants from
Fujian served to ignite a national debate about Canada's refugee policy
– specifically, about whether that policy was too 'soft' on refugees and
asylum seekers. It is especially noteworthy here that although upwards
of 30,000 claimants seek asylum in Canada each year (without much success), these particular migrants were singled out as exemplars of a 'crisis' of national security.

The second mode of address concerns what Hay terms *visual evidence*.
Arguably, media projections of the migrants precipitated moral panic in

a way that other mechanisms simply could not. Continuous and extensive news coverage of the migrants being escorted in handcuffs onto prison buses by armed, masked guards, and of the migrants being held in military barracks while awaiting processing (photographing, fingerprinting, interrogation, and so on) contributed to the static visual construction of the migrants as exhausted, weakened, unkempt criminals. The public's general helplessness (Hay, 1995) served as the basis of their mobilization, recruiting them as participants to this process by way of their resentment of the migrants' unconventional means of travel and the refusal of the migrants to use 'the proper channels' to gain entry to Canada. The images thus became the very objects of mobilization. Ironically, it was only through the signification of these images that questions of national security and collective identity came to be articulated as worthy of the public's attention and concern.

The third mode of address pertains to the importance of *the broader social, political and economic context* in which the event was located and, consequently, in which the locus of moral panic must be sought. It is our argument – developed most fully in the final section – that the migrants' arrival tapped into a reservoir of social anxiety pertaining to the escalating presence of Chinese people in Canada; this threatened a deeply entrenched nostalgia for tradition and heritage, for cultural and aesthetic values, and for political habits (Li, 1994, 1998). The Chinese have always generated uncertainty and fear in Canada; they have never gained full acceptance as 'true Canadians.' Immigration from Asian countries now constitutes over 50 per cent of all immigrants to Canada, and most of these immigrants are of Chinese origin. Canadians' collective anxieties are intensifying in the face of a growing and upwardly mobile Chinese-Canadian community.

**Materials and Sampling Procedures**

Given the strong attention the media paid to the arrival of the migrants, 'hard' news reports form the basis of our analysis.[9] Opinion pieces, editorials, guest columns, and letters to the editor, though they provide useful insight into each newspaper's ideological preferences, have been excluded from this study because they are not bound by the conventional journalistic standards of objectivity and balance.[10]

We analyzed four mainstream daily newspapers: *The National Post*, the *Vancouver Sun*, the *Times Colonist* (Victoria), and the *Toronto Sun*. Our discussion has two main components. The first component is based on van

Dijk's finding (1986, 1988, 1994) that newspaper readers tend to remember only a few 'striking details' of a newspaper story, and consists of a numeric analysis of terms used to characterize the migrants in titles, headlines, and hard news stories. In particular, headlines have the important function of summoning historically derived, culturally shared models and scripts about people and events. In this sense, headlines serve as 'retrieval cues' (van Dijk, 1988: 228) that activate the relevant knowledge of readers so that they can better understand the point of the news report. To put it simply, there is a huge difference in impact between headlines referring to 'human cargo,' 'illegal aliens,' a 'human avalanche,' or an 'invasion,' and those that read, say, 'oppressed people arrive to freedom.' Furthermore, headlines serve to attract readers' attention; they do a great deal to sell newspapers and their ideas. So it can only expected that news reports about minorities will reflect prevailing ideological values and also reflect the attitudes toward ethnic groups of the newspaper's core audience (229) – and that headlines will reflect the same.

It has also become conventional in media analysis to show that the themes of news texts are organized in specific ways. So the second component utilizes critical discourse analysis (CDA) to discuss the semantic macrostructure, or thematic mapping, of the news discourse. It is mainly through CDA that we can begin to see how news coverage constructs societal narratives that speak to the present experiences of Canadians. However, we do not attempt to establish a clearly defined set of mutually exclusive categories, since a crucial characteristic of news coverage is that its themes often contradict and blur into one another.

The news coverage of the migrants assumed two distinct patterns. The first related to how the migrants were portrayed: from the arrival of the first ship, they were narrowly defined as 'illegal Chinese' or 'illegal Asians' who presented a significant threat to Canada's integrity. They were racialized within the parameters of a discourse of illegality, objectified as 'human cargo,' and used to amplify the 'problem' of uncontrolled, illegal Chinese migration to Canada. The second pattern related to the construction of a 'crisis' centred on the Canadian immigration and refugee systems. Once racialization took hold, it gave way to objectification, a discursive transformation that probably fostered the perception that the migrants were a serious threat to Canadian sovereignty. This in turn evolved into a debate over Canada's policies for dealing with refugees and undocumented migrants. This debate found expression mainly in terms of the health risks, and in terms of Canada's exposing itself to crime by letting these 'illegal Chinese migrants' stay in the country. Interestingly, interwoven with these concerns was the additional perception that the migrants were *victims* in an international human smuggling network.[11]

## Problematizing the Migrants

In the following two sections we argue that as soon as the first boat arrived off the coast of British Columbia, the migrants were racialized in the news media, prematurely branded as 'illegal,' and lumped into a homogenous category: the Chinese/Asian 'other.' Once further boats began arriving, and once rumours of still more boats began to circulate, the migrants were objectified within a racialized discourse of illegality, through the use of terms such as 'boat people,' 'human cargo,' 'aliens,' 'detainees,' and 'illegal Chinese.' This did much to amplify the 'problem' among the Canadian public: fewer than 600 people arriving on four boats over two months came to epitomize 'waves' of illegal Chinese/Asian refugee claimants.

### Racialization and Illegality

Two predominant themes comprised the central was discourse about the migrants: racialization and illegality. Immediate news coverage of the migrants made repeated reference to the fact that they were of 'Chinese' or 'Asian' origin; this created an instant epistemological distinction between 'Chinese' and 'Canadian,' 'Orient' and 'Occident,' 'us' and 'them' (see Said, 1978). A process of racialized 'othering,' reflected in headlines such as '*Chinese* Face Immigration Hurdle' (*Times Colonist*, 23 July 1999), 'Illegal *Chinese* Migration Flowing Around the World' (*National Post*, 29 July 1999) and 'Latest Shipload of *Asians* Lands to Mixed Reception' (*Vancouver Sun* 13 August 1999), served to homogenize the migrants in a narrow and stereotypical fashion. These migrants were never referred to as potential or would-be Canadians, though they were often referred to as would-be refugee claimants. The news coverage they generated relied on historically laden, homogenizing racialized imagery – 'race tagging.' This served to construct a perception of international human migration predominately in terms of a Chinese/Asian phenomenon.

Linked to this racialization process was the heavy use in the media of 'illegal' and related terms in reference to the migrants. Nearly 20 per cent of the headlines labelled them as illegal or referred to them as having violated accepted standards and norms of due process, and 24 per cent of hard news coverage characterized them as such (see Tables 7.1 and 7.2).[12] Consider the following passages:

- 'By mid-afternoon Tuesday, government bureaucrats and enforcement officials began moving into the area, preparing for the expected boatload of illegal Asian migrants' (12 August 1999, *The National Post*) ...

- 'A special team of immigration officials had rehearsed the scenario many times: a mystery ship filled with illegal aliens is discovered off B.C.'s coast' (21 July 1999, *Vancouver Sun*) ...

- 'An estimated 190 illegal Chinese migrants landed on Canada's West Coast yesterday aboard a battered, rusty ship, the third and largest boatload to arrive in the country this summer' (1 September 1999, *The National Post*) ...

In these passages an ontological identity is being forged based on racialized imagery of the migrants; any passengers on any future ships will be *ipso facto* 'illegal' and 'Chinese/Asian.' The dangers of prejudging the migrants based on vague perceptions of illegality became evident in early September 1999, when refugee hearings for some of the migrants were initiated. After weeks of news reports claiming that the migrants had *all* failed to produce proper identification papers, and that they *all* had plans to make bogus refugee claims, one of the migrants, Lin Juen Li, presented not only a copy of her People's Republic of China identification card, but also a certificate for forced abortion issued under the auspices of China's one-child law.[13] Despite what seemed to be a valid refugee claim, Lin Juen Li was still detained in handcuffs on the assumption that she 'would attempt to go underground and resume a perilous and *illegal* journey to the U.S.' (*Vancouver Sun*, 8 September 1999: A1).

The discourse of racialized illegality served to homogenize the migrants, and to pigeonhole them into the category 'Chinese/Asian Other' – illegally in Canada and with no legal right to stay. News coverage characterized them as law-breaking Chinese/Asian foreigners – a portrayal that culminated in a series of questionable 'findings' derived from opinion polls. For example, under the headline 'Most Say Migrants Should Go,' the *Times Colonist* wrote: 'Send them back. That's the opinion of the majority of callers who responded to Friday's Times Colonist phone poll on the 123 Chinese migrants who arrived here last week ... A total of 1,272 callers urged the federal government to give the newcomers a return trip home. And 44 indicated that they should be allowed to stay' (12 July 1999).

This report was accompanied by a discussion of the results of a second poll conducted one month later, carrying the headline: 'Go Home: Yes 3362 No 105.' The latter found expression in *The National Post* (16 August 1999) under the headline, 'B.C. Residents Tell Newspaper Poll They Want 250 Migrants Returned to China,' and in the *Toronto Sun* (16 August 1999) under the headline: 'Send *Chinese Illegals* Packing: B.C. poll.'[14]

*Objectification and Amplification*

In each of the sampled newspapers, racialization of the migrants, coupled with a discourse of illegality, pervaded the news coverage. As the number of news stories multiplied, the racialized imagery of illegality was supplemented by the objectification of the migrants and the amplification of the number of 'refugees' coming to Canada. More and more often the migrants were branded 'boat people,' 'detainees,' 'aliens,' and 'human cargo,' within the context that 'waves of Chinese' were entering the country illegally. This intensified the polarity between 'legitimate citizens' and 'devious illegals,' 'Canadians' and 'Chinese.'

As Fleras (1994) outlines, the media convey information about who racial minorities are, what they want, why they want what they do, and how they propose to get it. In essence, the media not only shape reality in a reciprocal ideological process with the wider sociopolitical affairs of the state, but also codify reality, encapsulating various phenomena in what DuCharme (1986) calls 'newsspeak': language that distorts, confuses, or hides reality. One way this is accomplished is by naming phenomena, that is, by objectifying reality. Table 7.1 indicates that 24 per cent of headlines objectified the migrants using pejorative terms other than direct reference to their actions and agency as illegal. As shown in Table 7.2, these terms accounted for nearly 26 per cent of hard news reporting.[15] Examples:

- 'Esquimalt shelters *boat people*' (*Times Colonist*, 22 July 1999)

- '*Boat people* prepared to test their refugee claims' (*Vancouver Sun*, 7 September 1999)

TABLE 7.1
Terms used in 'hard' news headlines to characterize Chinese refugees arriving to
Canada (20 July – 30 September 1999): Frequency of occurrence

| Terms | Vancouver Sun | Victoria Times Colonist | Toronto Sun | National Post | avg. % |
|---|---|---|---|---|---|
| 'Migrants' | 37.6 | 39.9 | 73.3 | 47.1 | 49.48 |
| 'Illegal migrants' | 8.6 | 9.4 | – | 10.0 | 07.00 |
| 'Boat people' | 15.1 | 7.2 | – | 1.4 | 07.90 |
| 'Chinese/Asians' | 9.7 | 23.2 | – | 14.3 | 11.80 |
| 'Refugees' | 6.5 | 6.5 | 9.7 | 8.6 | 07.83 |
| 'Illegal aliens' | 4.3 | 5.1 | – | 7.1 | 04.13 |
| 'Detainees' | 4.3 | 1.5 | – | – | 01.45 |
| Other/negative* | 2.1 | 4.3 | 13.3 | 8.6 | 07.08 |
| Other/neutral** | 3.2 | 2.9 | 3.7 | 2.9 | 03.18 |

*'Other/negative' refers generally to transgressive terms (e.g., queue jumpers, stow-
aways), for which there were fewer than three total counts (there were five such terms)
**'Other/neutral' refers to non-transgressive terms (e.g., passengers), for which there
were fewer than three total counts (there were six such terms)

TABLE 7.2
Terms used in 'hard' news articles to characterize Chinese refugees arriving to Canada
(20 July – 30 September 1999): Frequency of occurrence

| Terms | Vancouver Sun | Victoria Times Colonist | Toronto Sun | National Post | avg. % |
|---|---|---|---|---|---|
| 'Migrants' | 49.0 | 43.9 | 42.0 | 45.8 | 45.18 |
| 'Illegal migrants' | 8.1 | 8.7 | 17.6 | 21.7 | 14.03 |
| 'Refugee claimants' | 14.1 | 12.7 | 4.2 | 7.2 | 09.55 |
| 'Boat people' | 4.8 | 5.5 | 3.4 | 6.3 | 05.00 |
| 'Passengers' | 3.3 | 2.3 | 8.4 | 3.9 | 04.48 |
| 'Refugees' | 2.6 | 2.4 | 6.7 | 4.1 | 03.95 |
| 'Persons/People' | 5.0 | 5.5 | – | 1.7 | 03.05 |
| 'Human Cargo' | 2.3 | 3.9 | 3.4 | 2.9 | 03.13 |
| '(Illegal) aliens' | 3.3 | 5.0 | 2.2 | 2.2 | 03.18 |
| 'Chinese nationals' | 2.8 | 3.8 | 6.2 | 4.8 | 04.40 |
| 'Detainees' | 2.1 | 1.4 | – | – | 00.88 |
| Other/negative | 2.6 | 2.2 | 5.9 | 1.4 | 03.03 |
| Other/neutral | 2.4 | 2.5 | – | 1.0 | 01.48 |

- 'Ship Dumps *human cargo*' (*Times Colonist*, 12 August 1999)

- 'Snookered again by the *boat people*' (*Toronto Sun*, 15 August 1999)

  In terms of thematic coverage, news reporting conveyed to readers that

- 'The first boat with 123 passengers was intercepted near Nootka Sound, its human cargo taken into custody and escorted to Gold River.' (*Times Colonist*, 10 September 1999)

- 'Although human smuggling operations have been found before in B.C., this is the first time in recent memory a ship has been intercepted before it could get rid of its cargo.' (*Vancouver Sun*, 21 July 1999)

- 'RCMP confirmed Thursday night that its emergency response team had boarded a boat with human cargo of smuggled Chinese migrants at Nootka Sound.' (*Times Colonist*, 10 September 1999)

- 'After 72 days at sea from China, the vessel crammed with smuggled human cargo was being escorted to the west coast of Vancouver Island when officials concluded it could go no farther safely.' (*Toronto Sun*, 1 September 1999)

In these news headlines and passages, the migrants, human beings, are subsumed under codified, depersonalizing tropes and homogenized and objectified as 'things' subject to packaging, transportation, and disposal. Racialized imagery serves to accommodate 'commonsense' ideological rationalizations of the migrants as 'illegals,' who are infringing on the boundaries of the state and who exist outside the landscape of Canada's imagined community.

With the arrival of the second boat on 11 August 1999 – the 'next wave' – racialized imagery under the codified discourse of illegality was qualitatively enhanced. This stimulated the construction of a discourse centred on dramatic visions of an 'influx' or 'flood' of illegal Chinese migrants.[16] Table 7.3 illustrates that nearly 14 per cent of all thematic coverage of the migrants concentrated on 'overwhelming numbers of Chinese' coming to Canada. Though this percentage seems statistically insignificant, it should be noted that the theme of an influx was often cross-articulated with other themes relating to the weakness of Canada's immigration and refugee policies (which comprised 27 per cent of thematic coverage). Thus, various themes entrenched and legitimized one

TABLE 7.3
Themes of concern about Chinese Migrants: Frequency of Reference (%)

| Themes | Vancouver Sun | Victoria Times Colonist | Toronto Sun | National Post | avg. % |
|---|---|---|---|---|---|
| Victimization | 11.6 | 10.6 | 13.8 | 14.7 | 12.7 |
| Documentation and identification | 9.3 | 8.9 | 11.9 | 12.1 | 10.6 |
| Illegitimate (i.e. economic) refugees | 6.8 | 4.4 | 9.9 | 6.3 | 6.9 |
| Threat to public health and security | 15.0 | 13.1 | 20.8 | 20.6 | 17.4 |
| Int'l problem–int'l solutions | 7.5 | 5.4 | 2.0 | 4.8 | 4.9 |
| Overwhelming numbers of Chinese | 21.5 | 18.1 | 7.0 | 8.7 | 13.8 |
| Negative impact on welfare state | 8.6 | 15.8 | 9.9 | 6.7 | 10.3 |
| Repressive Chinese state | 7.8 | 1.1 | 2.0 | 6.0 | 4.2 |
| Creating anti-immigrant climate | 1.6 | 7.2 | 0.0 | 2.6 | 2.9 |
| Weak immigration/ refugee legislation | 9.8 | 11.8 | 17.7 | 15.2 | 13.2 |
| Other* | 1.5 | 3.6 | 5.0 | 2.3 | 3.1 |

*The category 'other' comprises references to four minor themes: (1) claims of corruption among Chinese government officials in facilitating illegal migration; (2) the treatment (negative and positive) of migrants at the hands of Canadian authorities; (3) deliberate attempts by the migrants to disrupt the refugee determination process; and (4) positive economic spin-offs of migrant influx in local areas.

another, and thus gave rise to an inflationary ideological effect of thematic significance. Under headlines such as 'Waves of Migrants: Canada's Door Stays Open' (Times Colonist, 12 September 1999), 'Smuggling: Mounties Find It Tough to Keep Up with Influx' (Times Colonist, 29 July 1999), and 'Third Wave Hits Red Tape (Toronto Sun, 2 September 1999), the news coverage revealed:

- 'Authorities are bracing for an onslaught of migrants circumventing Canada's normal immigration process by seeking refugee status' (10 August 1999, Times Colonist).

- 'A third wave of smuggled Chinese migrants is believed to have arrived in Canadian waters Monday.' (31 August 1999, *Times Colonist*).

- 'The flood of illegal immigrants that is increasingly coming ashore in Canada is being fed by a Chinese system so corrupt army vehicles have been used to shuttle people to smuggling ships.' (6 September 1999, *National Post*)

- 'Thousands of Chinese migrants have landed on the British Columbia coast in the past few years ... The traffic predates by several years this summer's influx of immigrant ships from China.' (11 September 1999, *Vancouver Sun*)

Clearly, the migrants' arrival precipitated the social construction of a rapidly escalating phenomenon of *illegal* transnational *Chinese/Asian* migration to Canada. Arguably, the processes of objectification and amplification, playing on racialized imagery of illegality, rationalized the continued detention of the migrants in a makeshift military prison. As hooks (1990) argues, racialized stereotypes are formulated to serve as substitutes for reality. Codified language objectified the migrants by assigning a name to a particular event (Fujanese citizens migrating to Canada); this elevated four marginal events to the status of a 'phenomenon'; this phenomenon was then amplified to serve as the basis for transforming a 'problem' into a 'crisis.' In the process the people who made these voyages were stripped of their human agency, depersonalized as 'illegal cargo,' and problematized as a threat to the Canadian immigration and refugee systems. Indeed, when it was revealed, on the arrival of the second boat, that a dog named Breeze had made the sixty-day journey, the Victoria SPCA was inundated with calls from prospective owners voicing their concern for Breeze's well-being. Meanwhile, the people on board the ship were handcuffed, fingerprinted, and processed for detention.[17]

**From Problematization to Crisis**

Around one month after the arrival and subsequent problematization of two boats carrying 254 people, 'Canada's Weekly Newsmagazine,' *Maclean's*, carried a seven-page exposé of the events behind the cover headline: 'Canada's Open Door' (23 August 1999). The coverage in *Maclean's* represented a turning point for news reporting on the migrants. With the arrival of the second boat (accompanied by rumours of more to come), the discourse stopped focusing exclusively on illegality, and began to consider the state of Canada's immigration and refugee policies. The question in play now was whether the migrants posed a health risk and whether their intentions were criminal. The arrival of fewer than 600 migrants stimulated a nationwide debate about whether Canada's admission standards should be tightened.

In the next two sections we consider whether the migrants posed a health risk to Canadians and whether they did in fact have criminal intentions. The latter question in particular will demonstrate how the 'problem' of the migrants resulted in the social construction of a discursive crisis centred on the need to detain, criminalize, and ultimately deport the migrants.

*Health and Crime*

Although not as prominent as the discourses of racialization, illegality, objectification, and amplification, an attendant theme found in the news coverage revolved around fabricated health and security risks that the migrants allegedly posed to Canadian citizens. As we argue elsewhere (Greenberg and Hier, 2000), this portrayal encompassed three particular features: first, that the migrants were bringing with them infectious diseases; second, that their arrival would prompt a dramatic increase in organized crime; and third, that Canada was a stopover to their ultimate destination – the United States.

As a sort of early priming mechanism for things to come, *The National Post* (21 July 1999) quoted an RCMP spokesperson on the arrival of the first boat: 'There are concerns about *infectious diseases* because of the conditions they've been living under and we have been prepared to deal with that, to make sure it's safe for our people to go aboard.'

Table 7.3 demonstrates that the perceived threat to national security, encapsulating public health threats, accounted for just over 17 per cent of all thematic representations of the migrants. Again, the ideological significance of this theme was greater than its relatively small percentage would suggest. This is because it was linked discursively to the theme of victimization in particular, and in general to concerns about the capacity of Canadian legislation to curb the number of asylum seekers and other 'undocumented aliens.' For example, directly under the headline 'Reform Sees AIDS Risk,' the *Times Colonist* (3 September 1999) introduced this paragraph: 'Canadians could be at risk from terrorists and communicable diseases such as AIDS if action isn't taken soon to toughen Canada's immigration law, the Reform Party warned Thursday.' The article then proceeded to grant Reform Party leader Preston Manning a central voice alongside a photograph of the boat that the third group of migrants travelled on. It quoted Manning as follows: '*Immigration law* should ensure would-be *refugees* are properly screened, but if people can't get around all those provisions, then you expose yourself to all those *dangers* ... *criminal elements* and people with violent political habits and *communicable diseases.*'

The above passages introduced to the public the unsubstantiated notion that immigrants and refugees in general, and these *Chinese* migrants in particular, are/were carriers of communicable diseases. More importantly, they linked the threat of disease to immigration and refugee policy, and thereby lent credence to the growing perception of a wider crisis in Canada's national security. This technique is often found in the literature produced by racial supremacist organizations such as the Heritage Front (see Hier, 2000). Indeed, Leon Benoit, the immigration critic for the Reform Party (now the Canadian Alliance) and co-chair of the House of Commons Standing Committee on Citizenship and Immigration, was quoted as saying:

> Canadians face increased threats of contracting *AIDS* and *tuberculosis* from poorly screened *immigrants* and international criminals and terrorist groups find Canada an easy country in which to operate. (3 September 1999, *The National Post*)
>
> The consequences [of the migrants' arrival] are Canadians facing *increased health risks* though *diseases* like *tuberculosis* and *AIDS*, which are coming to our country increasingly through various types of *immigration*. (3 September 1999, *Times Colonist*)

As summer descended and rumours of more boats destined for Canada continued to spread, a discourse of criminalization began to play a central role in the news coverage. At the same time, the migrants' landing was being constructed as a wider crisis in Canadian immigration policy. the *National Post* carried a front-page story titled 'China Warned about Alien Smuggling,' which opened with this paragraph: 'Chinese officials warned Canada in June that smuggling of *illegal aliens* to Canada would increase because of our *refugee policies*' (16 August 1999).

The news stories that followed over the next month consistently linked the migrants to organized crime:

- '*Drug ship* could be next, police fear' (26 August 1991, *Times Colonist*)

- 'Organized *criminals* bringing paying customers to Vancouver Island are dealing in humans now, but tomorrow it could be heroin, credit cards or counterfeit money.' (26 August 1999, *Times Colonist*)

- '*Organized crime* groups in China are providing false documents to people interested in obtaining student visas as a back-door way to *illegally* enter Canada.' (27 August 1999, *The National Post*)

- '*Chinese gangs* operating out of the Caribbean and South America are warehousing *illegal migrants* by the *thousands* before helping them enter Canada.' (16 September 1999, *The National Post*)

Henry and colleagues (2000) contend that the criminal activities of racialized minorities, although perpetrated by isolated individuals, are often interpreted as 'group crime.' The news coverage was constructing a Chinese criminal element in the context of a racialized and objectifying discourse of 'us' and 'them,' 'Canadian' and 'Chinese.' For example, after items such as pens, safety pins, combs, and a dinner plate with a 'sharpened edge' were found among some of the migrants' belongings, news reports multiplied around the 'seizure of makeshift weapons from *123 Chinese* refugee-claimants detained at Victoria, B.C.' Furthermore 'a *similar group of illegal Chinese* immigrants broke out of an Australian jail' (28 July 1999, *The National Post*).[18]

*The Birth of a Crisis*

By the end of two months' news coverage, the media has succeeded in constructing a social crisis centred on Canadian immigration and refugee policy. Table 7.3 indicates that just over 13 per cent of all hard news coverage was concerned with perceived problems in the immigration and/or refugee systems. Examples:

- 'The federal government has come under fire over its immigration policies since the recent arrival of the *illegal* migrants. Polling indicates Canadians want a tougher system for dealing with *smugglers* and the *immigrants*.' (3 September 1999, *The National Post*)

- 'Two of Canada's *top political leaders* called for *tough* and fast action on the migrants ... *Illegal* migrants should get a speedy hearing and be whisked out of Canada within a week if they can't prove their refugee claims are genuine, says reform leader Preston Manning.' (17 September 1999, *Times Colonist*)

After the arrival of the second boat, the *Times Colonist* often published a 'HAVE YOUR SAY' response form on the front cover of editions that discussed the migrants. This 'coupon' informed readers: 'Here is your opportunity to call for action on the *chaotic* situation that has seen hundreds of illegal migrants arrive in unsafe ships on Canada's shores this summer. Fill out this coupon indicating your view on the best way to deal with the *crisis*' (emphases added).

At this point, news reports of the *crisis*, which till now had focused on weaknesses in the Canadian immigration and refugee systems, began targeting the cost of dealing with the migrants. As Fleras (1994) notes, media reporting on refugees often sets sights on processing and detention costs. Here, for example, headlines in *The National Post* declared, '*Military Exceeds Budget* by Tracking Migrants' (15 September 1999) and 'Ottawa Has Spent *$2-million* So Far on Food, Lodging for 600 Migrants (24 September 1999). The *Vancouver Sun* (1 September 1999) reported that care for each of the seventy-five 'migrant children' under the custody of British Columbia's Children and Families Ministry was costing taxpayers *$8,200* per month. The *Times Colonist* (29 July 1999) informed its readers that the 'migrant bill reached *$200,000* in two weeks.'[19]

In early September, motivated by the escalating perception that a crisis existed, Foreign Affairs Minister Lloyd Axworthy announced that he might send Canadian authorities to China to deal with *the crisis* in China-to-Canada population movements. In April 2000, the immigration minister, Elinor Caplan, visited Fujian to try to stem the 'flow' of would-be migrants. Shortly after that, in an especially bizarre event, after eight months' incarceration ninety migrants were suddenly repatriated to Fujian by force under heavy police security, which included a police riot squad, guard dogs, and a black-garbed emergency-response team (11 May 2000, *The Globe and Mail*). As of late July 2000, only sixteen of the migrants (fewer than 1 per cent) had been granted refugee status.[20]

The preceding analysis reveals that over a period of two months, the Canadian news media did a great deal to construct a crisis centring on Canada's immigration and refugee systems. The discourse drew heavily on notions of racialized illegality, objectified identities, amplified migration patterns, health risks, and criminality – notions that were heavily idealized and often fabricated. Meanwhile, politicians, government representatives, and various factions of the lay population mobilized to confront the phenomenon of *illegal* migration by unwelcome foreigners. The result was moral panic.

Especially noteworthy about the data we have presented is that although many of the percentages representing various patterns rarely exceeded 20 per cent of total news coverage, all of the data in Tables 7.1, 7.2, and 7.3, and many of those in Table 7.4, are negative. Furthermore, as shown in Table 7.4, the points of view most often presented in the newspaper coverage of the migrants were those of politicians, government representatives, and police personnel. Only 1.3 per cent of all the news coverage we analysed used the migrants as a news source. The figure for police personnel was nearly 20 per cent; for domestic government representatives it was 42 per cent. In other words, by far most of the news coverage was based on the opinions of politicians, government officials, and the police, who characterized the migrants as health risks, financial burdens, and criminals.

### Racial Exclusionism, Postmodern Capitalism, and the Chinese in Canada

One question demands immediate attention: How did the arrival of fewer than 600 migrants over sixty days mushroom into a crisis of national security? Goode and Ben-Yehuda (1994) discussed what they call the grassroots model of moral panic, which is based on the supposition that neither politicians nor the media are capable of fabricating social anxiety where none actually exists. According to the grassroots model, moral panic must be based on genuine public anxieties and concerns. We contend that the moral panic over the arrival of the migrants derived its particular strength from the fears and anxieties many Canadians hold concerning the growing presence of the Chinese in Canada, and from related uncertainties stemming from globalization and the rise of neoliberal ideology. In this section we argue that in the era of postmodern capitalism, which is characterized by globalization, capital consolidation, and a political shift to right, Euro-Canadian economic and cultural hegemony is increasingly being challenged by an upwardly mobile and steadily rising Chinese-Canadian population. The arrival of the migrants agitated a reservoir of social anxiety pertaining to whether Canada's national identity was resilient enough to withstand social transformation in this increasingly inhospitable world (see Husbands, 1994; Feredi, 1997: 59-70).

TABLE 7.4
News sources and point of view (POV): Frequency of reference

| | Source (%) | | | | POV (%) | | | |
|---|---|---|---|---|---|---|---|---|
| | Vancouver Sun | Victoria Times Colonist | Toronto Sun | National Post | Vancouver Sun | Victoria Times Colonist | Toronto Sun | National Post |
| Government (domestic)* | 39.9 | 40.9 | 60.5 | 33.1 | 38.0 | 40.2 | 58.0 | 31.9 |
| Government (foreign) | 7.2 | 5.2 | 0.0 | 11.2 | 7.4 | 4.1 | 0.0 | 10.1 |
| Police** | 19.0 | 18.3 | 18.2 | 28.1 | 20.0 | 20.4 | 20.2 | 29.0 |
| Political opposition | 13.3 | 14.7 | 10.0 | 9.4 | 18.8 | 18.6 | 10.3 | 9.5 |
| Lawyers | 7.3 | 9.0 | 3.8 | 6.5 | 7.8 | 8.9 | 4.6 | 7.6 |
| Migrants | 1.4 | 1.7 | 0.0 | 2.1 | 1.6 | 1.7 | 0.0 | 1.5 |
| Non-governmental orgs | 5.7 | 4.9 | 1.8 | 2.5 | 3.6 | 2.9 | 2.3 | 2.9 |
| Other/mixed | 6.2 | 5.3 | 5.7 | 6.1 | 2.8 | 3.2 | 4.6 | 7.5 |

*Government (domestic) = federal, provincial, and municipal, including Ministry of Immigration, Citizenship and Immigration Canada, and Immigration and Refugee Board
**Police = RCMP, Military (i.e., Navy), Canadian Security Intelligence Service (CSIS), and Coast Guard

*Postmodern Capitalism, the New Middle Class, and Racist Backlash*

During the period of Canadian nation building leading up to the Second World War, the experience of the Chinese in Canada was one of manual labour, exploitation, public resentment, institutional discrimination, and outright exclusion (see, for example, Li and Bolaria, 1983; Anderson, 1983; Boyko, 1995; Li, 1998). Not until after the war did the siutation begin to improve for them, and for non-Europeans in general. Canadian immigration policy has always attempted to control the volume and type of immigration (Li, 1996). At least since 1980, a large part of that policy has been to attract immigrants who are willing and able to invest in and contribute to the Canadian economy. Asian immigration to Canada was 71,421 between 1954 and 1967 (around 4 per cent of total immigration); between 1985 and 1992 it was 692, 782 (around 50 per cent of total immigration) (Li, 1996). In 1994, 223,875 immigrants came to Canada and 63.9 per cent of them were from Asia, nearly half of these (64,066) from China, Hong Kong, and Taiwan. Based on current immigration rates, by 2005 a significant percentage of urban Canadians will be visible minorities, and most of them will be of Chinese origin. Canadian immigration policy has undergone a profound shift: the Chinese are no longer summoned *by* capital, but summoned *for* capital.

As Karl Marx (1976: 932) went to some lengths to affirm, 'capital is not so much a thing, but a social relation between persons which is mediated through things.' This suggests that reliance on foreign capital involves the movement of not only money but also the 'agents' of capital (Miles and Satzewich, 1990). In terms of Canada, increased immigration from Asian countries – especially Hong Kong, Taiwan, and mainland China – since the 1980s has resulted in substantial investment capital for the country, but it has also led to the rise of 'the new Chinese middle class.' The new Chinese middle class, which is characterized by considerable wealth, education, and capital holdings, has stimulated significant social and economic change in Canada's largest cities (Li, 1998).

With the growth and success of this new middle class, many Canadians are feeling increasingly uncertain (Simmons, 1997). The racist stereotypes that all Canadians hold about the Chinese have been strongly challenged by the exceptional achievements of Chinese Canadians over the past three decades. Yet at the same time, old racist phobias are being reinvoked in the form of conflicts over 'inappropriate houses,' 'conflictual cultural values,' 'substandard social integration,' and 'criminality.'

The result has been a racist backlash against Chinese-Asian immigrants.
For example:

- The Canadian news media regularly highlight the involvement of
  'Asian or Chinese gangs' in drug trafficking, violence, and general
  criminal activity (on the racialization of crime in the Canadian news
  media, see Henry and Tator, 2000). In their study of Canadian news
  coverage of the ethnic Chinese community, Ma and Hildebrandt
  (1993) found that reporting of 'Asian crime' in the *Vancouver Sun* and
  *Toronto Star* increased more than 300 per cent between 1970 and
  1990.

- Chinese students entering the public school system are perceived as
  speaking English so poorly that they damage the learning environment for other students. Also, there is a general assumption that university students from China are actually migrants who are using
  exchange-student programs to enter the country, with no intention of
  leaving (Laquian and Laquian, 1997).

- Asian immigrants are accused of exploiting the welfare system by
  sponsoring relatives and then abandoning their promises. They are
  also accused of being 'parachutists' and 'astronauts' – that is, of com-
  muting to Asian countries to attend to business affairs while evading
  Canadian taxes (Laquian and Laquian, 1997).

- In 1993, when *Miss Saigon* opened at Toronto's Princess of Wales Theatre, protests against the production mounted. Resistance to *Miss
  Saigon* was based on the argument that the production eroticized
  racial difference(s) and played on rigid and demeaning stereotypes of
  Asian women (Tator, Henry, and Mattis, 1997). At a time when resentment of the Asian-Canadian presence in the country was building,
  *Miss Saigon* carried particular symbolic currency, in that it reinforced
  the socially constructed barrier between 'true Canadians' and the
  'Oriental other.'

- Members of the new Chinese middle class tend to move into neigh-
  bourhoods traditionally occupied by Canadians of European descent.
  Also, a number of Asian 'mega-malls' have been built or are being
  planned to cater specifcally to Chinese by offering Chinese goods and
  services. In the late 1980s and early 1990s this led to tensions in the
  suburbs of Richmond (near Vancouver) and Agincourt (on the edge
  of Toronto). In Agincourt, the public resentment took on a racial

character, though it expressed itself through grievances over traffic congestion, noise pollution, and parking (Li, 1998).

- In the past decade, popular stereotypes of the Chinese have abounded in everyday discourse. The University of British Columbia has been called the 'University of a Billion Chinese,' and the epithet 'Chinks Go Home!' has been inscribed on benches around the UBC campus (Laquian and Laquian, 1997). Vancouver has been nick-named 'Hong-couver,' and Toronto's Agincourt, 'Asian-court.' Such stereotyping sends an unambiguous message regarding who 'belongs' and who does not; more prominently, it speaks to the perceived threat to Euro-Canadian hegemony.

- The Chinese have been accused of creating 'unneighbourly houses' in residential areas of Vancouver. Vancouver residents (i.e., the White ones) point to the social and cultural characteristics of the Chinese in their efforts to block the construction of 'monster homes.' Interest-ingly, as Li (1994) demonstrates, often it was not the Chinese who bought up many of these houses, whatever the popular belief. None-theless, a racialized discourse has marginalized the Chinese commu-nity in areas such as Shaughnessy, and reinforced the perception that foreigners are taking over the city and destroying its European char-acter.

The growth of the new Chinese middle class has heightened fears about the Chinese in Canada. Ever since its inception in the mid-1980s, the Canadian Business Immigration Program has enabled Chinese Cana-dians to grow and prosper. This prosperity has created a racist backlash, which has taken a variety of forms, including (but not limited to) stereo-typing, resentment, marginalization, discrimination, and exclusion.

Canadians are reluctant to talk about their own racism; in the same vein, they hesitate to discuss immigration policy for fear of being accused of harboring racist sentiments (Laquian and Laquian, 1997). Henry and Tator (1994) explain this reluctance in terms of conflicting ideological value systems. Many Canadians are committed to the liberal-democratic principles of justice, equality, and fairness, but also to racist values that take the form of resentment against minority groups. This suggests that though many Canadians endorse basic human rights in *philosophical* terms, in practice they would prefer to maintain the status quo. This ideological conflict was reflected in the public's reaction to the migrants after the arrival of the second boat. The Angus Reid Group surveyed 1,502 Canadian adults (31 August 1999) and found that 49 per cent of Canadians believed the migrants should be returned to China immediately, and 49 per cent believed they should be allowed to apply for refugee status. Nonetheless, as Laquian and Laquian (1997: 11) correctly point out, more and more Asian immigrants consider it so much academic hair splitting to discuss whether they are the target(s) of 'symbolic,' 'backlash,' 'systemic,' or 'democratic' racism. The principles which underpin democratic liberalism were undermined by the racialization, objectification, and criminalization of the migrants. This in turn led to deportation proceedings and to the igniting of a national debate on the state of Canadian immigration and refugee policy.

## Conclusion

As a result of the rise of the Chinese new middle class, racial tensions have been mounting in Canada. The perception that Chinese Canadians are a foreign race possessing cultural values and habits incompatible with Occidental traditions stems from the history of Canadian nation building, and continues to generate hostilities against the Chinese in Canada (Li, 1998). At the same time, globalization and postmodern capitalism are continuing to create socioeconomic fractures on an international scale, and to reinforce divisions between 'have' and 'have-not' countries. The world's migrants are more skilled and better educated than they used to be. That being said, in the face of shifting investment, production, and employment patterns, a sizable non-White, 'unskilled' labour pool continues to circulate around the globe. When migratory populations circumvent existing immigration policies and enter Western capitalist nations 'illegally,' as happened in this case study, they often come to embody a wider resentment of the minority population residing in the host country (Husbands, 1994). In less than two months, the Canadian print media constructed a discursive crisis that resulted in a public debate focused on national security and state sovereignty. As a consequence, there was a hardening of attitudes and policies relating to undocumented migratory populations. All this, as a result of the arrival of only 599 migrants.

One year later, the migrants were still making headlines in Canadian newspapers. On 3 June 2000, facing immediate deportation, seven migrants escaped from Prince George Regional Correctional Centre.

The following day, RCMP officers, police dogs, and a helicopter equipped with an infrared camera were tracking them. In a scene straight out of a Hollywood movie, the migrants were represented in news reporting as criminals and wrong-doers, as escapees on the run from the law. Globalization, it seems, is not without its ironies.

# 9

# The Racialization of Crime

The strategies employed by the media to construct crime reflect the selectivity of news personnel and the news media to crime, the role of news values – that is, which crimes have higher news value (typically, murders and other violent offences) – and the routines and practices established in the industry. The public's view of crime reflects what the media think is newsworthy. Members of the public do not ordinarily have first-hand experience or knowledge of crime. It follows that the world of criminal activity is constructed for them by the media.

Hall et al. (1975, 1978) note that news making and crime are related in the sense that crime has always been considered dramatic, even sensational, as well as disruptive of society's social fabric. The 'news' is supposed to report such incidents. Crime is one of the oldest news categories. Crime news can be either routine or sensational. Routine crimes involve ordinary people and are given little if any newspaper coverage. The sensational crimes are the ones that involve personalities, or take place under unusual circumstances, or involve more than one victim, or, in our increasingly heterogeneous society, are interracial or intercultural.

The media raise the public's anxiety about crime. The well-known discourse on crime statistics and whether those statistics (or any other kind) should be compiled on the basis of race) was largely media driven. Moreover, the media, in line with their traditional news values, often find ways to keep sensational stories in the news. The term 'media feeding frenzy' is often used to describe this phenomenon. The extended coverage given to the Just Desserts case is only one example. There are many others, including events that have nothing to do with crime but only with charges of racism.[1] These 'over-eventized' incidents have led to moral panics about the crime rate, drugs, race, youth violence, the need to control immigration, and so on.

### The Construction of People of Colour by the Media: 'Blacks'

One of the most important factors in the racializing of crime is the over-reporting of crimes allegedly committed by people of colour – especially Blacks.[2]

There has been considerable concern about how the media represent people of colour, and especially Blacks, as having criminal propensities. However, it should also be noted that the media construct them in ways that are, furthermore, damaging to their personal identity and to their social status in the community. One of the first major studies to demonstrate this was that of Hall and colleagues (1978) in the United Kingdom. The resulting book, *Policing the Crisis* (1978), showed that the media not only played a crucial role in generating public fear about crime, but also isolated a specific type of criminal, who was supposedly responsible for the new wave of crimes called 'muggings.' The media were largely responsible for implanting the idea that young Black males were enemies of society rather than the products of depressed socio-economic conditions. Most working-class crime develops from such conditions.

Black youth are being criminalized in the U.K., and increasingly in Toronto, where Asian youth gangs are also being targeted. The findings of the Hall study are in accord with those of Ericson (1987) and colleagues, especially when deviance is broadly defined as difference from socially accepted norms. Ericson (1987) suggests that deviance is the 'defining characteristic of what journalists regard as newsworthy' (4). Moreover, the concept of deviance influences how journalists go about their work: how they choose stories, how they select and use sources, and how they finally write stories.

In the United States, there is considerable evidence that the media construct Blacks as criminally disposed. They do this through three particular strategies. First, they use racially coded language and images that portray African Americans as more 'dangerous, less deserving of sympathy, and less capable of rehabilitation than Whites' (Center on Crime, Communities and Culture, 2000). Examples include the use of the terms 'superpredators, maggots and animals' to refer to inner-city Black youth crime; White young criminals are not described with such hyperbole. Entman and Rojecki (2000) found that Black suspects were four times more likely than Whites to be shown in mug shots and in handcuffs. Second, the media 'search for the "newsworthy" victim.' This results in sensationalized overreporting of incidents involving Blacks. The media frenzy surrounding the O.J. Simpson trial is an example from the United States. In Canada, the overzealous reporting of the Just Desserts murder is a case in point. Third, the media report crime through 'the narrow lens of law-and-order.' Studies indicate that the American media are more likely to report the killings of Whites. It is suggested that a 'Black or Latino corpse is perhaps "less newsworthy" than a White one' (ibid). This strategy can be seen in Canada as well. More coverage was given to the trial of the Black man convicted of the killing of a bank teller in Brampton, than there ever was to any murder of a Black by another Black.

There is plenty of evidence that television reinforces racism and racist stereotypes (Howitt, 1998). There are hardly any Black news readers or on-air reporters, and very few in behind-the-camera decision-making roles. Twelve per cent of Americans are Black, yet Black men account for only 4 per cent of major roles, Black women for only 2 per cent. When Blacks are shown, they often appear in groups, which suggests that Blacks associate only with members of their own race. TV also reinforces stereotypes of Blacks in more subtle ways. For example, it shows more White people in positions of authority or demonstrating superior knowledge. Whites are also shown dispensing goods and favours, whereas Black people do not seem capable of giving anything to anybody else. A familiar stereotype about Blacks is that they are good at sports and entertainment. As a result, all the media devote a considerable amount of attention to Black people in sports and entertainment.

A study of Canadian TV news – specifically, of the evening news on CBC and CTV – analysed news stories to determine whether the people interviewed were White, racial minorities, or Native Canadians (Perigoe and Lazar, 1992). Of 756 interview subjects, 4 per cent were visible minorities and 3.1 per cent were Native people; the remainder were White. Statistics Canada data show that that same year, visible minorities accounted for 6.4 per cent of the population and Native people for 3.6 per cent; so it seems that they participated in news stories in rough proportion to their numbers. However, when consideration was given to the content of the stories in which visible minorities and Native people were seen, it was found that almost all the stories in which non-Whites appeared were about non-Whites. There were only twenty stories on general topics – political issues, taxes, and so on – in which non-Whites were interviewed.

In another study, Grenier analysed how Montreal's *Gazette* covered Native issues over six months in 1991 and found that of 357 articles, 206

(58 per cent) dealt with 'protest' issues, such as the Oka seige. He also found that headlines dealing with Oka contained a large percentage (71 per cent) of conflict-based terms and references to race or Native status. These headlines – which readers see first and which are sometimes the only part of the article they do read – associated Native people with conflict.

With respect to race and news reporting, Campbell (1995) has shown that even mainstream reporting can harbour and reproduce racism. He suggests that when news organizations in the United States publish stories of successful Blacks and other minorities, they feed the myth that success is open to everyone. When the majority of news accounts focus on criminal behaviour, such as 'killers of pizza parlor employees, mothers who leave their children home alone to die in fires, and so on – the implication is that these people had the same options and preparation necessary to seize The American Dream, yet chose a life of savagery and/or destitution instead.' In another significant study of racism in television news, Entman and Rojecki (2000) posit three aspects of racism in the news:

1. An anti-Black effect – or emotive hostility towards Black people results from the emphasis on crime-related activities of Black people often showing them in mug shots or being handcuffed and led away by White police officers.
2. Resistance to political demands of Black people – this comes about as a result of the belief that Blacks demand more rights and benefits then their work deserves. The media reinforce this belief by showing Black politicians addressing only Black audiences and Black issues. On TV, the use of sound bites, which show the anger of the individual or his '*emotional*' tirade, sustains the image of Black political figures as more emotional and angry than others.
3. The belief that racism is dead and no longer an issue is ironically promulgated by the use of Black journalists and authorities, however infrequent.

A definitive study about the relationship between race and perceptions of criminality was conducted in 1996. In an experiment, Peffley and colleagues showed two videos of a crime story to a group of subjects (in Kidd-Hewett and Osborne, 1998). The videos were identical except that in one, a White suspect was led away in handcuffs, and in the other, it was an African-American. The participants were then asked a series of questions about the suspect, for example, whether he was guilty or not and whether he was likely to commit more crimes in the future. They found that the more racist viewers thought the Black suspect was guilty and likely to commit more crimes. The researchers concluded that racist stereotypes are activated by media reports showing Blacks involved in criminal activities.

Although the research evidence is still scanty, there is general agreement that media reporting produces, reproduces, and reinforces racist stereotyping. But so far there is little evidence that media reports actually *cause* crime, either by or against minorities.

Most of these research findings speak to the situation of racism in the United States and Britain. In Canada, the similarities are stark and the trends much the same. In the next section we present a quantitative analysis of articles reporting on two ethnic groups: Jamaicans and Vietnamese.

**The Construction of 'Jamaican' and 'Vietnamese'**

We used quantitative methods to capture an overview of how these two groups were reported on in the press. We created two databases. For the first, we downloaded from the Canadian News Disks for 1994–97 all articles published in the *Toronto Star*, the *Toronto Sun*, and the *Globe and Mail* in which Jamaica or Jamaicans and Vietnamese were featured. This yielded 2,622 articles featuring Jamaicans and 386 articles featuring Vietnamese. For the second database, we downloaded from the same disks all articles on all crimes committed by everybody, not just people of colour. However, we did this for only three time periods: April–May 1994; April–May 1996; and September–October 1997. These two-month periods and years were chosen at random. We categorized crimes by type: sex crimes, murder, break and enter, fraud, and so on. This second database held 2,840 articles, of which 443 were from the *Globe*, 1,506 from the *Star*, and 876 from the *Sun*. We then analyzed this database to ascertain how many articles identified people of colour.

Forty-five per cent of the 2,622 articles mentioning Jamaica or Jamaicans fell into the categories of sports and entertainment. This overemphasis perpetuates the stereotype that Black people excel at running and singing but cannot perform competitively in other arenas of life. Rarely is there any reporting on Black professionals in other fields. In the *Star* and the *Sun*, 39 per cent of all the articles dealing with Jamaicans in the randomly selected periods concerned social issues such as crime and justice, immigration, and deportation. The remainder fell into food and travel, events in Jamaica (including a number of articles on crime, policing, and corruption in Jamaica), and other categories. Positive stories about Jamaicans accounted for only 2 per cent of all articles. Thus, the media have constructed Jamaicans as people from a crime-ridden and poverty-stricken country who are good at sports and entertainment but who consistently present Canadian society with myriad social problems. In other words, they have been constructed quite clearly as problem people.

Regarding the Vietnamese, 37 per cent of the articles related to crime and justice issues. Another 37 per cent fell into the 'social problem' category. So it seems that the Vietnamese are being constructed in the media as criminals, though to a lesser extent than the Jamaicans.

*The Use of Racial Identifiers*

When newspapers identify crime suspects or their victims by racial identifiers, the term 'Black' is encountered most often – at least twice as often as 'White.' In fact, 46 per cent of all crime articles in the *Globe* that used a racial or ethnic descriptor involved Blacks or people of Caribbean origin. In the *Star*, the figure was 38.5 per cent, and in the *Sun*, 25.6 per cent.

Regarding articles about deportation, by far the largest number deal with Blacks and/or Jamaicans: 44 of 102 articles analyzed in the *Star*, the *Sun* and the *Globe*. Whites were mentioned 16 times in these stories, Nazis 15 times.

Almost one-third of the pictures used with crime stories depicted people of colour – roughly equal to their percentage in the GTA population. However, Blacks were overrepresented. They constitute less than 7 per cent of the population, yet they were depicted in 44 per cent of all the photos of racial minorities used in the three papers during the study period. More than half of the photos of alleged Black criminals appeared in the *Sun*.

We now conduct a critical discourse analysis (CDA) of two specific case studies. The Just Desserts café killing, and a murder in a Chinese restaurant.

**Discourse Analysis of Just Desserts**

On the evening of 5 April 1994, three young Black men entered the Just

Desserts Café in midtown Toronto demanding money and jewellery from the patrons. Around twenty people were held at gunpoint, and when several of them resisted, one of the assailants pulled out a sawed-off shotgun and, seemingly at random, shot one of the patrons. A young White woman, Georgina Leimonis, was gravely wounded and died shortly afterwards in hospital. The robbers fled in a waiting car driven by a fourth man. The trial of three men concluded in December 1999 with two found guilty and one not guilty.[3]

This case generated widespread media coverage, including articles, features, editorials, and many photographs of the assailants. The main reasons for this amount of coverage and media commentary was that Just Desserts went far beyond a shooting of a helpless victim: it raised a 'moral panic' of enormous dimensions and led to public discourses about a number of social issues, such as the importance of tighter gun control and the need to get tougher with young offenders. Most importantly, the case inspired a heated debate over immigration and the deportation of alleged criminals. In addition to all this, the shooting occurred in a supposedly safe area, in an exclusive café frequented mainly by the fashion and design crowd. So it therefore raised the issue of rich people's safety.

Race became a focus of all these controversies. The victim was White, and the alleged shooters were young Black men of Jamaican heritage. This is an ideal case to analyse, since it highlights important social issues. It also provides powerful examples of newer forms of racism, such as those that invoke the supposed inferiority of 'foreign' cultures. Moreover, the substantial media attention paid to it, and to another case involving a person of Jamaican origin, contributed significantly to changes in the law by tightening the rules for relating to the deportation of alleged criminals. This is an unusual case in that we can directly trace a cause–effect relationship between media reporting and policy changes. It was the uproar created by the Just Desserts shooting – and to a certain extent by the Baylis shooting – that led to a bill to strengthen Canada's provisions on deportation.[4]

*The Major Discourses*

We downloaded all articles about the Just Desserts case in the three mainstream Toronto newspapers for the period 1994–7. All told, we analysed 210 articles using critical linguistic analysis. This analysis revealed, first of all, that besides reporting 'just the facts,' the papers developed three discourses about some aspect of law and order:

- The discourse of gun control appeared in fifty-one articles.
- The discourse of the young offender appeared in eighteen articles.
- The discourse of immigration/deportation appeared in thirty-four articles (see Table 8.1).

Our database comprised 201 articles: 37 from the *Globe*, 88 from the *Sun*, and 76 from the *Star*.

### The *Globe and Mail*

During the eight weeks of coverage of the Just Desserts case included in our analysis, the *Globe* published thirty-seven articles. Eleven of these related to gun control, seven to young offenders, and eight to immigration/deportation. Three (8 per cent) of the articles could be categorized as 'minority' articles.

In the first article in the *Globe*, which was published *before* the suspects in the Just Desserts killing had been identified by the police, the murder was likened to crimes in Chinatown and to similar crimes in New York City (Gay Abbate, 7 April 1994: A1). Crime was thus represented in the very early reporting as un-Canadian – as an imported deviant practice. For example, Michael Valpy wrote in his first of three columns on the Just Desserts case: 'Getting robbed in an Annex restaurant is alien enough ... Mindless, gratuitous violence belongs to New York, to Los Angeles ... not Toronto and Ottawa' (7 April 1994: A2). Four of the other five articles that were published within three days of the event drew comparisons between American and Canadian crime rates.

On the following day, 8 April, the police released descriptions of the alleged perpetrators. In subsequent reporting in the *Globe*, these were often generically identified as 'young Black males.' For example, on its front page on 8 April, the *Globe* reported: 'For some, the fact that it was a Black man who shot Georgina Leimonis underscored what appears to be growing involvement of *young Black men* in violent robberies in the city' (Abbate and Hess, 8 April, 1994: A1, emphasis added). By the end of the first week of reporting, what Valpy termed Toronto's 'empirical problem' had been more specifically identified as 'a growing tendency toward random violent crime ... particularly among young Black people of Jamaican origin' (12 April, 1994: A2). Furthermore, explicit associations between crime and Blacks and/or Jamaicans were made in fourteen of the thirty-seven *Globe* articles we analysed. Three of the fourteen articles were what we consider 'minority' discourse articles on racism.

This 'empirical problem' could not be substantiated, because race-based statistics on criminal activity are not gathered in Toronto. This did not stop John Barber, in his column opposite Valpy's, from insisting that the relationship between Blacks and crime had empirical validity: 'Although statistics are banned, everybody knows the tale they tell: Young Black men are responsible for a disproportionate amount of violent crime in Toronto' (12 April, 1994: A3). The *Globe*'s editor-in-chief, William Thorsell, in fact, published a plea that such statistics be collected and that they be included in media reports:

> A rising incidence of armed robbery with violence may be traced in signifi-
> cant part to a particular immigrant community, but the media will almost
> never investigate the possibility – as was apparent this week in coverage of
> the awful restaurant killing in Toronto ...
> In not reporting on the unusual pathologies of [ethnic groups other
> than aboriginals], we are failing in our duty to inform society of significant
> social facts.' (9 April 1994: D6)

*Young Offenders and Gun Control:* During the first weeks of reporting, almost one-third (eight of twenty-three) of the articles relating to the Just Desserts case made reference to youth crime and/or the young offender laws. The connections the *Globe* made between youth and gang-related criminal behaviour bear out Schissel's assertion that references to gangs are generally racialized (Schissel, 1997). Indeed, every reference made to gangs in the first two weeks of reporting in the *Globe* was inflected with a racial designator, either Chinese, Black, or White. Eventually the discussion focused specifically on the 'culture of violence among Jamaican-Canadian youth' and how these cultural attributes are passed on to other Canadian youth: 'If there is a culture of violence among Jamaican-Canadian youth, why is it so? Why ... are their dress, patois and behaviour being imitated by other young Canadians?' (Valpy, 12 April 1994: A2).

The second law-and-order discourse revealed in our analysis of the *Globe* coverage was that of gun control. In the first three weeks of its coverage, the *Globe* raised the issue of gun control in eleven (48 per cent) of its twenty-three articles. On 9 April the *Globe* published a background article on Black youth's problems with crime and the criminal justice system (Kirk Makin, 9 April 1994: A6). This article featured interviews with 'young Black males,' who explicitly linked membership in gangs organized along racial lines to gun possession. '"Everything these days is gangs," according to one of the young Black men. "You don't see them, but you know they probably have guns."' Another informant, 'Mr Idris,' said that guns and intimidation were commonplace among both Black and White youth. This suggestion, which would dominate the media coverage of this case until the end of the year, was first attributed to one of these young informants. 'Mr. Lunan suggested tightening up legislation so it would be less costly and difficult to deport criminals' (Makin, 9 April 1994: A6). Thus, not only were the young perpetrators of violent crimes from somewhere else, but so were their guns, according to Makin's article and another by Abbate, MacLeod, and Philip (7 April 1994: A1).

All the sources for these articles, whether expert or non-expert, contended that handguns were being smuggled in from the United States, often though Montreal. The weapon used in the Just Desserts robbery, however, was a shotgun, and shotguns can legally be purchased legally at many sporting goods stores. Admittedly, the specific origins – domestic or otherwise – of the one used in the Just Desserts case are unknown (W. Cukier, 15 April 1994: A5). The gun control issue, which dominated the early reporting on this case, sparked a weapons amnesty campaign intended to rid the city of excess weapons. Unfortunately, according to the police most of those handing in their weapons were 'average Joes' who happened to have guns in their basements (J. Smyth, 18 April, 1994:A6). These 'average Joes,' though they distinguished themselves by having guns in their basements, were presumably not 'the young Black people of Jamaican origin' at whom the 'turn in your guns' campaign was directed.

In this way, the crimes, the criminals themselves, and finally even the weapons used to commit these crimes were symbolically 'othered.' That is, crimes, criminals, and weapon ownership were perceived as deviating from social norms, and this deviance was perceived as foreign to 'our social fabric, here in Canada' (Valpy, 7 April 1994: A2).

*Immigration and Deportation Issues:* The discourse of immigration and deportation was the most explicitly racialized of the three we analysed. From 28 April till the end of our study period, neither young offender nor gun control issues were discussed again in relation to the Just Desserts case. On the other hand, half of the articles published till the end of May discussed deportation issues. In its initial discussion of the stay of deportation against Grant, the *Globe* focused on the specific discourses of family and cultural background that we noted earlier:

> Mr. Grant, 22, was raised in Jamaica by his grandmother and came to Canada when he was 12 ... He changed school three times in five years and quit halfway through Grade 9 when he was 16 ... Mr. Grant had fathered two children. Immigration authorities were looking for the mother of his four-year old daughter and Mr. Grant's own mother was caring for the child, although she did not have legal custody ... At the time of the hearing, Mr. Grant was in a common-law relationship with another woman, who was eight months pregnant.' (Lila Sarick, 28 April 1994: A1)

In a column a few days later, Michael Valpy focused on what he perceived to be the failures of the Immigration and Refugee Board panel. He repeated Grant's personal history and asked, 'Whose responsibility is Mr. Grant? Canada's or Jamaica's?' He also claimed that an Iranian who had been convicted of raping an eighteen-month-old girl had been granted refugee status. 'Very few crimes,' he wrote, 'are more repulsive to Canadian values' (3 May 1994: A2). He later admitted that this information was erroneous (18 May 1994: A2).

### The *Toronto Sun*

The *Toronto Sun* published 88 articles with explicit references to the Just Desserts case in its first weeks of coverage. Of these, some seven articles referred to young offenders, twenty to gun control, and sixteen to immigration and deportation. Two articles (around 2 per cent) of the eighty-eight were devoted to 'minority' discourses.

The coverage of the Just Desserts case in the *Toronto Sun* began 6 April 1994. In the initial article, the 'shotgun-toting bandit' who had wounded two of the restaurant patrons was identified as one of 'three Black males' (Lamberti, 6 April 1994: 7). By the following day, Georgina Leimonis had died from her wounds. Her face featured prominently on page 1 of the *Sun*'s 7 April edition, under four fuzzy freeze-frame prints of the 'thugs' taken from a video of the robbery. The headline read: 'In Cold Blood.' On page 4, the paper posed a question for phone-in comments that more or less mirrored the *Globe*'s preliminary framing of the crime as deviant, alien, and American: 'Do you think the horrific murder-robbery at Just Desserts means brutal, American-style crime is now in Canada's future?' Later, in a letter to the editor, a reader claimed she was afraid that 'Canada [will] turn into another Los Angeles, Washington, D.C., Miami and New York City all rolled into one' (C. Hinds, 19 April 1994: 10).

On the following page, in 'Good and Evil,' the first of her columns on the Just Desserts case, Christie Blatchford gave the event epic proportions. She suggested that an 'epic contest' was being waged in Toronto between 'the forces of good' and 'evil' – more specifically, between victims of crime, like the 'perfectly innocent young woman named Vivi,' and their armed attackers (7 April 1994: 5). 'Metro Police Chief Bill McCormack [said he'd] never seen a more senseless or wanton murder of an innocent victim' (Lamberti, 7 April 1994: 18). The theme of wanton corruption was pursued in the item next to Blatchford's initial column, where the headline 'T.O.'s Innocence Lost' was superimposed on two photographs that captured the innocence of Georgina Lemonis at age twenty-three and as a young three-year-old (7 April 1994: 5). Much was made of the fact that as an unmarried Greek woman, Vivi would be ritually buried in her wedding dress. She was going to God as a virgin bride (Thana Burnett, 8 April 1994: 4; 10 April 1994: 10; George Christopolous, 12 April 1994: 14). Blatchford elaborated her epic motif in additional articles on 7 and 8 April, titled 'Innocence Lost' and 'The Day Toronto Changed': 'It's not the end of the world, and there will always be much to like about Toronto. But changed it is and a city's safety and self-confidence, like a woman's virginity, is lost only once and is never retrieved' (8 April 1994: 5). Thus, the demise of 'pretty, blonde ... Vivi' was to become a symbol of 'Toronto the Good's' ruined reputation (Blatchford, 7 April 1994: 16–7). In other words, according to Blatchford, good Torontonians were succumbing to an evil, American-style crime wave, just as the innocent Vivi had been vanquished by 'young Black males,' who had already been cast as the antagonists in this Greek tragedy.

Echoing her other colleagues' sentiments (see, for example, Bob MacDonald, 8 April 1994: 36; Raynier Maharaj, 15 April 1994: 11; 29 April 1994: 11; editorials, 30 April and 1 May 1994), Blatchford blamed this modern urban degeneration on a too lenient justice system combined with 'two decades of choosing too many of the wrong immigrants' (8 April, 1994: 5).

Raynier Maharaj didn't shy away from exposing the 'racial' identity and criminal attributes of these 'wrong immigrants': 'Unfortunately, these days most of the murderers seem to be Black ... Given the society we live in, racial conflict is often the result when there is Black-on-White crime ... Are we a society of racists? Certainly not. It's just that White Canadians are understandably fed up with people they see as outsiders coming into their country and beating and killing them' (15 April, 1994: 11). Having identified what he perceived to be racial and cultural differences in the commission of crimes, Maharaj concluded that it would be useful to collect statistics on the involvement of various ethnic groups in criminal activity. Minority groups with a propensity to commit crimes could then be targeted for special assistance (for similar recommendations, see also Blatchford, 12 April 1994: 5; L. Armstrong; 20 April, 1994:11). Writers in the *Sun* proposed various solutions to this perceived increase in crime, among them capital punishment ('Readers,' 8 April, 1994: 18), increased sentences (e.g., MacDonald, 8 April, 1994: 36), boot camps (Robert Payne, 1 May, 1994:30) for young offenders, and changes to Canada's gun laws.

*Young Offenders and Gun Control:*  The day after the killing, a bystander at the crime scene was quoted as follows: 'The cause of all this goes back to those kids getting away with lax laws as children and then as teens' (Sharon Lem, 8 April 1994: 18). The same day, columnist Bob Mac-Donald took the same position, calling on politicians to implement a tougher Young Offender's Act (8 April 1994: 36). These calls were later repeated by a letter writer, who complained about the 'unjust system with YOA, and armed punks who laugh at security cameras' (Harris, 16 April 1994: 13).

Next to a story on Leimonis's funeral, the *Sun* disclosed that in response to these demands, Justice Minister Allan Rock planned to introduce a bill to increase sentences for young killers (Durkan, 12 April 1994: 15). Columnist Robert Payne suggested that boot camps might be the solution to youth involvement in crime (1 May 1994: 30). Kids join gangs, Payne contended, paraphrasing the director of the Toronto YMCA's Black Achievers Program, because they are seeking the kind of discipline they aren't getting at home. Payne cited an American judge who said that 'the problem will never go away until we learn to deal with what's happening – or NOT happening – in these young people's homes.'

This American judge was articulating what Errol Lawrence (1982) refers to as the 'commonsense' view of the world, in which the family is the primary purveyor of cultural norms and moral values. According to this view, the misbehaviour of young adults is the result of lack of disci-

pline and moral guidance in the home. This view has been reinter-
preted in the 1990s as a call to return to 'family values,' which among
other things means reinstating two-parent, male-headed families.
According to Lawrence, this hegemonic 'commonsense' view, more or
less assumes that Black families are reproducing a culture of deprivation
that leads to criminal behaviour among their children. It is in this context that the *Sun*'s intersecting commentaries on the family, cultural
background, and criminal behaviour of the accused make sense.

Like the *Globe*, the *Sun* elaborated on the connections between the
background, 'dress, patois and behaviour' of the accused and the supposed pervasive 'culture of violence among Jamaican-Canadian youths'
(Valpy, 12 April 1994, above). For example, the day after the primary
suspect had been identified as a Jamaican-born landed immigrant
named Lawrence Brown, or 'Brownman,' the *Sun* ran the headline
'Rappers on the Run' (Godfrey and Stewart, 13 April 1994: 5). In this
article, it was reported that the four suspects wanted in the killing
belonged to 'a reggae-funk-rap group called the 'Black Supreme Crew,'
which performed at westend clubs.'

When the first suspect, Lawrence Brown was finally arrested and
appeared in court, he was described as being a 'tall lean man with short
dreadlocks and a shadowy moustache and beard ... Wearing a hip length
hot mauve vest over cream-colored shirt and trousers ... he stood with
his hands deep in his pockets, his head swaying back and forth' (Ian
Robertson, 15 April 1994: 4). Later, when the second suspect, O'Neil
Grant, appeared in court, the reporter remarked that Grant was 'speaking in Jamaican patois' and that he too was moving oddly, 'bobbing and
weaving like a boxer' (Lem, 26 April 1994: 2). The *Sun* also reported
that in the search for the suspects in the Just Desserts case, two more
Jamaican 'gangsters' had been arrested, one of whom was 'associated
with Jamaican organized crime groups called "posses" and the other is
an illegal resident in the country' (Godfrey, 14 April 1994: 16).

On the day that Brown first appeared in court, in a featured Letter of
the Day, a reader made explicit the connections being established in the
*Sun* between rap, gangsters, and crime:

My heart went out to the family of beautiful young Vivi Leimonis ... I want
murdering punks locked up forever. I was wondering why it's getting so
bad here when this stuff used to happen mostly in Los Angeles ... I was
flicking through the channels and stopped on Much Music's Rap City. All
of a sudden I got a feeling of déjà vu. There on the screen was a group of
young Black men singing about robbing people ... I found out later that

this is called 'gangsta' rap ... I want 20 years in jail for possession of an unlicensed firearm. I want gangsta rap banned everywhere and to heck with so-called creative freedom ... We live in a democratic country and we are only truly free when we draw the line somewhere    to protect the freedom of the good people. (Eugene Forsey, 15 April 1994: 11)

In this letter, the writer was implying that gun possession, like rap music, was among the cultural attributes of the accused. Drug trafficking was also connected with this 'violent culture.' For example, in an article outlining the types, origins, and numbers of weapons used in robberies such as the Just Desserts case, a police source warned that 'a lucrative business in illegal firearms – especially easily concealed handguns – has sprung up to supply the druggies with weapons for their crimes' (Don Wanagas, 9 April 1994: 27)

Like other writers (e.g., Blatchford, 8 April 1994: 5) who wanted to focus more on the racial and cultural background of the perpetrators than on the issue of gun control, columnist Dick Smyth insisted that 'jumped-up Black punk[s]' alone were responsible for the supposed increase in urban crime. He wrote: 'The clamour for gun control in the wake of this shooting is misdirected. There should be a clamor for narcotics control! Drugs are responsible for half the crime in this city. There is reason to believe they were a factor that night in the Annex' (14 April 1994: 12).

The connection between drugs and handguns was further reinforced by how the *Sun* articles were laid out. Beside the article 'Drug Suspect Shot in Shoulder by Cops' (Lem, 9 April, 1994: 6–7), the paper published the first of many articles that discussed the availability of guns: 'Handguns Are a Snap to Get' (Wanagas, 9 April 1994: 27).

In the early weeks, articles on gun control dominated coverage of the crime. Of the eighty-eight articles published in total, twenty referred to gun control. Like the *Globe*, the *Sun* was interested in where the weapons came from that were being used to commit violent offences. According to a police source quoted in the *Sun*, it was simple and inexpensive to buy guns in the United States and smuggle them into Canada. Therefore, 'the best way to control the criminal use of guns [was] to cut the supply ... at the border' (Wanagas, 9 April 1994: 27; Lem, 12 April 1994: 17). In an effort to cut off the supply of guns in Toronto, after several citizens offered money for guns turned in to the police, the *Sun* launched a 'Turn in Your Guns' campaign, modelled after a similar initiative in New York. The symbol for this campaign was a handgun with a line through it. The news article that announced the Sun's 'War on

Guns' (Ian Harvey, 13 April, 1994:4) was accompanied by a photo of a police officer holding two handguns.

*Immigration/Deportation*: After the *Sun* had established that O'Neil Grant was truly an outsider – a landed immigrant whose deportation had been stayed – it published an editorial about his background and troubled youth:

'He came to Canada from Jamaica with a kindergarten level of education and was placed in Grade 6. In other words, from the very beginning he was set up to fail. He changed schools frequently and quit when he was 16. He took drugs, he fathered two children out of wedlock and ... had ... 'a criminal record as long as your arm.' If this whole sorry mess was a rare incident, it would at least be understandable. But it is not rare at all. It is simply yet one more nail in the credibility of the immigration and refugee system that Marchi alleges is basically sound.' (1 May 1994: 14)

According to later commentaries, Canadians had been 'betrayed by the system' (editorial, 1 May 1994: 14). Canada had become 'a sucker nation' with a 'crazy system that was softened up for political reasons ... making our society even more dangerous for law-abiding Canadians' (MacDonald, 20 May, 1994: 22).

Like the *Globe*, then, the *Sun* was apparently constructing an argument that the Just Desserts case represented the arrival in Toronto of American-style inner-city crime. Supposedly, the perpetrators of such crime were 'young Black males,' who were involved in drugs and arms offences in Canadian urban centres. Furthermore, the problem was seen as imported rather than homegrown.

**The *Toronto Star***

Between 6 April and 31 May 1994, the *Star* published seventy-six articles that made direct reference to the Just Desserts case. Twenty of these related to gun control, four to young offenders, and ten to immigration/ deportation issues. The *Star* published far and away the greatest number of 'minority' discourse articles: twenty-one (2 per cent) of the seventy-six articles it published in this period reflected a 'minority' perspective.

*Race, Crime, and Culture*: The first and second articles published on 6 and 7 April reported that 'all the robbers are Black' (Edwards and De Mara,

6 April 1994: A10; Hall and Stancu, 7 April 1994: A1). On the front page of the 7 April edition, two fuzzy, freeze-frame video photos were juxta-posed with a photo of Georgina Leimonis, under a headline that described the attack as 'urban terrorism' (Hall and Stancu, 7 April 1994: A1). According to Chief McCormack, 'urban terrorism' and its counter-part, 'home invasion,' were 'appearing increasingly in the Metro area after leaving big U.S. cities like Miami and Detroit' (Phil Mascoll, 7 April 1994: A6).

Barclay described the criminals as predators (Linwood Barclay, 8 April 1994: A2). In an editorial on 8 April, the call went out to 'govern-ments at all levels ... to ensure that our streets and neighborhoods con-tinue to belong to us, not drug-crazed, gun-toting criminals' (A22). On 8 April Rosie DiManno wrote the first of several articles criticizing the discourses reflected in this type of reporting (see also Antonia Zerbiasis, 8 April 1994: A21; Thomas Walkom, 9 April 1994: B1; David Lewis Stein, 10 April 1994: A6; Rosie DiManno, 12 April 1994: A6; Rita Daly, 14 April 1994: A3). These journalists rejected the sensationalizing and racializing of the incident in media reports – especially those in the *Sun* – as well as the 'urban terror rhetoric' of the police.

The *Star*'s second editorial on the Just Desserts case was something of a turnaround from the first, in that it dialed down the rhetoric and tried to consider the social factors that lead to criminal activity among youth. This effort was somewhat similar to those made in both the *Globe* and the *Sun*:

> It is not the killers' skin colour that explains this abhorrent act. Criminals come in every colour and from every race and ethnic background. Instead, we should be asking where these youths got the sawed-off shotgun they used in this robbery. We should be concerned about what contributed to their criminal behavior and if drugs were involved. Where did they grow up, what kind of families do they come from, what kind of educations did they get, and what were their job prospects? (9 April 1994: B2)

In other words, race said nothing about why the killers did what they did. It was their families, as the purveyors of cultural and social norms, that had shaped their conduct.

*Young Offenders and Gun Control:* Of the three Toronto papers, the *Star* published the fewest articles on young offenders. Only four of seventy-six Just Desserts articles referred to young offender issues explicitly. All four of these articles were news reports about calls made by police (Rebecca Bragg, 10 April 1994: A6) and politicians (Sean McCarthy, 9 April 1994: A4; David Vienneau, 12 April 1994: A1, and 13 April 1994: A6) for the Young Offender's Act to be toughened up. In other words, no features, editorials, columns, or letters to the editor were devoted to the young offender issue.

As in the *Sun*, issues of gun control dominated the *Star*'s coverage of the Just Desserts case. Some twenty articles were devoted to this issue. The *Star* published calls from politicians (Bob Brent, 8 April 1994: A6; McCarthy, April 1994: A4; Vienneau, 13 April 1994: A6; Linwood Papp, 14 April 1994: A7), citizens (Peter Small, 9 April 1994: A4; Mark Zwolinski, 11 April 1994: A6; Marc Tedesco, 15 April 1994: A26; Sher Singh, 20 April 1994: A19), and journalists (editorial, 8 April 1994: A22 and 14 April 1994: A24; Clayton Ruby, 29 April 1994: A17) alike for changes to gun control laws. Some *Star* reports focused on the source of the guns; like the *Sun*, they located this in the United States. For example, 'Mullin, who works out of Metro's firearms registration centre, and calls handgun use in this city "epidemic," ... They are being smuggled here from the United States' (Joe Hall, 13 April 1994: A6).

Early on in the discussion of gun control, some attempt was made to downplay the supposed connections between the increase in crime in Metro and both illegal gun possession (Hall, 8 April 1994: A6) and the origins of the weapons used to commit crimes. Between 28 April and the end of May 1994, the *Star* published four articles dealing with the deportation issue. Three of these articles reported on the decisions made by the Immigration Board in the case of O'Neil Grant (Allan Thompson, 28 April 1994: A4; Henry Stancu, 29 April 1994: A1; CP, 19 May 1994: A10). One of the four articles was a 'minority' article in the 'Diversities' column of the paper that argued against making distinctions between Canadian society and immigrants (Andrew Cardozo, 16 May 1994: A21).

**Critical Discourse Analysis of the Racialization of Crime**

The following critical discourse analysis (CDA) of how the media reported the Just Desserts case is divided into four sections. Each of these sections represents a step in the racialization of the crime in the media. In the first section, 'Othering Crime,' we show how crimes are linked to the social other, and how in the Just Desserts case this *'other'* was assigned American origins. The second section, 'Racializing Crime, details how the dominant discourse surrounding the Just Desserts case focused on the relationship between Blackness and crime. In the third section, 'Guns and the Other,' we demonstrate how the alternative law-and-order discourse (in this case, gun control) became co-opted into the dominant discourse that associated race with crime. In 'Criminalizing Immigration,' the fourth and final section, we discuss how the journalistic practices of selection and combination produced a discourse that constructed Jamaican immigrants as inherently prone to criminality.

*Othering Crime*

We have already established that criminal behaviour is associated with 'deviants' who fall outside social norms. Once criminal behaviour is attributed to social outsiders, it is only a short conceptual leap to associating crime with foreigners and foreignness in general with deviant, criminal behaviour. In the first of his many columns on the Just Desserts case for the *Globe and Mail,* Michael Valpy focused on what he perceived to be the unique features of the type of criminal behaviour associated with this case. His particular take on the crime led him to speculate about the specific national origins of what he described in his column as 'alien slaughter.' 'Getting robbed in an Annex restaurant is alien enough ... Mindless, gratuitous violence belongs to New York, to Los Angeles ... not Toronto and Ottawa' (7 April 1994: A2).

Here, Valpy made several syntactic shifts that established his particular take on the Just Desserts crime. First, by using the phrase 'getting robbed,' Valpy was *passivizing* the sentence in order to delete the reference to the perpetrators of the crime; the action was then *nominalized* and moved to the *topical* position; this served to remove any reference to the victims as well. Thus, in this particular passage Valpy was downplaying the participants in the event in order to emphasize the event itself. In removing some of the specifics – that is, the 'who, when, and where' of the incident – and concentrating on the 'what,' Valpy was *generalizing* about the type of crime being committed. In this section of the column, then, the 'story' was not about criminals but about crime in general. It wasn't until the following day that any of the papers released descriptions of the perpetrators.

In this column, Valpy was *generalizing* from two recent crimes – a drive-by shooting in Ottawa and the Just Desserts robbery in Toronto – to what he saw as the changing nature of crime. He was maintaining that crime was becoming more 'mindlessly' and 'gratuitously' violent. In support of this stance, he provided two *sources of evidentiality*: comments made by Toronto's police chief, William McCormack, and statistical validation.

Valpy reported McCormack as lamenting, 'I thought what a terribly cowardly, senseless act it was, *in the presence of children*' (emphasis added). McCormack also offered what Valpy himself referred to as 'anecdotal' evidence to the effect that those displaying this 'growing propensity for [savage] violence in the commission of crimes ... do so as a kind of badge of pride. "They boast to each other about violence," the chief said.'

Although the comments made by McCormack were personal and anecdotal in nature, he was speaking from a position of authority. By including the remarks of an official – in fact, *the* foremost official police source – Valpy was lending credibility to a form of argumentation that played on the sentiments and moral outrage of his readers 'here in Canada.'

Another rhetorical strategy journalists commonly use is *the numbers game*. After citing McCormack's impassioned response to the crime, Valpy tried to support the claim that this particular type of morally reprehensible violent crime was on the increase by referring to quantitative evidence. The point of the numbers game is to alarm the reader with impressive figures so as to increase the significance of the writers' assertions. Valpy quoted statistics *gathered by a colleague of his*, which indicated that between 1989 and 1993 the presence of firearms in robberies in Toronto increased by 37 per cent. However, had Valpy chosen a different set of statistics – for example, those revealing how many deaths had been caused by gunshot wounds – he would have reported that these numbers had been declining nationally for twenty years (Peter Moon, 12 April 1994: A5). Thus, Valpy was 'playing' with numbers to add quantitative substance to his claims.

Furthermore, the use of this particular set of statistics served to *imply* that this new type of violent crime was distinguished from earlier types by the presence of guns and not, say, by the likelihood of being killed, which was no greater than in previous years. This *presupposition* on Valpy's part – that the presence of guns signalled a change in the nature of crime – tied the shootings in Ottawa and Toronto to the gun control issue. We will return to gun control in later sections, but for the moment it is interesting that Valpy's 'semantic moves' had at this point framed the crime as a gun control issue rather than, for example, a young offender or immigration/deportation issue.

One final point needs to be made about Valpy's *lexicon*. The lexicon he chose to describe the crime was important. Certain lexical configurations signal specific semantic domains, or domains of meaning. In the introductory paragraphs of this column, Valpy referred to the recent shootings in Ottawa and Toronto as 'alien' 'slaughter.' In the abbreviated passage cited earlier, he repeated the term 'alien.' It seems, then, that this lexical choice was not arbitrary. As 'alien' clearly does not refer to 'extraplanetary beings' in this context, we conclude that Valpy's preference for this lexical item signalled the legal semantic domain, as this is the only other semantic domain where the term 'alien' is commonly used. In the context of the law, 'alien' refers to foreignness in general and is often appended with the adjectival qualifier 'illegal,' as in 'illegal aliens.' McCormack's *hyperbolic* references to 'urban terrorism' which the *Star*'s early reports of the crime make much of, also support this conclusion (Hall and Stancu, 7 April 1994: A1; Mascoll, 7 April 1994: A6). The word 'terrorism' also conjures up images of invasions by foreign criminals. In a later section we will discuss how conceptual links were established between immigration and illegality and criminal behaviour. For the moment, we want to focus on Valpy's premise that violent crime is foreign to 'our social fabric, here in Canada.' In the quote above, it is clear where Valpy believes this alien behaviour originated: it 'belongs to New York, to Los Angeles.' 'Mindless, gratuitous violence' is, according to Valpy, an American import.

By isolating the criminal act, branding it qualitatively different, and then supplying statistics to support how he had branded it, Valpy was establishing the premise for the line of argument he wanted to pursue. Having provided evidence that these types of crimes were both novel and escalating, his next order of business was to offer explanations and solutions for the problem as he had conceived it. He wanted readers to conclude that for an explanation of the 'problem' they would have to look to its foreign source, the United States. In later articles and columns, Valpy and his colleagues offered 'solutions' to this 'problem,' some of which we will discuss below.

Valpy was employing many forms of argumentation to convince his readers to share his particular take on the crime, which he had already stated in the opening line of this column: 'The barbarians are inside the gate.' By fronting what was actually the conclusion of his line of argumentation – that is, by stating his conclusion in the opening line of his argument – Valpy was implicitly emphasizing its importance. He was contending that what was significant about this type of crime was that 'barbarians' – that is, foreign, savage, uncivilized people – were responsible for it.

On the same day that Valpy's column was published, the editorial staff of the *Sun* framed the issue in a similar manner – albeit with far fewer argumentative manoeuvres, when it posed this call-in question to its readers: 'Do you think the horrific murder-robbery at Just Desserts means brutal, American-style crime is now in Canada's future?' (7 April 1994: 4).

This question presupposed everything that Valpy had argued far more comprehensively in his initial column. Whether readers answered yes or no to this question, they were implicitly accepting the *presuppositions* underlying the question itself. First, in asking whether this type of crime was to be expected in 'Canada's future,' the *Sun* writers were presupposing that this 'horrific murder-robbery' was qualitatively different from – that is, more horrific than – other crimes in Canada's *past*. And, second, the question presupposed that such 'brutal' crimes were not only novel but also specifically American in origin.

Two days after the crime was first reported, the first editorial in the *Star* dealing with the Just Desserts case claimed:

'Random violence is on the increase ... Most of the violence is related to illegal guns and drugs ... The long-term solution lies in curbing the demand for drugs, and in tougher gun controls. Governments at all levels need to co-ordinate their strategies, urgently, to ensure that our streets and neighborhoods continue to belong to us, not drug-crazed, gun-toting criminals.' (8 April 1994: A22)

Thus, as early as the second day of reporting of the incident, 8 April, the assertion that violent crime was escalating had become an accepted premise. To support this sweeping statement, the editor relied on *intertextually* generated evidence. That is, the *particular understandings* of the issues generated by journalists themselves had become accepted as the *facts* of the case. In drawing on these intertextually generated 'facts' – that is, that this particular type of gun-related violence was on the increase – and then linking these 'facts' to drugs, the editor was evoking a familiar *topos*.

As noted earlier *topoi* are the standard 'commonsense' reasonings used to 'explain' specific recurring social issues. Here, the editor was clearly drawing on a contemporary 'law-and-order' *topos*: 'drug-crazed, gun-toting criminals' were making 'our' streets unsafe. In this particular *topos, they* (the criminals) were characterized as *threats* to *us*. Thus, once again, criminals were stereotypically othered: characterized as outsiders threatening 'our' social order. The editors again resorted to exclusionary pronouns in their closing remarks: 'Our streets and neighborhoods continue to belong to us' (emphasis added). It is important to note that no explicit connections between the Just Desserts killing and drugs had been reported up to this point in the coverage. Moreover, after the manhunt for Lawrence Brown ended in his arrest, he appeared in court on several past but still pending offences. *None* of the charges for which he appeared in court during our two-month study were drug charges. Nevertheless, the editors were able to introduce the drug issue in this context because of the standardized knowledge reflected in the *topos* from which they draw.

It is significant that this was an editorial rather than a news item or column. Editorials generally fall into one of the following schematic categories: a summary of the event; an evaluation of the event; or a pragmatic conclusion (recommendation, advice, warning) (van Dijk, 1996). With this 'law-and-order' *topos*, which by then was well established in the social imagination as providing the explanatory framework for the criminal event, the editorial was able to pass quickly from summary and evaluation to recommendation. The explanations for the event and the calls for governmental control of guns and drugs were easy to associate with the logic of the *topos* within which the editorial was reasoning. The explanations, arguments, and solutions offered for the event were coherent only to the extent that readers reasoned within this specific topical framework.

The columnists and editors of the various newspapers all added substance to a particular mindset – one that connected the Just Desserts crime to a broader social problem. The writers believed that an invasion of 'American-style,' 'drug-crazed, gun-toting barbarians' was imminent. Although none of these articles included *explicit* references to race, a composite image of the perpetrators emerged from these reports that seemed to trigger the racialized discourses of the following days and weeks. Within days, explicit references to race and nation begin to dominate the coverage.

*Racializing Crime*

As noted above, the presuppositions made by the *Sun* were logically argued by Valpy. Valpy at least attempted to apply the rules of evidential-

ity. It quickly became axiomatic that the Just Desserts crime was some-
how linked to the perpetrators' race. For example, on page 1 of *The
Globe and Mail*, less than forty-eight hours after coverage of the crime
had begun, and on the same day the police released descriptions of the
perpetrators, other writers are able to authoritatively frame the event in
the following way: 'For some, the shooting reflects an escalation of violence during the commission of robberies linked to the availability and
proliferation of firearms. For some, the fact that it was a Black man who
shot Georgina Leimonis underscored what appears to be growing
involvement of young Black men in violent robberies in the city'
(Abbate and Hess, 8 April 1994: A1).

These reporters had taken up and expanded the frames of reference
established in earlier news reports. Again, the rules of evidence being
employed in this extract were those of *intertextuality*. Moreover, the arguments and understandings being generated in the discursive exchange
between the various media were being generalized to the population at
large through use of the modifier 'For some.' At the same time that the
authors were generalizing about the pervasiveness of these particular
interpretations of the event, they were very *vague* about the specific referent 'some.' 'For some' acted as a *hedging device* – that is, it rhetorically
mitigated, the assertions about the relationship between guns, race, and
crime that might have been considered offensive by some of their readers. The hedge also allowed reporters to look like they were merely
recounting widespread consensus while distancing themselves – and
their newspaper – from the substance of those assertions.

It is important to remember that newspapers make strategic choices
about what to print. Every journalist knows that it is impossible to cover
every angle of a story. News writers and their editors include only the
information they consider significant to the story as they see it. Thus,
their angle of coverage reflects their particular perception of the event;
this in turn is based on a certain set of sources and their particular takes
on an event. This makes neutrality impossible. So if Abbate and Hess
selected these issues to focus on, it was not because they were reporting
on the incident in any objective sense, but rather because they had chosen to underwrite – and, more importantly, expand on – the premises
that had been established in the reports of the crime that had preceded
theirs. In what follows we show how the Just Desserts crime was explicitly
racialized in Abbate and Hess's article. It is interesting that gun control
– an issue we will return to later on – had already been bracketed off by
the twin concerns of 'availability' and 'proliferation,' which eventually

led to undocumented speculation about the source of the firearms. However, it is the second assertion – that there 'appears to be growing involvement of young Black men in violent robberies in the city' – that we wish to address next.

We have already noted the vagueness of 'for some' and suggested that although the reporters attempted to distance themselves from the assertions that followed its use, their inclusion and elaboration of the premises and explanations we outlined in the previous section marked a significant development in the reporting of this crime. In the two days of coverage preceding this article, the issue of the perpetrator's race was included in the reporting in all the papers, but this was in a more-or-less matter-of-fact fashion, in the form of police descriptions. Usually, race was mentioned near the end of the news item, so we can hardly say it was being emphasized in terms of *placement*. Moreover, the more generalized connections between race and crime being asserted in this article were not made explicit in any of the articles included in our study prior to 8 April. So the 'some' to whom Abbate and Hess were referring did not include any of the *Globe*'s, the *Sun*'s, or the *Star*'s journalists.

Among those cited by the authors as sources for the above assertions were unnamed 'Toronto residents.' However, on the same day that this article was published in the *Globe*, the *Sun* published responses to its call-in survey. Of the 'Toronto residents' who responded and were cited, all were concerned with 'the American-style murder.' None, however, was quoted making any explicit reference to race. So the vagueness of the source provokes curiosity about just whom the authors were referring to in their opening comments; so does the fact that even in the *Sun*, 'Toronto residents' were not focusing on the issue of race.

According to this article, the Police Services Board had discussed the Just Desserts case in an emergency meeting the evening before. The ex-chief of police and Norm Gardner, who at that time was a board member and who, the authors informed us, is 'White,' were *paraphrased* as claiming that based on impressionistic readings of the police blotter, a large percentage of perpetrators are Black. But in the next paragraph, 'board member Arnold Minors, who is Black,' was quoted as follows: 'To criminalize the whole Black society because of one action is awful and must not be done. Until we have a society where people can feel comfortable that everybody is respectfully and justly treated, I'm not happy with this attention to race' (8 April 1994: A1).

Clearly, within the Police Services Board opinion was divided about whether race was at issue. 'For some,' that is, for Minors at least – this crime had nothing whatsoever to do with the presupposed 'growing involvement of young Black men in violent robberies in the city.' The authors included racial *identifiers* for their sources because these descriptions of the actors explained and gave coherence to two racially located argumentative *topoi*. That is, in both cases the reader was being informed of the race of the source because the reporters felt it would clarify the arguments they were deploying. On the one, 'White' hand, Gardner was drawing on the standard argument that a relationship, possibly causal, exists between race and crime; on the other, 'Black' hand, Minors was countering with the familiar response that it is racism that is the real problem.

Once we have located the respective arguments within these racialized topoi, the reason why the referent 'for some' was used in the introduction to the article becomes clear. Of the general populace that makes up 'Toronto's residents,' it is specifically those who share the 'White' point of view who are represented. It is the 'some' who believe there is a 'growing involvement of young Black men in violent robberies in the city' whose comments form one side of the debate as it is put forward by these reports. Moreover, so far as placement goes, these specific comments and evaluations are moved to the topical position in the article, so that they themselves become the 'main event' – that is, the news. The 'Black' point of view in the article is referred to only later, in a 'comments' section of the article. This approach to placement seems to support van Dijk's claim that 'minority group speakers ... are seen as partisan, whereas White authorities, such as the police or the government, are simply seen as ethnically "neutral" – and thus, in this case, more "objectively" representative of 'Toronto's residents.'

Moreover, the article's introductory assertions were posed as *contrasts*, so it seems that the authors were implicitly staking out 'two sides of the debate on crime': race versus gun control. The rhetorical device of contrast implicitly blocked, or at least preempted, other discussions surrounding the event – for instance, Minors's concern with racism. It also set up these two points of view as opposing. On the Police Services Board, the two sides were represented by established rivals Norm Gardner, representing the race and crime issue, and chairperson Susan Eng, who claimed that the issue was not a race issue but a gun control problem (see also John Barber, *The Globe and Mail*, 8 April 1994: A9).

Another striking example of the use of racial *identifiers* can be found in a column by John Barber (12 April 1994), 'Good People and Bad People,' which began with a description of the funeral of Leimonis:

'Four young women in white each holding a single white rose, led a gleaming white coffin to the altar. A wedding dress and a veil [which were white]; a corpse pale as the moon.'

The repetition of the colour term 'white' evoked an image of purity and goodness. This was strongly reinforced by the headline. Although that headline was a quote from a source, the remainder of the text, which was about colour, strongly connected white with goodness and black with badness. Here, 'good people' were White. Later, Barber talked about Black people and crime: 'Everybody knows the tale they tell [crime statistics]: young Black men are responsible for a disproportionate amount of violent crime in Toronto.' These young Black men were, therefore, the 'bad people.'

In her column of 8 April, Christie Blatchford of the *Sun* reported on the board meeting as follows:

> This isn't the Toronto I saw when I came here in 1967 and I am tired of people blowing smoke and saying it is ... That's what they were doing at the Metro Police Services Board yesterday, where Susan Eng was saying, 'It's the guns that kill' (as though the guns are not held in human hands) and Metro Chairman Alan Tonks was saying the city was not 'falling into the pattern of large American cities' (when clearly it is), and Arnold Minors was noting that at such a time 'to pay attention to race is at best unfortunate and at worst malicious.' If only we could lock our doors as tightly as these people are locked into their self-made roles ... Metro Councillor Alan Ashton, who appears genuinely horrified by the Just Desserts shooting ... was the only member of the board to admit the city isn't safe anymore, to show fear, to mention the 'immigration laws that don't work,' to say, 'If we need more jails, fine – build 'em. It took two decades of choosing too many of the wrong immigrants ... too much of the police budget taken from the front lines and spent on what Bob Crampton, a wonderful metro cop now retired, calls 'armed social workers.' (5)

Blatchford touched on several issues that we wish to discuss. First, however, we address the issue of gun control.

*Guns and the Others*

Eng's statement, 'It's the guns that kill,' had a *cleft sentence* structure that focused the debate on gun control. Cleft sentences imply a contrast; the absent contrast in Eng's assertion was, of course, the perpetrators; in other words, she was insisting that guns, not the perpetrators themselves, or what cause death. It seems that Eng's statement was an argumentative move designed to divert attention from the perpetrators and their racial background. Unlike her colleague Minors, Eng had enough political savvy to avoid framing the issue in terms of a 'partisan' social issue such as racism. Instead she was drawing on another dominant law-and-order discourse, that of gun control, to argue her point. Minors's 'partisan' concerns with social issues were easy to undermine by drawing on an authoritative, 'neutral' police *source*. Blatchford took this tack in an earlier example. Her credible source, whom she even described as 'wonderful,' contended that when the police concern themselves with social issues such as racism, they become nothing more than 'armed social workers.' In general terms, in the coverage of the Just Desserts crime, the gun control issue became the dominant opposing discourse to the 'race and crime' discourse. Each of the papers picked up on the issue of gun control, and as we have already noted, each devoted a great deal of copy to this issue, especially in the early weeks of the coverage. Eight of the thirty-six articles in the *Globe*, twenty of the eighty-eight in the *Sun*, and twenty of the seventy-six in the *Star* referred to the gun control issue. However, each paper focused on this issue in its own way.

In the *Sun*, the headline of the first article to focus on gun control read, 'Handguns Are a Snap to Get' (D. Wanagas, 9 April 1994: 27). The opening sentence read, 'Metro police are battling a plague of illegal guns streaming into the Toronto area from the United States.'

This statement utilized the same metaphors and legal semantic domain that Valpy employed in his early comments on the case. In this article, however, the author was concerned not about an invasion of illegal aliens, but rather about a 'plague of illegal guns streaming in.' For both writers, however, the source of the problem was the same: the United States. The article on handguns was accompanied by a table detailing 'the weapons of choice' in armed robberies and violent crimes between 1992 and 1994. It showed that handguns were the overwhelming weapons of choice in armed robberies, having been used in almost four-fifths of all armed robberies. On 10 and 11 April the *Sun* featured a section called 'Blood and Tears' that highlighted a variety of violent crimes. The banner accompanying this section featured a drawing of a handgun. On 13 April, on page 1, the *Sun* announced its Turn in Your Guns campaign, with the announcement accompanied by a photo of two policemen holding handguns. The icon for the campaign was a handgun with a line through it. The *Sun* featured this icon prominently in the following weeks. On top of this, between 7, and 19 April one-quarter of the *Sun*'s fifty-seven headlines about the Just Desserts crime mentioned handguns in some way (gun, 11; handgun, 1; pistol, 1; gun down, 1).

A further analysis of word frequency in the headlines indicates that during this period, gun control was the dominant issue for the other two Toronto papers as well. Headlines are especially important units of analysis because they summarize the most significant information in an article and are often the only part of the article that is read. Between 7 and 18 April the *Globe* published five articles – out of a total of nineteen Just Desserts–related articles – with the word *gun* in the headline (gun(s), 6; shotgun, 1). One of the earliest articles on the gun control issue in the *Globe* asserted that the 'sudden clamour for gun legislation [is] an over-reaction' (Moon, 12 April 1994: A5). But in a later, favourable report on the weapons amnesty co-sponsored by the *Sun*, Justice Minister Rock's hyperbolic metaphor was cited: 'We're trying to deal with the disease of crime infestation ... We don't want to go the way of U.S. cities' (Smyth, 18 April 1994: A6). The crime-as-sickness ('plague'/ 'disease'/ 'infestation') metaphor was repeated in the above citation, and once again the problem was attributed to the same source: the United States.

In the *Star*, thirteen of the forty-four (29 per cent) Just Desserts headlines printed between 7 and 16 April contained the word (hand)gun or rifle (gun, 9; handgun, 2; gun-free, 1; rifle, 1). Two early articles that focused exclusively on this issue were 'Handgun Ban Being Studied' (Vienneau, 12 April 1994: A1) and, the following day, 'Handgun Ban Idea Wins Jeers, Plaudits from Various Sources' (Vienneau, 13 April 1994: A6). In both articles, Vienneau noted that Rock's call for a ban on handguns was a response to public perceptions, in the wake of the Just Desserts killing, that violent crime was increasing. On 13 April the Star devoted an entire page (A6) to this issue under the headline, 'Gun-Control Debate.' This page featured a photograph of a policeman holding a handgun and a sawed-off shotgun, with a caption reading 'DEADLY WEAPONS: Detective Mullin ... says U.S. is source of smuggled handguns.' Furthermore, two of the four articles on the page examined the smuggling operations that had resulted in the 'epidemic' of handguns in Toronto (Hall, 13 April 1994: A6).

There are two empirical problems with how the media linked the Just Desserts case to the gun control issue. First, the coverage of this issue, especially in the *Sun*, focused on handguns. Yet in the Just Desserts killing it was not a handgun but a sawed-off shotgun that was

used. Second, all three papers drew on the crime-as-sickness ('plague'/
'disease'/'epidemic') metaphor to describe what was perceived as an
alarming increase in the smuggling of guns in from the crime-infested
United States. Yet a 1994 report on the prevalence and source of handguns used in crimes in Toronto – a report based on the police's own
statistics – disputes this perception. In only *two of the 593 files* investigated in this study was the firearm found to be smuggled (Axon and
Moyer, 1994). Moreover, only 20 per cent of cases involving firearms
involved real firearms. And the data further indicate that a handgun
was used in only half of 'real' firearm robberies. The *Sun's* alarming
figures on the use of handguns in armed robberies seem to have been
based on the incidence of robberies using both real *and* fake firearms
of any kind. In other words, the *Sun* neglected to tell its readers that
the majority of handgun incidents involved robberies with fake weapons. So the *degree of completeness* of the information the *Sun* provided
was low. Given that in the Just Desserts case it was a shotgun and not a
handgun that was used, and given that there is little *empirical* evidence
to support the claim that guns of any type are smuggled from the
United States, the question is: Why did the papers choose to focus on
two gun control issues – the proliferation of handguns and smuggling
from the United States?

We suggest that the media focused so heavily on the proliferation and
origins of handguns because handguns smuggled from the United
States better fit the image of the 'American-style,' 'drug-crazed, gun-
toting' Black criminal – an image the media play up. The gun control
issue was initially raised in opposition to the race and crime evaluation
of the Just Desserts case; soon enough, however, gun control discourses
were co-opted into a more generalized 'law-and-order' discourse on
crime and the 'other.' Through the use of the hyperbolic crime-as-infes-
tation metaphor, journalists drew *false analogies* by symbolically associating illegal guns with illegal aliens. The associations established between
immigrants (i.e., Blacks) and illegal handguns in the above articles reinforced rather than subverted the dominant discourses on crime and the
racialized 'other.'

Let us return to Blatchford's comments. This citation was preceded in
the article by six stories about her own, her friend's, and her friend's
'dear young son's' personal experiences as crime victims. One of these
stories referred to Vietnamese neighbours of Blatchford's who had been
'busted for' gambling and drugs. She ended her tales by inquiring: 'Is
this too personal? Too bad. This isn't the Toronto I saw when I came

here in 1967 and I am tired of people blowing smoke and saying it is' (8 April 1994: 5).

Blatchford resorted to two argumentative moves in her testimonies and comments. First, she used personal stories as *sources of evidentiality* in a highly effective way. Personal experiences are much harder to challenge for their truth value than other kinds of 'factual' evidence, such as statistics. Moreover, 'concrete cases that engender pity or outrage are usually more memorable, more imaginable and emotionally stimulating, and hence more persuasive than statistics.'

Second, Blatchford set up a *straw man* who opposed her narrative evidence on the grounds that it was 'too personal'; then she defeated this fictitious opponent with another personal observation.

Blatchford repeated this pattern of setting up opposing arguments and then rhetorically defeating them three successive times in the following paragraph. In each case, she drew on her personal experiences and then *generalized* them to the greater population in order to argue *what everybody knows to be true.* For instance, to Tonks's insistence that an American crime wave was *not* overtaking the city, she offered her own evidence that 'clearly it is.' In the same way, she also dismissed Eng's take on the gun control issue and Minors's discussion of racism. In the final sentence of the paragraph, she used the pronouns *we* and *their* to exclude 'these people' (i.e., Tonks, Eng, and Minors) from the general population, who, like her source, Ashton, were 'genuinely horrified by the Just Desserts shooting.'

Having discredited the other Police Services Board members and Metro councillors, Blatchford established the credibility of her source by contrasting him with the others. Like the general population, but unlike his colleagues, Ashton was genuinely horrified. According to Ashton, the problem was 'immigration laws that don't work.' From her Vietnamese example, Blatchford was able to authoritatively generalize: 'It took two decades of choosing too many of the wrong immigrants' to change the city from 'the Toronto [she] saw when [she] came here in 1967' to a Toronto under 'siege.'

*Criminalizing Immigration*

It was not until the second suspect in the case, O'Neil Grant, was arrested and it was discovered that his deportation had been stayed, that any discussion about deporting criminal immigrants took place. Below, we deliberately juxtapose three articles – one from each of the papers –

to compare the various journalistic practices of selection and combination that went into constructing a particular view of Jamaican immigrants in the deportation debate:

> Grant came to Canada in 1983, at age 12 ... Hanger told the Commons that the deportation order against Grant was stayed 'despite the fact that he had a criminal record as long as your arm.' (*Toronto Star*, Allan Thompson, 28 April 1994: A4)

> Reform MP Art Hanger described Mr. Grant as having 'a criminal record as long as your arm' ... Mr. Grant, 22, was raised in Jamaica by his grandmother and came to Canada when he was 12 ... He changed school three times in five years and quit halfway through Grade 9 when he was 16 ... Mr. Grant had fathered two children. Immigration authorities were looking for the mother of his four-year old daughter and Mr. Grant's own mother was caring for the child, although she did not have legal custody ... At the time of the hearing, Mr. Grant was in a common-law relationship with another woman, who was eight months pregnant. (*The Globe and Mail*, Lila Sarick, 28 April 1994: A1)

> He came to Canada from Jamaica with a kindergarten level of education and was placed in Grade 6. In other words, from the very beginning he was set up to fail. He changed schools frequently and quit when he was 16. He took drugs, he fathered two children out of wedlock and ... had, as Reform MP Art Hanger told the Commons last week, 'a criminal record as long as your arm.' If this whole sorry mess was a rare incident, it would at least be understandable. But it is not rare at all. It is simply yet one more nail in the credibility of the immigration and refugee system that Marchi alleges is basically sound. (*Toronto Sun*, editorial, 1 May 1994: 14)

These three examples exhibit varying degrees of completeness. Journalists operate in accordance with the Grecian maxim of quantity, which states that one should neither include 'irrelevant' information, nor leave out any information that is needed for clarity. All three papers quoted Reform MP Art Hanger's colourful turn of phrase. And all three papers mentioned that Grant came to Canada when he was twelve. However, only the *Globe* and the *Sun* concluded that references to Grant's single-parent, female-headed family situation and to his poor educational performance were relevant to 'the story.' It seems that the journalists and editors of the *Sun* and the *Globe* were trying to reinforce the 'commonsense' links that had been made between 'inadequate family' situations in Black families, 'cultures of deprivation,' and 'criminal youth' since the Moynihan Report of the 1960s. In the *Star*, on the other hand, the only information that was considered relevant was that Grant had come to Canada as a young teenager.

Once the relationship between this Jamaican culture of deprivation and crime was established, the solutions to the problem of race and crime became clear. A common neoconservative solution to 'law-and-order' problems is to build prisons in which to house more criminals for longer sentences. The unique solution to the problem of race and crime that arose in the discourses surrounding the Just Desserts case was deportation.

**Parliamentary Debates on Deportation**

So far we have been making the case that pre-existing, dominant law-and-order discourses on gun control and young offender issues were taken up and reconfigured by the news media in response to the particular circumstances of the Just Desserts case. We have demonstrated that when these law-and-order discourses become racialized in the media – as they did in this case – the 'explanation' for this criminal deviance becomes obvious: foreign 'others' bring with them their criminal ways. This racialized chain of signification leads from the particularities of the Just Desserts incident, to the general cultural attributes of its (Black) perpetrators, to their specific national origins outside Canada. Once it is 'demonstrated' that this kind of crime is imported, the source of the problem can be pinpointed at 'the border' between us and them, and crime prevention becomes synonymous with immigration controls.

Controls on immigration can take two forms: preventing criminals/immigrants from entering the country, and deporting those who are already here. The latter controls were stressed in media reports and picked up on in the legislation to amend the Immigration Act (Bill C-44) that was tabled by the federal government on 17 June 1994, approximately two-and-a-half months after the Just Desserts shooting. The point of this bill was to make it easier to deport criminals who had been convicted of serious crimes. For support for our assertion that a link existed between media representations of the crime and the changes to the immigration legislation, we reviewed the transcriptions in the *Hansard* of the debates surrounding this bill, from its introduction to its adoption.[5]

We found that parliamentarians often cited 'facts' or 'statistics' reported in the news media in support of their arguments. For example, on one of the seven occasions that the *Globe and Mail* was cited, Reform MP Philip Mayfield paraphrased Michael Valpy's assertion 'that an unprecedented clear majority of Canadians ... thought immigration levels were too high' (19 September 1994: 5805).

Parliamentarians also have access to daily news clippings services. The Minister of Citizenship and Immigration, Sergio Marchi, referred to these in his introductory remarks on the bill (19 September 1994: 5796). Clearly, the dominant 'explanations' for the crime that were constructed by the media influenced the drafting of Bill C-44, as well as the debates surrounding it, as well as its easy passage.

As we pointed out earlier, the links that the media forged between the Just Desserts case and a particular type of crime – and later between crime and immigration in general – led to forceful calls in newspaper columns and editorials to reform the immigration system so as to make it easier to weed out and deport the criminal immigrant element. As a result of the focus on deportation among the public and in the media, and the moral panic around issues of immigration and deportation, the bill was agreed to by all parties. Both those for it and those against it focused on the need for 'enforcement,' or policing, of immigration. Not surprisingly, other policing issues related to the Just Desserts case – for example, gun control, and the tightening of the young offender laws – were mentioned on a number of occasions during the debate on C-44. This 'Just Desserts Bill,' as it was dubbed by one reporter, was passed on 7 February 1995 and enacted on 10 July 1995. Its impact on the Black community in general, and on the Jamaican community in particular, has been excessive.

### Discourse Analysis of a Chinese Restaurant Slaying

On 17 December 1995, a shooting took place in a Chinese restaurant on Gerrard Street in downtown Toronto. A man named Tommy Vo was ambushed and shot while leaving the restaurant with two friends. Vo died, and his friends sustained non-fatal injuries. The weapon used was identified as an AK-47 assault rifle.

This case created a substantial amount of news coverage, partly because it occurred in a public place, but also because of how the police carried out their investigations. Dozens of restaurant patrons were lined up outside the restaurant on a very cold evening and searched at gunpoint. They were forced to stand with their hands against the wall, and some were even handcuffed. They were later taken to a police station and questioned before being released. Several women hid in their car, too frightened to come out, and did so only when the police called to them through a megaphone. 'They were screaming at us. It was terrible. They were pointing their guns in our face, they made us hold our hands up over our heads' (Rosie DiManno, *Toronto Star*, 18 December 1995). The scene on the street was 'sheer pandemonium ... at one point it resembled a war zone ... Police officers carrying assault rifles and sawed-off shotguns ran around monitoring the area to make sure there were no more armed suspects around' (*Star*, 18 December 1995).

The police were quoted as saying that all the people in the restaurant had to be considered suspects until they were cleared, and that the exact same procedures would have been followed had the event taken place in a different location. It should be noted, however, that the police treated the patrons at the Just Deserts cafe with respect and defer-ence. Which brings us to this critical question: Had the shooting taken place at a White-owned restaurant patronized mainly by White middle-class customers, would the police have acted in a similar manner?

Members of the Chinese community voiced their concerns about the methods the police used. One Chinese organization sent a letter to the Police Services Board complaining that 'there is a blanket assumption of criminality of Asians who live or work in the Chinatown area.' After a private meeting between their spokespeople and the police, they expressed satisfaction with the explanations the police offered. Later, in January, a Chinese newspaper, *Ming Pao*, published the results of an informal poll of its readers with regard to how the police had treated the restaurant patrons. Eighty five per cent of those who phoned in said they supported the police action; only 13.5 per cent said there was 'a racial factor at play' (*Toronto Sun*, 3 January 1996).

We contend that the police acted in a manner consistent with their negative perceptions of Asian communities, and that the media dis-course on the case contained elements of covert racism.

*Stereotypic Assumptions about Asian Gangs*

The early reporting of the incident reflected the subtle use of stereo-types about the Chinese. For example, in a feature by Rosie DiManno (*Star*, 18 December), the four women who had hidden in their car were described as a 'hip, Generation X crowd, mostly Asian and mostly clique-ish.' The descriptor 'clique-ish' didn't seem at all relevant to the incident; also, four young women spending a night on the town usually wouldn't be described as clique-ish. These women could have been described, and more accurately, as friends rather than as members of a clique. This term reinforced a common stereotype about Asians and especially Chinese – that they are secretive and clannish.

Early on, the media made a definite attempt to report the crime as a gangland slaying. The assumption was clear: the killing of an Asian, by an Asian, in a Chinese restaurant, had to be gang-related. DiManno wrote of Vo's death, 'The hit, if that's what is was, occurred outside.'

The *Toronto Sun* made the same assumption. The day after the shooting it headlined its news report, 'Gang Slaying Fits Pattern: Murder Weapon Left by Body.' The article began by stating quite clearly that 'yesterday's slaying of a man ... was the first gangland-style murder this year' (18 December 1995). It then recalled that in 1994, a 'Big Circle Boys gang member' had been shot several times and a weapon left by his body. It also recalled an even earlier gangland slaying, that of Johnny Tran in 1991.

In a related article on the same date, Vo's friend was quoted as saying he was lucky to have escaped the 'assassin's AK-47' but that a bullet fragment had hit him. The article later described the weapon as 'An AK-47 assault rifle cut short into a traditional gang-style weapon.'

On 19 December the *Sun* headlined its article 'Vietnamese Racketeer's Violent End: Slain Goon Sold Protection.' Though it described the victim as a gangster, it also identified his friend as a 'hard-core gang member once linked to murdered underworld boss Asua "Johnny" Tran.' It also noted that this friend had once been implicated in a 1994 'home invasion' but had been released. The article then recalled that Tran, 'a ruthless boss of about 100 young Vietnamese gangsters was murdered in 1991,' and concluded that 'as in Vo's killing, an Ak-47 was dumped beside their bodies in what police describe as a Asian-gang execution calling card.'

In its report of 19 December, the *Toronto Star* was more circumspect. It quoted a police detective as saying that Vo was known to police; however, the detective declined to say what exactly he was known for. When asked – presumably by reporters – whether the victim had been a member of an organized gang, police spokespeople declined to comment. Even so, the report went on to say that 'Vo may have been the victim of a gang-style hit.' The Metro police, it continued, had summoned in the Combined Forces Asian Investigative Unit, which in the past had been

called in for killings with a 'gang' connection. Later, the article specu-
lated that many of Vo's friends were associated with the Big Circle Boys,
a 'well-known Chinese gang.'

For its article of 20 December, the *Star* seemed to have done some
investigating of its own. It noted that the police were searching for the
killer of 'Vo, a known criminal,' and went on to say that 'intelligence
documents obtained by the Star identify Chanh Thong Vo with links to
gang activity in Ottawa and Toronto.' Thus, although up to this point
the police were not admitting gangland connections, the newspaper was
going out of its way to obtain documents that associated the victim with
gangs. In an apparent rush to justice, the media – and especially the *Star*
in this case – were eager to associate the crime with gangs. Crimes by
gangs of Asian immigrants – particularly gangs of Vietnamese immigrants – was the theme of a column by Bob Macdonald headed, 'Immigrant Gangs Out of Control: Bring Back Capital Punishment, Work
Camps' (*Sun*, 20 December 1995). After again describing Vo as a mobster, he noted that he himself has been a patron of this particular restaurant, so he shares the concerns of many Torontonians accustomed to
patronizing restaurants and shops in the area. Thus began the familiar
discourse of immigration. Macdonald said that violence in the Chinese
community surprised people, because when Chinatown was smaller it
did not produce violence and the Chinese were known as hard working
and law abiding. The fault lay with the loose immigration system established by the Liberals under Trudeau, which was allowing people to
enter Canada from crime-prone areas of the world. Macdonald identified gangs from China, Vietnam, Jamaica, Somalia, and Russia.
Although he agreed that most immigrants are decent people, he
indicted Canada's loose system, which enabled many criminal types to
enter the country easily and stay there. He then added that when immigrant gangs were added to the activities of homegrown gangs, 'Canada
has an increasingly threatening criminal future.' He called for Canadians to demand that 'our gutless politicians' tighten immigration and
criminal laws. Thus, four days after the crime, the *Sun* was already linking crime to immigrant gangs and to the immigration system itself. The
idea that immigrants cause crime was being planted deep in the minds
of readers.

Meanwhile, stories published in both the *Sun* and the *Star* continued
to focus on the gangland character of the incident. On 20 December
the *Sun* began its main article, 'A Vietnamese gangster cut down by a
high-powered assault rifle.' The rifle was described as 'An AK-47, with a

cut-down handle favored by hitmen.' Under the paragraph heading 'Gang Member,' one of Vo's friends was described as a 'hard-core gang member.' In a second article on this case, DiManno called the incident a 'gangland-style shooting' (20 December 1995). More gang-related comments appeared in the following days.

It seems that press reports of this slaying were heavily coloured by stereotypic assumptions. Because it was an Asian crime, it had to be a gang crime. The notion that it might have been a personally motivated crime was nowhere to be found in any of the early coverage. Here, as in the case of Just Desserts, the media were following the police lead – that is, investigating not the possibility but the *probability* that Vo's death was gang-related. All of this raises the issue of how stereotypes are applied in crime reporting about racial minority perpetrators. It is highly doubtful that the same stereotypic assumptions would have influenced the reporting of a 'White' murder, even in a public place.

It is also apparent that Vo as an individual was of no importance to the reporters, who cared only about his gang and mobster associations. On 19 December the *Sun* quoted 'sources' describing him as a 'half-assed dai lo ... dai lo or elder brother is an Asian term for gang leader.' It described his arrest record, but noted that he was never convicted. The reader never learned anything about this man, or his friends, other than that they were Vietnamese, probably criminals, and affiliated with gangs. The only item of personal information reported was about his sexuality. Several reports wrote that he was known as 'Tommy No Dick' since he had shot off the top of his penis while pocketing a gun.

Neither Vo nor his associates were treated as individuals; they were discussed only as members of ethnic groups. The *Star*'s article of 19 December complained that the police had released no photo of Vo, and no information about his address and occupation. Yet the same newspaper went to considerable lengths to access confidential documents indicating that he and his associates were ganged up. Refusal to acknowledge individuality is part of the same 'othering' process we described earlier in the Just Deserts case. The perpetrators were members of groups, and these groups are certainly not *us* but *them*. This 'othering' process was reinforced by language differences. Citing the police, the media noted that language became an issue when it came to interviewing patrons who did not speak English. Interpreters had to be brought in for those who spoke Cantonese, Mandarin, or Vietnamese. The same point was made in a *Star* article, which stated that eleven translators had been brought in. All these items of information reinforced in readers' minds that these people were outsiders. When the issue of immigration controls was added to the discourse, these people were marginalized even more strongly.

A few days later the police arrested a man in connection with the shooting of Vo, along with two of his 'gangland associates.' Vo was again described as a 'street punk' who loved violence (*Sun*, 21 December). The *Star*, in reporting the same event, described Vo's killing as a 'wild Chinatown East shooting' (21 December 1995). Yet it also quoted a police detective as saying, 'There's no gang relation here that we see.' The next day the *Star* reported that a suspect had been apprehended, again described Vo as having connections to an Asian criminal gang, and reminded readers that he had been shot by an assault rifle. It also noted, near the very end of the article, that 'investigators believe the attack was personally motivated and did not involve Asian gang rivalries.' Nevertheless, Vo's alleged connections to an Asian gang continued to be cited in this article, and the murder weapon was again described as an assault rifle. Eventually 'three Asian men' were arrested, according to a *Sun* article on 22 December. This article again tried to link the crime to gangs, reporting that the three men were connected to a Winnipeg gang and that Vo had a record for extortion and violence.

The media had information that the attack was personally motivated, but they chose to ignore it. The underlying assumption being made here was that gang rivalries, and the ensuing violence, were the norm for these communities. Again, this reinforced the stereotypic assumptions made by the police and the media about alleged Asian criminal behaviour.

*Links to Other Communities*

In the aftermath of Vo's slaying, the *Star* published a story about the use of ethnic police squads (28 January 1996). This story noted that there were mixed feelings about ethnic police squads. The police credited their success in the week-long manhunt for Vo's killers to the 'great community support' they had; without it 'the situation itself would be far more complicated and frustrating from both sides.' The article then shifted to a discussion of another shooting, this one in the Black community, regarding which witnesses were reluctant to come forward. 'When turf wars by drug gangs catch innocent victims in the crossfire, witnesses are often loath to come forward'; the main reason was 'the poor relations, be they real or perceived, between the black community and the police.' The article went on to say that a similar situation existed in the Asian community, within which 'robberies and extortions were rampant' until more Asian officers were recruited. 'Improving community relations has had a direct impact on crime in the Asian community.'

In raising the issue of 'turf wars by drug gangs,' the article was linking the restaurant slaying to the Black community and drugs. It was comparing the Asian community's positive attitude toward the Asian police units with the Black community's often negative attitudes toward Black crime squads. To the casual reader, turf wars about drugs in the Black community and about extortions, robberies, and shootings in the Asian community, and relations between these communities and the police, had become the central issue. What was being reinforced here was the notion of racialized crime. No attempt was made to compare police methods for apprehending Whites who had or allegedly had committed crimes. The issue of crime was being treated solely through the perspectives of race and ethnicity. The message being communicated was that people of colour were the ones committing crimes. The 'facts' of White criminality, though obviously there, were not mentioned even in passing, and the view that crime is a function of race was probably reinforced in the minds of casual readers, and certainly in those of bigoted readers.

**Conclusions**

The two case studies in this chapter reveal just how much power the media have to disseminate 'facts' and to generate specific discourses based on those 'facts.' In the Just Desserts case, the media helped significantly to create a moral panic about the need for law and order. Gun control was elevated to a key issue. The 'truth' being promoted was that young Black foreign men were responsible for the escalating violence in this society and had to be deported in greater numbers. It is also quite apparent that the media strongly influenced parliamentary debates on the new legislation. The case therefore illustrates the media's great power to influence attitudes and policies. More specifically, it shows how the media can target specific groups in society for marginalizing. This distinction between *us* and *them* was especially clear in the case of the restaurant murder: allegations of violence and gang warfare were used to isolate the Chinese community from mainstream Canadian society.

# PART IV
# FIRST NATIONS PEOPLE IN
# THE PRINT MEDIA

In this section we analyse the misrepresentation of First Nations People in some of the print media. Native groups and communities have tried many strategies to reduce bias and achieve some form of more balanced news reporting in the Canadian print media, but with little success. The Native Action Committee on the Media (NACOM) has pursued a number of avenues to deal with racism in the press, including petitioning the courts, lobbying 'power-brokers,' and utilizing government regulatory bodies whenever possible. NACOM has urged newspapers to move away from 'self-serving, negative, or racist commentary to more equitable and balanced reporting and editorial writing' (Linklater, 1986).

In the early 1980s, the Peguis Band Council laid complaints against the *Winnipeg Sun* and its owners for contravening the Manitoba Human Rights Act. NACOM, for its part, was concerned about how First Nations peoples were being portrayed in the *Toronto Sun*. It argued that the *Sun* had gone beyond the moral and legal conventions of society in its coverage of Native peoples, and that its coverage resulted in representations that would result in 'hatred and misunderstanding' toward Native peoples.

In 1993 the British Columbia Organization to Fight Racism (BCOFR) was appalled when it learned that the Governor General of Canada had presented Doug Collins with an award that honours Canadians who have made a significant contribution to their fellow citizens, their community, or Canada. Collins was described as a controversial columnist for the *North Shore News* and the *Vancouver Sun* who forced people to think for themselves. Actually, Collins had a long history of maligning Aboriginal people, racial minorities and immigrants. Anthropologist Robin Ridington launched a complaint against the journalist with the

British Columbia Press Council. The complaint was dismissed (Riding-ton, 1986).

Maurice Switzer (1998), director of communications for the Assembly of First Nations, contends that the Canadian media 'have declared open season on Indians.' He notes as well that the progress that First Nations people are making in key areas such as treaty and land claims has cre-ated an even more hostile relationship between the mainstream media and First Nations peoples. Also, that the once-clear lines between sensa-tional tabloid journalism and the more respectable press have 'blurred beyond recognition;' and that newspapers like the *Ottawa Citizen* 'have been literally thumbing their noses at First Nations peoples and their issues' (8). He cites the example of a publisher in British Columbia who publishes sixty weekly newspapers in the province, who ordered all his editors to carry only editorials or columns critical of the Nisga'a treaty.

The Royal Commission on Aboriginal Peoples (RCAP, 1996) found that most coverage in the mainstream media was being written in the context of Aboriginal peoples as pathetic victims, angry warriors, or noble environmentalists. The commissioners were so concerned about media indifference to their findings that they distributed to community newspapers a series of articles dealing with various aspects of the ground-breaking report. As Switzer observes, this media indifference to Aboriginal issues, is reflected in polling results which indicate that 40 per cent of the public believe that First Nations peoples enjoy a standard of living as good as or better than their own.

Researchers such as Roth and colleagues (1995) and Skea (1993–94) note that First Nations peoples are commonly portrayed as a significant threat to the social order. Roth and colleagues (1995) make the point that the Oka crisis created a media frenzy, during which negative stereo-typing of First Nations peoples was never more blatant. Headlines in the national media revealed the depth of racialized discourse that placed all Mohawks 'within a system of categories of violence' (see Roth et al. chapter 2).

Fleras and Kunz (2001) observe that the mainstream news media frame First Nations peoples as problem peoples who either have prob-lems or create problems. Media depictions of Aboriginal initiatives that seek to challenge historic and current inequities tend to focus on the conflictual and confrontational aspects rather than on the historical and social contexts underpinning the issues at stake.

The following two case studies provide a clear demonstration of media bias in the coverage of Native issues.

# 10

# Media Discourse Involving First Nations Peoples

**Case Study 1: Ramsay's Assault on a First Nations Woman**

In this case study we present a discourse analysis of an event in Saskatchewan involving the sexual assault of a young, unidentified First Nations woman several years ago by Jack Ramsay, a member of Parliament. We analyse three newspapers: *The Globe and Mail*, the *Saskatoon Star Phoenix*, and the *Regina Leader Post*.

In central and eastern Canada, media coverage of minorities has generally focused on 'immigrant' minorities; in contrast, in the Western provinces such press coverage has generally focused on First Nations peoples, in particular, their alleged criminal behaviour. All minorities suffer from roughly the same ill treatment at the hands of the press; as we will show, any differences are found mainly in the specifics.

*Background*

Late in 1999 a story about Jack Ramsay, an Alberta Reform MP, appeared in the media. A Native woman had accused him of sexually assaulting her thirty years earlier, at a time when he was an RCMP officer in Pelican Narrows, Saskatchewan. The assault allegedly took place in 1969, but the victim had reported the event only recently. After her evidence was heard, Ramsay was charged with sexual assault. His trial was scheduled to begin in November 1999.

*A Critical Discourse Analysis of the* Globe*'s Coverage of the Case*

The *Globe* published the first of its articles on the Ramsay case on 22

November 1999. It had dispatched a reporter to Melfort, Saskatchewan, to cover the story. This first article, which ran on page 1, was headlined, '*Sexual Assault Trial Begins for ex-Mountie, Now Reform MP.*'

> The native reserve of Pelican Narrows was no dream posting for a veteran in 1969. The 600 Crees who lived there, rammed into log shacks on the rocky brush sloping up from the lake, made do without running water or telephones.
>
> The Roman Catholics lived on the west side, the Anglicans on the east; at one time, they would meet in the middle to fight with slingshots.
>
> A gravel road had reached the village two years earlier, but the nearest town, Flin Flon, was 120 kilometres away.
>
> White trappers had named the town after the pelicans that flocked to the bay in summer. The Crees call it 'Narrows of Fear,' after an old battle.
>
> Ramsay arrived in 1969 to be the RCMP corporal in charge of a two-man detachment. He was 32 years old, still a year away from marrying his wife, Glenna, two decades from his first run at politics.
>
> He'd been a Mountie for 12 years, lured off his father's Alberta farm by the 'fair and square' postcard image of the red serge. He'd served in about a dozen small communities across Manitoba and Saskatchewan.

The trial was to be about an alleged assault committed by Ramsay, yet the article's first four paragraphs focused exclusively on the Native community where he had been stationed. The article *fronted* with a description of the community – a description that included a significant number of *stereotypes* commonly associated with Native communities.

Poverty was presented graphically in the phrase 'crammed into log shacks.' The verb 'crammed' suggested a shortage of housing space, and the noun 'shack' was used instead of house or building. It was also noted that the shacks were made of logs. The poverty found in Pelican Narrows was further highlighted by the comment that the villagers made do without 'running water or telephones.'

The hostility between Catholics and Protestants was then noted: they lived in separate parts of the village, and 'at one time, they would meet in the middle to fight with slingshots.' No *attribution* or *source* was offered for this. The next paragraph reinforced that the village was isolated. The writer then pointed out that the Cree had their own name for the village: 'Narrows of Fear' ... after an old battle. Again, this suggests aggression and violence. Thus, within a few lead paragraphs, the writer was *stereotyping* the Native community of Pelican Narrows as impoverished, isolated, given to religious factionalism, and prone to violence. The only stereotype missing was that of drunkenness, but that would come later in the article!

Presumably, the writer was making these points to establish that this was no 'dream posting' for a Mountie. The hardship of the social and physical environment was beginning to emerge as an excuse for Ramsay's behaviour.

After discussing Ramsay's arrival there, and describing something of his personal life, the writer quickly made the point that Ramsay has been a strong critic of the RCMP. The paragraph that continued the article overleaf (A2) noted: 'He would later write publicly about the Mounties who walked into reserve homes without knocking, who used drunken Indians to pad their arrest statistics.' The writer was making the point that Ramsay was criticizing the Mounties, but she still managed to slip in the infamous stereotype 'drunken Indian.' The full complement of commonly held *stereotypes* against Native people had thus been provided.

Toward the end of this very long article, Ramsay's piece condemning the RCMP, published in *Maclean's* in 1972, was cited at length. Ramsay in the article made many strong criticisms, and offered many reasons why he was leaving the force, but the *Globe* writer chose to highlight one particular criticism that included yet another stereotype of Native people. As the *Globe* writer noted, Ramsey wrote 'about a close friend who was prosecuted internally for having an extra marital affair with a 16-year-old native girl – an act, he said he "could not condone" ... He then remembered "a similar story about a native constable accused of getting a white girl pregnant – charges he says were hushed up "because if an Indian was discharged, people might think the force was prejudiced."' In citing this particular incident, the article was reinforcing Ramsay's own point: Native constables were treated better because the Mounties feared being labelled as prejudiced. The argument that RCMP policy was 'politically correct' was thus invoked, though without being specifically identified.

Most of this long article, which covered *all* of A2 and included two photos of Ramsay – the first in full colour as a young man in full Mountie uniform, and the second, on the following page, showing him in the present day – was about Jack Ramsay. His long history of service to Canada, first in the Mounties and later as an elected parliamentarian, was cited in great detail. As well, the article made much of the fact that he was a strong critic of the RCMP – in fact, that he was a champion of Native rights who had served as an ombudsman for Native people in Alberta, in which office he was outspoken in his criticism of the Mounties.

The article ended with a detailed commentary on how Ramsay had helped a Native family after one of its members had been charged with murdering a White woman. The man was imprisoned for five years, and after his release wandered into the woods, where he died of exposure. This case was presented to show Ramsay's attempts to help the family; even so, it involved a Native person accused of a crime, and again the reader was being presented with the stereotype of the *Native as criminal.* On the whole, the article was written with a strong *us* and *them* perspective: Ramsay and his family were the good guys, and Natives and their community were the othered *them.* In this very long piece, not one positive image of the Native experience in Saskatchewan or the rest of Canada was presented.

The next article, published one day later, on 23 November, began with this statement: 'By his own account, he was young, single and stupid.' This set the tone that allowed the writer to introduce some of the testimony that the victim had raised against Jack Ramsay. Even by his own testimony, Ramsay had committed some inappropriate acts. Yet the very next paragraph described the Native victim as follows: 'She was 14 years old, from a home where her mother was a drunk and her father beat her.' Another set of *stereotypes* was thus being established to convey the image of drunkenness and violence. The article continued: 'Testifying tearfully in Court of Queen's Bench, after 30 years of silence, the woman bowed her head, and described how Mr. Ramsay told her in his office to pull down her pants. He undid his. Then he raped her, she said, standing up, pressed against the office desk, and left her to walk home alone.' Here the Native woman was being portrayed as a victim, which is appropriate. However, the phrase 'after 30 years of silence' is problematic. By inserting this phrase, the writer was reminding us that the incident had taken place many years earlier. This is an example of *irrelevance*: this insertion did not add anything to her testimony and in fact detracted from it by suggesting that her memory might be at fault, given the long lapse of time.

The article continued: 'While the conversation was played for the jury, Mr. Ramsay, 62, sat in the oak prisoner's box, staring at the floor over his reading glasses. His wife, Glenna, his four grown children, and his three brothers – even his campaign manager – filled the rows behind him. Without Mr. Ramsay's supporters, and minus the media, the public gallery would have been practically empty.' In this paragraph, the writer was invoking sympathy for Ramsay by mentioning that his family was present in the room. By noting that without Ramsay's supporters the gallery would have been empty, the writer was again resorting to the technique of *irrelevance*, since this added nothing to the unfolding story. That the woman was now living in Edmonton and was employed was the first information the reader received about the victim other than the repeated stereotypes about Natives and their lives.

The article continued: 'She had just finished telling the jury – collapsing once in tears, pausing at every question – how Mr. Ramsay had turned up at her home in uniform and asked her mother whether he could take her back to the police station, two blocks away.' It was not necessary to state again that the victim cried. This is yet another example of *irrelevance*. The article continued by describing the woman's testimony as well as a taped conversation that had taken place between herself and Ramsay.

On 24 November the *Globe* carried another article that began with straightforward writing about the testimony that has thus far been presented. Then it went on to speculate about the hurdles the case presented to both the Crown and the defence: 'The Crown has the harder case to hoe. What the jury has seen is this: an unsteady, alcoholic Native woman who can't remember whether she was wearing underwear the day she says she was raped, whose testimony has changed, in little details, from one statement to the next, and who waited three decades to come forward – until the man she is accusing was famous.'

The writer was describing the victim in very unflattering terms. The word 'unsteady' hardly belongs in objective reportage, and this was supposed to be a news report, not an editorial or feature piece. She was described as 'alcoholic,' although she had testified that she was going to AA, had successfully completed a 12-step recovery program, and was now fully employed. The writer continued the use of *stereotypes* against Natives by describing her at present as an alcoholic. She was also charged with not remembering – although admittedly in 'little details.' In the final sentence, the fact that she had waited for three decades was juxtaposed in a *contrastive* strategy with an evaluative opinion statement: 'until the man ... was famous.' The reader was expected to get the message that the woman had waited deliberately until this man was famous. The reason for this strategy was strongly suggested in the next paragraph: 'Perhaps, Mr. Ramsay's lawyer, Morris Bodnar, hinted yesterday, she is hoping to get some money out of his client? I'm not interested, the woman said, a statement made somewhat less convincing when she added "It is a good idea."' The phrase 'made somewhat less convincing' was being used to underscore that perhaps the lawyer was correct in his assessment.

The next few paragraphs were devoted to the strengths of the defence: 'a gem of a client, a respected politician, whose loving family sits in court ...' Ramsay was being described in glowing terms. In particular, his loving family was noted.

The writer concluded with her description of the victim's weaknesses: 'The woman, who cannot be identified, has not been the best of witnesses. She has been vague on many details, changing her version ... tossing in new elements that she never mentioned before testifying at trial.' During questioning by defence counsel, she finally agreed to a statement of his. To this, the writer appended: 'and in a rare instance, her voice rose above a whisper.' This statement added little to the story other than that the witness perhaps felt harassed by counsel. By implication, her raising her voice once brought into question her earlier testimony, which was apparently delivered in a whisper. Thus, a value judgment was being made about her testimony – a judgment based on a factor that was *irrelevant* to the matter at hand.

In the final paragraph, the article predicted the outcome of the trial, noting that the witness's newfound assertiveness was unlikely to prevail over the forceful Mr. Ramsay, who was facing 'a complainant who cannot, for whatever reason, keep her story straight.'

The long article ended with yet another indictment of the victim, who, it was implied, could not keep her story straight and who might well have a hidden agenda for not keeping it straight.

These articles painted a classic *us* and *them* image for the reader. While admitting that Ramsay did behave inappropriately, the writer of these articles was going to great lengths to marginalize the Native victim as untrustworthy, unreliable, forgetful, and alcoholic. This may well have been the image the defence counsel was trying to establish; our point is that by selecting and choosing various elements of testimony, making assumptions and value judgments, and resorting to powerful and emotive language to describe the inadequacies of the Native woman, the writer was reinforcing the image of 'otherness.'

On 25 November, the article headlined 'MP Ramsay Found Guilty of Attempted Rape in 1969,' was mainly about the fact that the jury had found him guilty. Yet, in terms of frontage, the article began: 'It took a solid second for the guilty verdict to sink in. Then, in the front row, Jack Ramsay's daughter, Jackie, put her head in her hands and began to weep silently.' Immediately, the reader was aware that Ramsay has a devoted daughter who was in tears about the verdict against her father. The point of mentioning the daughter's tears was to instil some sympathy for the accused. A little later, the article noted: 'Mr. Ramsay did not move in the prisoner's box ... did not glance back at his wife, Glenna and their four grown children.' Then, Mrs Ramsay was described as wandering the courthouse 'with weepy eyes,' while Ramsay's three brothers 'talked taxes in the hallway.' Again, the inference was that Ramsay had his family's support. The victim was not referred to, nor were any members of her family. Even their presumed absence was not mentioned. When the victim was mentioned, around the middle of the article, the poverty of her community was highlighted once again: 'A poor reserve so cut off that it did not even have telephones. Her mother was mean when she was drinking, and her father was just plain mean.' Another significant mention of her was made toward the end of the article: 'Her story changed and her memory is more than foggy – perhaps, Mr. Bodnar suggested to the jury, her years of "injecting herself" with drugs and drinking herself unconscious fried her brain.'

Although the article did not blame the victim, and although Ramsay's inappropriate behaviour was described several times, and although Ramsay's own words of regret were noted, a clear dichotomy was being established between how Ramsay and his family were presented and how the victim was presented. Ramsay was surrounded by a supportive and weeping family. The victim's past as a beaten, poverty stricken, and drug and alcohol addicted woman was again recalled, thereby perpetuating these stereotypes once more. Once again an *us* and *them* dichotomy was being presented.

The article of 26 November was headlined, 'Ramsay and Family Still Insist He's Innocent.' On A2 the article continuation was headed, 'Family Rallies Round Ramsay.' The main point of this article was to show how supportive Ramsay's family, friends, and neighbours were and how they believed in his innocence. In the second headline the strategy used was *alliteration* – that is, the constant repetition of sounds: 'family rallies round Ramsay.' This served to enforce meaning and provide evaluation. Here, the meaning to be reinforced was the strength of Ramsay's family network.

The article described Ramsay's home, and noted that his neighbours had sent flowers and offered other kinds of help, and provided details about his two daughters, who believed in his innocence. The article also noted that Ramsay believed his behaviour had been inappropriate rather than criminal. There was no mention of the victim, who had become virtually invisible.[1]

*Summary of the Main Discursive Strategies Used by the* Globe and Mail

The *Globe* followed several linguistic strategies in its coverage of the Ramsay case. Most common throughout was the use of *stereotypes* about Native peoples, stereotypes that were repeated over and over again and established a particular and usually negative image. Native people were described as poor, drunken, drug taking, violent, and hostile. Nowhere in any of the articles was there a mention of the legacy of colonialism – the enforced reserve system, the resident school program, or any other aspects of the history of the relationship between Native peoples and mainstream Canada. Stereotypes about Natives were often repeated, but never was there even a small attempt, in a phrase or an aside, to explain what might have brought about the situation that was described in these articles.

Other strategies included *alliteration* in headlines to enforce meaning, the frequent use of *irrelevant* descriptors, and the use of *fronting* to establish stereotypes.

In terms of the general perspective and tone of these articles, there was a distancing between Ramsay and the Native victim and her community. Ramsay's family and network, his respected position as a former RCMP officer, and his current position as a parliamentarian were mentioned repeatedly. A victim of uncertain memory and past was repeatedly contrasted with an upright defendant who was willing to acknowledge a moment of inappropriate behaviour. The articles reported Ramsay's bad behaviour in great detail, as well as his refusal to accept the verdict; nevertheless, the reader was left with the impression that he had made one mistake in an otherwise worthy and blameless career. The fact that the woman has rehabilitated her life was stated in one sentence in one article and never mentioned again. Even in the present, she is still identified as a drug-using alcoholic.

The *us* and *them* distancing mechanism was firmly established. Readers were encouraged to identify with Ramsay and his family, notwithstanding his one mistake, but never with the victim.

*Local Coverage: The* Saskatoon Star Phoenix *and* Regina Leader Post

We downloaded the coverage of the Ramsay case from the *Saskatoon Star*

*Phoenix* and the *Regina Leader Post* to examine how the local press dealt with the trial. In all, we analysed from articles from the *Star Phoenix* and seven from the *Leader Post*.

It was immediately apparent to us that the local coverage differed significantly from that of the *Globe*. Both local papers provided more details of the trial. There was far more material about the legalities of the case, and court personnel were cited more often. For example, in several articles pretrial motions were discussed. One dealt with the defence's effort to have the charges stayed, another with the possibility of mounting a Charter challenge. The presiding judge was quoted at length saying that he did not believe the fact that some documents were missing made a fair trial for Ramsay impossible: 'Missing documents and destroyed police records do not make it impossible for Reform MP Jack Ramsay to get a fair trial, Justice Ted Noble ruled Wednesday. Noble dismissed a defense application to stay the 30-year-old rape charge against the 62-year-old former Reform Justice critic. Defence co-counsel.'

Both papers also paid far more attention to Ramsay's political position. Several articles dealt at length with his dismissal from the Reform Party's caucus and the general effect of his trial on his constituency, and questioned whether he was still able to serve the interests of his constituents. Members of the party and residents in his riding were quoted. The *Leader Post* reported: '"The board is still standing solidly behind him," Perreault [President of Ramsay's riding association] said. "We are withholding our judgment until justice has run its course. There isn't much else we can do."' Perreault said the verdict meant that 'every male in Canada should check the skeletons in their closet because what this means is any lady can accuse you of rape, and even when you haven't done it, it's your word against theirs.'

Members of Ramsay's constituency were also quoted: 'It's unfortunate,' said Mary Durand, a city councillor and life-long resident of Camrose, Ramsay's home town in the Crowfoot riding. 'I really feel bad. It should not have happened ... He's done a good job representing us.'

One article also cited an expert witness brought forward by the Crown: 'It's not unusual for sexual assault victims to stay silent for years because many distrust the ability of the criminal justice system to effectively deal with the matters.' This was compounded when the victim was Native because 'Aboriginal distrust runs quite deep.' After the trial concluded: 'Defence lawyer Morris Bodnar said he was obviously disappointed with the verdict.'

The possibility of an appeal was also discussed. The local coverage also included more commentary from the victim. In one article her cousin was also quoted.

On 24 November, the *Star Phoenix* wrote:

> The woman, now 44, wanted the RCMP to press rape charges against the man two years ago when they were investigating her allegations against the Alberta Reform MP ... She is angry the matter never proceeded.
>
> 'All I know is I got a call saying there was not enough witnesses and they have to close it for now,' she said. The woman alleged that she was raped by the man in 1969.

The woman would not discuss the details of the alleged assault because she did not know the legal status of the matter, and because of her experiences with the media during the Ramsay trial. Her cousin, however, said she recalled from the summer of 1969 when three teens, aged fourteen, sixteen, and eighteen, ran away from home. They hitch-hiked to another northern community and ended up at a house party, where the alleged assault occurred. 'When you get there, half the people you don't even know. Over half the people you don't even know, and then everybody just ends up partying and then shit happens.'

The cousin said she did not witness the alleged rape. The fourteen-year-old victim told her about the incident with Ramsay but did not raise the allegations against him with her until 1992. 'I don't know when she figured out it was him. She didn't tell me about him until about 1992, when my husband died. We were out of touch for about 17 years, and then all of a sudden there she was.'

Notably absent in local reporting was commentary about social conditions in Pelican Narrows and especially about the victim's substance abuse problems. There was no discussion of Native poverty or of the violence that allegedly characterized relations in Native families. In short, the local coverage did not resort to stereotypes about Native people. There was no discussion about the woman adding new details to her story, or having memory lapses, or changing her story – about anything that would detract from her testimony. There was extensive coverage of the graphic details of the rape as described in Ramsay's taped conversations; there were also detailed excerpts from the victim's trial testimony. The local press covered the incident largely from a legal perspective and relied on quotes from officers of the court.

The second major focus of the local coverage was the impact that

Ramsay's conviction would have on his political career. The tone and perspective of these articles differed significantly from what was found in the *Globe and Mail*, which focused strongly on Native life and experience and used many linguistic techniques to present its particular slant.

What is responsible for these differences? Perhaps the local papers were serving communities that were already well familiar with the facts of Native life. Perhaps they wanted to avoid perpetuating stereotypes that Saskatchewan's Native people would criticize. The *Globe*, in contrast, is a national newspaper published in Toronto, where the Native population, though large, is not as significant as in the West. These arguments don't really speak to the differences. It is more likely that the *Globe*'s coverage was coloured by its conservative ideology, which is often characterized by the 'othering' of disadvantaged peoples.

*Conclusions*

*The Globe and Mail* resorted to stereotypes in its presentation of Pelican Narrows and the Native woman who pressed charges against Jack Ramsay. In contrast, the local press was more interested in objectively reporting the legal events and arguments.

One of the striking elements in this case study is how racism, sexism, and classism intersected so consistently throughout the *Globe*'s coverage of the trial. The identity and gaze of the White journalists who covered this story acted as a filter screening out the historical, socioeconomic, and political context of this narrative. The mediated image of the passive, alcoholic, indigent, inarticulate Native woman, who was perhaps sexually promiscuous, appeared as a familiar figure to readers within the dominant discourse. Her family and her community were represented through denigrating images that highlighted their poverty and their social dysfunction.

Jack Ramsay was found guilty of a serious crime, yet readers of the *Globe* were provided with many strongly positive images of a White, middle-class, morally upright family man with a loving wife and daughters who contributed to the community for many decades. The juxtaposition of the two protagonists established the superiority of Whiteness over the racialized '*others*.' Consistent with colonial discourse, the journalists covering this story for the *Globe*, presented a narrative that supported, validated, and preserved the dominance of White, Anglo-European culture.

**Case Study 2: Mi'kmaq Fishing Rights at Burnt Church**

Between 2 February and 25 September 1999, *The National Post* published fifty-six news articles and editorials about the controversy surrounding fishing rights in Atlantic waters. The disputes the paper covered took place between the Mi'kmaq people and non-natives. Thirty-six of the articles were straight news stories that recounted events as they took place. Fourteen were essentially crime stories, that is, stories that focused on violence and/or alleged criminal activity. Examples: 'Native Fisherman Arrested as Dispute Heats Up in N.S.'; 'Fisheries Officer Injured by Rock in Lobster Dispute.' In addition, there were seven editorials on the subject.

This extensive coverage of this issue by the *Post* suggests a high level of interest on the part of the newspaper. It may well be that it was so interested in the dispute for the platform it offered for launching partisan attacks on the Liberal government.

In this case study we analyse the editorials published on Burnt Church in the *Post.* Using critical discourse analysis (CDA), we offer some evidence of racialized discourse. Before turning to the actual editorials, we examine the powerful role of editorials in newsmaking.

*The Nature of Editorials*

The common assumption is that editorials express the perspectives and opinions of the management and/or ownership of the newspaper. They help readers make up their minds about national and international events. In fact, editorials are ideological statements intended to convince the reader to embrace a particular point of view, as well as the ideology that underlies it.

It follows that editorials have important discursive properties. In transmitting ideological messages, they perform important social, political, and sociocultural functions. These messages do a great deal to shape public opinion on events and to set political agendas. Editorials are closely heeded by political decision makers and sometimes influence political and legislative action. Conservative and right-wing editorials have an especially strong impact because the shared social representations and beliefs of dominant hegemonic groups – that is, White upper-class males – are usually imbedded in them.

Most papers tend to be associated with particular ideologies, and *The National Post* is well known for its conservative, even right-wing perspective on many issues. As a conservative paper, it is, of course, strongly critical of the Liberal government and that government's ministers and policies. So it takes every opportunity available to it to criticize government policy. We saw this in its analysis of the Tamil community: the *Post* published so many editorials on that issue in part because it saw a unique opportunity to criticize the government – several of its ministers, including a senior minister, had attended a function hosted by a Tamil organization. In a similar way, the *Post* used the controversy surrounding fishing rights in Atlantic Canada to criticize both the government and the Supreme Court of Canada.

*Background*

The controversy surrounding fishing rights for Atlantic Canada's First Nations people goes back to 1760. In 1990 the Supreme Court of Canada decided that Indians in the Maritimes had the right to fish for ceremonial and social purposes only – not for their economic livelihood. That decision was challenged successfully in the fall of 1999, when Supreme Court Justice Ian Binnie ruled that a treaty signed in 1760 between an Indian chief and the then governor of Nova Scotia indicated that Indians in the present day had the right to hunt and fish to order to achieve a 'moderate livelihood,' and that they did not have to conform to licensing fees and other regulations. This decision generated considerable controversy in the Atlantic fishing communities. Predictably, non-native fishermen were outraged, while the Mi'kmaq considered the ruling a victory. Binnie's decision had several important consequences. The two groups been confronting each other on the water, and outside mediators had to be brought in to help settle disputes that the new policy had created.

The *Post* covered this issue intensively; only regional papers devoted more resources and space to it.

*The Editorials: Analysis*

Its first editorial, on 11 April 2000, jeeringly titled 'Fishing for Trouble,' the *Post* made heavy use of *ridicule* and *humour* to make its point. In the second paragraph, Justice Binnie was identified as coming from 'the great fishing city of Toronto.' The suggestion, of course, was that a Justice from a non-fishing area had neither the knowledge nor the right to begin changing fishing laws. Such an *unwarranted assumption* is naturally absurd when one considers the range of issues the Supreme Court is called upon to adjudicate. It is akin to saying that a justice who is a heterosexual cannot make a decision on homosexuality!

The sentence continued: '... tried his hand at re-writing centuries of Atlantic law.' Here we encounter the linguistic strategy of *implicitness*. The phrase 'tried his hand' implied that the justice was new to the idea of changing old laws. It also implied that there is something inherently wrong with changing or 're-writing' old laws. This line of reasoning presents a rather static view of history and is inherently critical of change.

In its next paragraph, the decision was *ironically* described as 'ingenious' in that apparently the word 'fish' did not appear in it. The treaty was described as a 'document of surrender' on the part of the chiefs and their people. It was also described as a 'scrap of paper.' Here, the *Post* was hurling *ridicule* at the treaty and its contents. Yet the justice was able to rule that Indians can fish for a moderate livelihood 'no matter how depleted the fish stocks, or how many non-Indian fisherman already must leave the sea to make room for them.' Here, the real criticism of Justice Binnie was made clear: the decision was reducing the traditional rights of non-native fishermen. The *Post* did not perceive the livelihood of Mi'kmaq as an issue. Nor the fact that Atlantic fish stocks are being depleted for many reasons (e.g., the incursion of American and Japanese fishing trawlers is doing far more damage to those stocks than a few hundred native fishermen ever could). The editorial went on to discuss the many effects of Justice Binnie's decision, which included 'race riots in Burnt Church, N.B.' In this way the spectre of 'race' was introduced.

The editorial then shifted to its main objective – to criticize the Liberal government. It noted that the federal fisheries minister, Herb Dhaliwal, was dealing with the situation for the government, and described his plan as 'the increased racialization of the Atlantic Fishery. Where Judge Binnie gave the natives the right to enter the fishing business, Mr. Dhaliwal has decided to buy them a fishing business, complete with licenses, boats, nets and even docks.' It further noted that the Atlantic fishery was worth only $1.5 billion, and then pointed out, 'Mr. Dhaliwal is spending $159 million to equip Indian fishermen to compete against their predominantly white neighbours.' Again, the editorial was evoking *racialization*. The editorial criticized the granting of licences and other federal regulations in this dispute, and concluded that 'a Toronto judge and a Vancouver minister are putting Canada's fishery in greater jeopardy than any foreign fishing fleet.' By evoking their areas of origin, the *Post* was sending a *coded message* to the reader: people who are not from the area involved could not know anything about how to regulate the fisheries industry. Such editorializing, however coded, made little sense, given the practice of choosing ministers often without regard to their particular areas of expertise. The editorial ended by criticizing both the judge and the federal government – the two primary targets of this piece – 'Judge Binnie's interpretation of the Nova Scotia treaty was ... questionable,' and the minister's 'expansion ... has compounded the problem, not mitigated it.'

The *Post*'s next editorial on the issue, dated 14 August 2000, titled 'Lobster Trap,' briefly described a 'clash' between the police and Aboriginal lobster fishermen. The latter were described as 'camoflage-clad aboriginals; and as 'staring down the law? 'Camoflage-clad' was an example of *alliteration*, 'staring down,' a strong and *hyperbolic verb-adverb* combination, was intended to instil fear and apprehension in the reader. The *Post* now reminded readers that similar confrontations had occurred in the past, citing specifically the seige at Oka, Quebec, and the murder of a policeman. Although a 'maritime Oka' has not yet developed, the paper noted that 'a small scale race riot [had broken] out in Burnt Church, N.B.' The editorial continued by comparing this current situation with that of Oka and suggesting that the fishing dispute was more important because the livelihood of '25,000 East Coast fishermen and their 400 year old tradition' was being threatened. The livelihood of the Aboriginal fishermen was not considered worth noting. At this point the editorial writer was including only that information that was vital to the understanding of his point of view. When information is left out that would help *contextualize* the conflict, the reader is left thinking that only one party to the dispute is at fault. Clearly, the editorial was championing the rights of White fishermen over those of Native people. Because several Indian bands had not taken up the federal government's offers of free licences, boats, and training, they were described as having a 'militant approach' and identified as 'rogue bands' that should be treated like 'any other law-breaking gang.' The identifier 'rogue,' meaning scoundrel, knave, or outlaw, carries strong connotations of law breaking and violence. The same with 'gang.' The editorial concluded by reverting to its main themes: predicting violence, describing natives as 'militant,' and criticizing the government, which now had 'the most supine Indian Affairs Ministry' while the Assembly of First Nations had a 'militant new Grand Chief.' The 'supineness' of the government was *juxtaposed* against the 'militancy' of the Natives – a situation that would inevitably lead to further escalation and a 'showdown.'

The next editorial, 17 August 2000, 'Law Enforcers Take Sides on Miramichi Bay,' dealt with the issue of law and law breaking. It is worth noting that only alleged Native lawbreaking was discussed. Whatever violence had taken place, any that had been initiated by non-Natives was not taken into account. The editorial was concerned mainly with how Native groups were breaking the law. It began or *fronted* with the notion that this incident had elicited a 'far more powerful indictment of self government.' It noted that federal fisheries officers had been cautious about administering the law despite the 'taunting and gamesmanship' of 'native provocateurs.' Native law officers were labelled negatively, and their efforts to assume some authority were described *mockingly* as gamesmanship. These words – especially 'provocateur' (which means 'agitator' or 'rabble rouser'), were being used to impugn the integrity and validity of Native law officials.

The editorial continued by stating that the local struggle had escalated and that 'extra muscle' had been imported from Quebec. 'Muscle' carries strong connotations of violence. As if that weren't enough, the editorial then stated, 'muscle that bears the uneasy imprimatur of authority.' These Native fish and game officials from Quebec were described as 'wearing dark blue uniforms with black caps,' and their speedboats as having 'Ranger emblazoned on their sides.' The tone being established through the use of these *hyperbolic* descriptions was one of fear and apprehension. The darkness of the uniforms implied that these officials were *threatening* as well as authoritative. All of this was further reinforced by the allegation that they were 'claiming' to provide 'safety and protection' for Native fishermen who were, of course, 'fishing illegally.' The verb 'claim' raised doubts that they had really come to protect Native fishermen, and suggested that some ulterior motive – probably involving further escalation of violence – was in play.

The editorial then began reverting back to its fronted message by emphasizing that the Native officials were breaking the law and by their actions '[throwing] into question the loyalty of all Native police forces and fish and game officials in the country. Do they regard it as their duty to uphold the law, or are they simply enforcers for the Native community in whatever endeavour it chooses?' Again, the use of the strongly *hyperbolic* term 'enforcers' implied a highly derogatory understanding of the role of Native officials. The piece ended by stating firmly that there could only be one set of laws, which had to be enforced by a 'clear and consistent chain of command. Native self-government cannot be allowed to set peace officers against each other.' All told, this editorial painted an extremely negative picture of Native self-government and its officials. Its aim was to convince the reader that the incidents surrounding the fishing controversy had escalated into violence solely as a result of the actions by Natives and their 'peace' officers. This point was sharply reinforced by the total absence of any concerns about non-Native law breaking or the role of non-Native officials. The editorial was presenting a *biased* and *one-sided* perspective on the issue of law and its violation in this controversy.

Ten days later, on 24 August 2000, the *Post* published another editorial, 'Bait and Switch.' It discussed a plan to hold discussions with Native groups and Maritime governments, as well as 'what are politely called First Nations rights.' This description *ridiculed* the Native groups. But it also went beyond ridicule by deliberately promoting *vagueness* and *ambiguity*, in that it did not make clear to the reader whether the writer was joking. Were the rights of First Nations people being mocked? If they were, the *Post* was pointedly suggesting that they have no rights.

In paragraph three, Native leaders were referred to with the term 'leader' in quote marks. In effect, the reader was being told that these people were not really 'leaders.' Moreover, the use of quote marks cast doubt on whether Native people really have 'leaders.' Continuing on the theme of violence, the writer referred in *inflammatory* language to 'violent aboriginals' who were still doing illegal fishing in Atlantic waters. Nevertheless, Native spokespeople, now referred to as 'negotiators' rather than 'leaders,' were still willing to hold discussions with federal officials. By choosing the term 'negotiators' the writer seemed to be admitting that his own, earlier *hyperbole* had gone to extremes.

But in the next sentence, the editorialist *trivialized* the events by writing, 'But wait a minute.' If the negotiators could not control the 'rebellious aboriginal fishermen' (again a *negative* and *violence*-prone description) 'what is the point in talking to them? They have nothing to offer.' In a strong *denigration* of the Native negotiating team, the editorial added that they could only come to the negotiating table if 'they are in a position only to pocket government concessions, not to guarantee the Native bands will stick to their side of the quid pro quo.' It was strongly implied – but not, of course, clearly stated – that Native peoples and their negotiators were there only to 'pocket' more concessions, and that they weren't there to deal with the situation in good faith.

The editorial concluded by alluding to the 'bad faith, or worse leadership, of the native bands.' Here again, both the intentions and the competence of Native leaders were being questioned. The real point at issue, however, according to this editorial, was that any Native who dropped a trap without a proper licence was breaking the law and should be arrested like any other citizen. It concluded with a clever use of the strategy of *reversal* by noting: 'Appeasement of lawbreaking Native fishermen is fundamentally racist, for the premise beneath it is that minority aboriginals cannot really be expected to behave properly like the rest of us.' Here, the editorial was claiming to be a champion of Native equality. This, even though this editorial and others like it had done everything possible to denigrate and ridicule Native people and question their enshrined rights. By using the descriptor 'racist,' it was attempting to disassociate itself from those who were making 'us and them' distinctions. Yet throughout this editorial and others on the subject, the *Post* had consistently reinforced precisely that dichotomy.

An editorial on 14 September, 'Wrong Man, Wrong Job,' was an attack on Bob Rae, the former premier of Ontario, whom Dhaliwal had appointed to mediate the dispute. The editorial opined that this was an 'odd' choice, unless one believed that a mediator who had himself disregarded the law for the 'benefit of natives' was the best person for this job. It recalled that Mr Rae had been arrested in 1989 for participating in an 'illegal blockade to protest native rights in Northern Ontario.' Thus, the mediator's record was suspect. Also, Rae was accused of having 'a weighty track record of favouring the most extreme expansions of native "rights" and a history of elevating Native rights above those of other Canadians.' Note that the *Post* again placed the term Native 'rights' in quotation marks. This had the effect of challenging and questioning those rights. The *Post*'s position seems to be that Natives do not have any 'rights.' The *Post* recalled that during Rae's time in office, Ontario became the first province to acknowledge the Native right to self-government, and concluded, 'This is not an impartial broker.'

The last paragraph of this editorial stated, '[Rae's] unsuitability is not the main point.' Too late – several hundred words had already argued that it was the main point. The element now being described as secondary had already been embedded in the reader's consciousness as primary; both Rae and the federal government's choice of him as mediator had already been thoroughly criticized. The *Post* now tried to argue as its main point that there was no reason to negotiate with Native fishermen because dropping a trap without a licence was against the law: 'To negotiate with lawbreakers is foolhardy; to appoint Mr. Rae to do the negotiating is frivolous.' *Exaggerated* and *hyperbolic* language was being used in this last sentence. The adjective 'frivolous' is inherently *ambigu-*

*ous* and *unclear.* Were we to believe that Rae was frivolous – that is, 'fool-hardy' – or was the entire process 'foolhardy'? Thus, the editorial concluded on an unclear but basically derogatory note. The reader was being told once again that the federal government was wrong and that Native fishermen were lawbreakers who did not deserve any attention.

The anti-government editorial stance taken in this controversy by the *Post* was further reinforced by two guest columns. The first (26 September), titled 'The Next City,' was by Lawrence Solomon of the Urban Renaissance Institute. In it, Solomon wrote in favour of the Native fisherman and spent considerable column space describing the violent actins of non-Native fishermen, who had destroyed '$250,000 worth of native property' after Justice Binnie's initial decision. Earlier editorials in the *Post* had omitted the facts about non-Native aggression from their discourse. Solomon concluded, 'Burnt Church natives, far from acting illegally, were only exercising their legitimate property rights.' However, the thrust of this guest piece was that the federal government has been ill advised in its fishing policies; specifically, it had been the regulating lobster fishery only on a seasonal basis and thereby creating 'closed' seasons. He blamed these policies on the government's desire to court the votes of Atlantic Canadians who were not fishermen: 'The white fishermen's refusal to accept the law of the land and the government's fear that it could lose the Maritimes – and its majority government – if it alienates the white vote, explains the fishery department's sudden concern for conservation.'

The publication of this guest feature served two particular functions. It demonstrated that the *Post* was prepared to publish articles supporting Native fishing rights; also, that it was willing to publish guest columns supporting its partisan attacks on the Liberal government.

The next guest article, published on 30 September, was by William Hipwell and was titled 'Ottawa's War Against the Mi'kmaq.' Hipwell was generally supportive of Native rights, but sharply critical of Liberal policy. His language was stronger and given more to *hyperbole*: 'firing the first shot ... inflame the anger that has been smouldering ... triggering violence ...' and so on. Apparently, he was afraid that the conflict could 'culminate ... in a protracted and bloody civil war.' However, he focused his argument on the government's change in policy: it had now declared Native fishing illegal despite the Supreme Court's decision to the contrary. Hipwell accused the government of 'arrogance' in contravening its own Constitution and in defying the Supreme Court, and concluded, 'All citizens have reason to be afraid.' He too noted that a federal election was imminent and that 'Liberals are gambling that the violent suppression of Mi'kmaq rights will go unopposed by the public.' He concluded that a peaceful resolution to the conflict had to be found.

Again, it seems that Hipwell's column was published because it was anti-Liberal, notwithstanding its support for the Native fishing industry. These two articles concluded the *Post*'s discussion of the Burnt Church controversy. It seems that the final message was that government policy must be attacked by any methods available.

**Conclusions**

Our discourse analysis of the editorials in *The National Post* dealing with the Burnt Church indicates that the editors racialized the issue, and constructed a number of dominant discourses that had strong similarities to those we delineated in earlier case studies. The *Post* strongly denied any form of bias. But at the same time, it portrayed First Nations communities as problem people who posed a threat to law and order. Misinformation and misrepresentation characterized the *Post*'s central narratives, as well as its interpretations of the events at Burnt Church.[2]

It is also important to emphasize that much of the racialized discourse that appeared in the *Post* was clearly linked to the neoconservative ideology of its former publisher, Conrad Black, and the political agenda of his newspaper. Our three case studies based on *Post* news coverage and editorials, taken together, made it clear that the *Post* sees First Nations peoples, the Tamils, and other immigrants of colour as existing outside the symbolic boundaries of the imagined community of Canada, and thus as posing a significant threat to 'our' way of life.

# Conclusion

In this book we have explored in a number of ways the nature and extent of racialized discourse in the media. We have incorporated the following approaches: a review and analysis of Canadian research over the past two decades on racism in the media; a review of the body of literature emerging from other countries, drawing on the work of scholars in the United States, Britain, Australia, and the Netherlands; and empirical study of the perceptions and experiences of minorities working in the media. Finally, we have employed critical discourse analysis to explore several discursive events and crises that received wide coverage in Canadian newspapers. In this final chapter we discuss a number of the central themes that have emerged from our study. Our analysis of the dominant racialized discourses that often appear in a number of newspapers in this country is consistent with Stuart Hall's view (1979) that dominant discursive formation is not a single, monolithic process; rather, it includes a plurality of texts, narratives, and everyday conversations among the media and other members of the cultural, social, and political elite. The core ideas emanating from the dominant mainstream culture – ideas that are reproduced in newspaper columns, editorials, and features – constitute a 'field of meanings' (Hall, 1997) through which situations and events are constructed, interpreted, and communicated to the reader. In this study we have attempted to uncover the racial filters the media use when selecting particular 'facts' and 'events' and transforming them into today's 'truths' – today's 'news.' As is evidenced in every case study (and documented in much of the research cited throughout this book), this process is largely unconscious. It seems that racialized discourse works silently within the cognitive make-up of individual journalists and editors, and within the collective culture and professional norms and values of media organizations. Journalists and editors often deny strongly that racism exists in newsrooms, and sometimes refuse to validate the voices and views of those they have represented as 'others.' As a result, the discursive and institutionally structured forms of bias and discrimination remain unacknowledged and invisible. Media representations are discursive formations. Furthermore, they are so much a part of the everyday normative culture – including the material fabric of media institutions – that racist ideologies and rhetorical practices seem natural to those immersed in this environment.

A number of the case studies offered powerful examples of this process. The White media's strong defence of Avery Haines, and Haines's own comments following the event, demonstrated a lack of reflexivity. Haines seemed unwilling to acknowledge the harm her words caused to those whose identities she had so glibly denigrated. The remarkable solidarity expressed by almost all her colleagues was an excellent example of the group-think and group-speak that often operate within and across many media organizations. Similarly, the many editorials against employment equity in *The Globe and Mail,* the campaign against immigrants and refugees in *The National Post* and other papers, and the racialization of crime in many of the newspapers we examined, show clearly that the press often cannot imagine non-dominant peoples as part of the 'imagined community' of Canada.

The notion of an 'imagined community' (Anderson, 1983) is a useful concept in the context of our research, because it underscores how the Canadian media so often construct a discursive sketch of Canadian society that silences, erases, and marginalizes a significant proportion of this country's population. We see this process at work in media discourses on immigrants and refugees, and on state policies that are intended to foster greater access and participation, such as employment equity and immigration. We witness the practice of denigration in the media's discourses of crime, cultural differences, deviance, and national identity. The media select, interpret, and communicate subjects through a series of filters that reflect the social identities and social experiences of those who produce media discourse. In everyday media discourse there are very few preferred 'ethnic' topics (van Dijk, 1991). Yet many subjects are available to journalists in their coverage of the dominant culture.

The repeated use by the press of the rhetorical strategies of invective, censure, and deprecation against immigrants and ethnoracial communities suggests a pervasive and systemic bias. This bias was obvious in each of the case studies: Tamil Canadians were represented as terrorists and gang members; the Black community was represented as culturally deficient and crime ridden; the Chinese migrants were categorized as invading hordes; and First Nations communities and cultures were stigmatized. Furthermore, anti-immigrant narratives were strongly reflected in headlines and press coverage. On every occasion the press created the perception that a moral, social, and in some instances political crisis was at hand. Both readers and journalists, editors, and publishers should be asking themselves this question: Would this particular event, condition, or issue have been seen as contentious, threatening, or dangerous, without first having been constructed as such in public discourse, and especially in media discourse?

Many scholars (Fiske, 1994; van Dijk, 1998; Hall, 1997) have noted that the discourses and misrepresentations that permeate much of the press are not haphazard and isolated, but rather part of a deep and complex ideological process. In a racially divided society, the assumptions and beliefs that underpin the dominant discourses of much of the media and other members of the power elite serve an important function: they explain, rationalize, and resolve insupportable contradictions and tensions in society. For example, employment equity profoundly upsets the understood balance of relationships in society at the psychological, social, and economic levels. It threatens the infrastructure of White organizational space, as well as the sense of entitlement of those who have unrestricted access to employment and who have benefited from systemic discrimination. In the same way, by stereotyping people of colour and First Nations communities, the dominant culture is able to preserve the myth that Canada is a White settler, Anglo-European culture.

In this book we have identified some of these take-for-granted beliefs. In this final chapter we revisit and highlight some of the most common, overlapping dominant discourses as they are reflected in the print media. It is important to remember that these discourses resonate with very dissimilar meanings and consequences for both the producers of the text and the diverse communities of readers. However, based on the findings of these case studies, it seems that some of the print media largely see their readers as sharing a single, monolithic belief and value system – an ideology that, presumably, they share with the White world of journalism.

In our introduction and in the theory chapters we introduced the concept of democratic racism and described it as a formulation that

helps explain new forms of racism (distinguished from the more traditional construct of biological racism). We argued that democratic racism arises when 'democratic' societies retain a legacy of racist beliefs
and behaviours. Democratic racism is an ideology in which two conflicting sets of values are made congruent with each other. Democratic principles such as equality, fairness, and justice conflict with, but also but
coexist with, racist attitudes and behaviours – including negative feelings about minority groups and differential treatment of them (see
Henry et al., 2000). One of the consequences of democratic racism is a
lack of support for policies and practices that might improve the status
of people of colour. Any organized public intervention – except perhaps
as a response to overt expressions of racial hatred and/or violence – is
deemed to be in conflict with the values of liberal democracy. Efforts to
limit the spread of democratic racism, and any attempts to change society's fundamental power relations, lack legitimacy and support within
the dominant culture.

Democratic racism (see Tator et al., 1998) is most evident in the
everyday discourse we encounter within our cultural, social, economic,
and political institutions. In its discursive form, it[1] draws on the language of liberal values and principles, among other ideologies (see
Wetherell and Potter, 1992). It is an elusive concept because the rhetoric of dominant discourses is hidden within the mythical norms that
define Canada as a White, humanistic, tolerant, and accommodating
society. However, as all of the case studies have shown, beneath the reassuring notions of liberal arguments and justificatory lines of reasoning
remain deeply problematic ideas about minority populations. Though
the discourses of democratic racism are found in all Canadian institutions, it is through the press (and other forms of mass communication)
that everyday discursive racism has its most significant impact.

**The Discourses of Democratic Racism**

The following are some of the dominant discourses that structured the
press coverage of each of the discursive events analyzed in this book. In
earlier works (see Henry et al., 2000) we identified these discourses as
the discourses of democratic racism.

*The Discourse of Denial*

Within this discourse, the principle assumption is that racism simply does not exist in a democratic society. In each of the case studies, a persistent and pervasive rhetorical theme was the media's refusal to accept the reality of racism, despite the overwhelming evidence that racial prejudice and discrimination were damaging the lives and life chances of people of colour. The assumption is that because Canadian society upholds the ideals of a liberal democracy, it cannot possibly be racist. The media deny their own racism so habitually that even to allege that they are biased and to raise the possibility that their biases influence social outcomes is a serious social infraction – one that brings down the wrath and ridicule of many journalists and editors.

*The Discourse of Political Correctness*

Among many of the mainstream media this discourse has become a central rhetorical strategy. It functions as an expression of resistance to social change. The demands of marginalized minorities for inclusive language and proactive policies and practices (e.g., employment equity, non-biased cultural representation) are discredited as an 'overdose of political correctness.' Those who are opposed to proactive measures to ensure the inclusion of non-dominant voices, stories, and perspectives dismiss these concerns as the wailings and whinings of radicals whose polemics – and actions – are a threat to the basic principles of democratic liberalism. For example, journalists, editors, and columnists often used the term 'political correctness' in the case studies on employment equity and Avery Haines.

*The Discourse of Colour Evasion or Colour Blindness*

Colour blindness or colour evasion is a powerful and appealing liberal discourse that involves White journalists contending that skin colour is irrelevant to their journalist practices. In the case studies, journalists and editors repeatedly claimed that it was racial minorities, not the media, who were obsessed with racial identity. In the commentaries by Diane Francis and the journalists and editors writing about Just Desserts, the Vo killing, the Tamil community, the Chinese migrants, the Mi'kmaq, and First Nations people living on reserves, the code term 'race' was concealed within the narratives on immigration, crime, fishing rights, and land claims. Some of the news media made strong efforts to justify the pervasive use of demonizing and denigrating language. At the same time, many editors and columnists remained fixed in their own White mediacentric gaze. These journalists and editors seemed to share a common sense of White entitlement – an entitlement reinforced by their experiential frameworks. This enabled them to engage in colour evasion. We found little evidence that the media recognize their awesome power to construct people of colour as deviant populations.

### The Discourse of Equal Opportunity

The discourse of equal opportunity was most clearly articulated in the debate around employment equity in the second case study. However, it clearly reflects the collective mindset that underpins many of the discourses we have identified in this book. *The Globe and Mail*'s editors argued repeatedly that to ensure fairness to everyone, all we need to do is treat all individuals the same. This notion is based on an ahistorical premise – that we all begin from the same starting point, and that every group competes on a level playing field. From this cherished myth, it follows that society's only obligation is to provide the conditions within which individuals differentially endowed can make their mark. All have the same rights and an equal opportunity to succeed. Individual merit determines who will have access to jobs and promotions, to the media, to educational advancement, and so on.

The *Globe*'s unconditional support for equal opportunity and opposition to employment equity reflects an ideology that rejects the need to dismantle White institutional spaces and power. The argument against employment equity is based on the premise that there is no need for White social capital to be redistributed.

### The Discourse of Blame the Victim, or White Victimization

If equal opportunity and racial equality exist, then when a minority population fails to thrive in Canada it must be for reasons other than a lack of such equality. Some of the media have suggested as a reason that certain minority communities are culturally deficient. This explanation was most clearly articulated in the case study on the racialization of crime. In this form of dominant discourse it is assumed that certain groups (e.g., African Canadians, immigrants of colour) are more prone than others to deviant behaviour – that they lack the motivation, education, or skills to participate fully in the workplace, the educational system, and other arenas of Canadian society.

Alternatively, it is argued that certain groups fail to integrate themselves into the mainstream dominant culture mainly because recalcitrant members of these groups refuse to adapt their 'traditional,' 'different' cultural values and norms to those of Canadian society, and make unreasonable demands on the 'host' society. The media lashed out against minorities who raised concerns about Avery Haines's 'light-hearted' joke about Blacks, lesbians, and people with 'gimpy legs.' When people of colour demand media representations that do not demean their experiences, histories, and sense of identity, they are viewed as 'irresponsible,' 'undemocratic,' 'a threat to our core values.' The media repeatedly describe minorities as 'special interests groups.' According to many media accounts, the real victim of the Haines controversy was Haines herself, and not those who had been hurt by her words.

In the case study of the Aboriginal woman sexually assaulted by Jack Ramsay, the *Globe*'s discourse focused largely on Ramsay, who was portrayed as a man of strong principles, a champion of Native rights, a family man. At the same time, the *Globe* racialized Native culture and community life and raised to prominence all the familiar stereotypes. It was suggested that the bleak social and physical environment in which the assault took place was a contributing cause for Ramsay's behaviour.

Throughout the media discourses we analysed – and especially in the discourse of employment equity – White victimization was expressed in terms of 'reverse racism,' 'reverse discrimination,' 'the abandonment of the merit principle,' 'quotas,' and 'preferential treatment.' Those associated with the dominant culture are now contending that they are the victims of a new form of oppression and exclusion. Antiracism and equity policies are seen as undemocratic and are discredited in strong, emotive language. As a consequence, positive and proactive policies and programs are aligned with a creeping totalitarianism that incorporates the antidemocratic, authoritarian methods of the extreme right.

*The Discourse of 'Otherness'*

This discourse was pervasive in each of the case studies. The ubiquitous *we* represents the White dominant culture or the culture of the organization (i.e., the newspaper, or the radio station, or in other contexts the courts, the police, the schools, the museums); *they* refers to the communities that are the *other*, and that possess 'different' (i.e., undesirable) values, beliefs, and norms. In the Ramsay case study, the First Nations community and members of the victim's family were described in extremely negative stereotypes – as drunks and drug users, as violent and mean.

The *Post*'s reporting on the dangers posed by the Tamil community, and its coverage of the arrival of the Chinese migrants, and its editorials about Mi'kmaq fishing rights, were charged with racial stereotypes and images. The discourse was often framed in terms of a clash between majority and minority values and norms – in effect, in terms of cultural superiority or inferiority. *We* meant those who belonged to the 'imagined community' of (White) Canadians: 'We are the real Canadians' ... 'birthright Canadians' (Cyril Dabydeen 'Citizenship Is More Than a Birthright,' *Toronto Star*, 20 September 1994, A23). '*They*,' that is, the '*Other*' (including First Nations peoples, Tamils, Asians, Blacks, immigrants, and refugees of colour), were viewed as outside the boundaries of the symbolic Canadian community. As Hall (1996b) points out: 'A nation is a symbolic community ... a national culture is a discourse – a way of constructing meanings, which influence and organize both our actions and our conceptions of ourselves' (612–13). Thus, the discourse of 'otherness' becomes bound to the discourse of national identity.

*The Discourse of National Identity*

The debate over national identity is fundamental to Canadian print media discourse. In each of our case studies this debate manifested itself in the narratives, core ideas, and codes of meaning that journalists and editors constructed. However, the discourse of Canada's national identity as shaped by some of the press is marked by erasures, omissions, and silences. Our review of the literature and the case studies has demonstrated that the print media often place ethnoracial minorities outside the national vision of Canada, and exclude them from the mainstream of Canadian society.

Our case studies, and our review of the studies of the Canadian national press by other scholars, show how often the voices, views, beliefs, and experiences of African Canadians, Muslim Canadians, East Asian Canadians, South Asian Canadians, and other ethnoracial communities are ignored, deflected, or dismissed. Too often omitted are the historical background and the social, economic, and political contexts that would help explain how and why these events occur. Our analysis of the Ramsay case illustrated powerfully how the voices, feelings, and experiences of First Nations women are of little interest to the media. This particular Native woman's experience of sexual assault was reported on as a single, isolated event, only worthy of attention because it involved a widely respected individual with a high public profile. In the same way, the *Post*'s coverage of Burnt Church highlighted the lawlessness of the First Nations fishers and made little mention of over-fishing and illegal poaching by non-Aboriginal fishers. Only when a situation or event creates an opportunity for the media to construct a discursive crisis do minorities become a focus of attention.

*The Discourse of Moral Panic*

The concept of 'moral panic' (Cohen, 1972) or discursive crisis (van Dijk, 1998; Fiske, 1994) suggests that often, a particular event is not seen as contentious until it has been constructed as such in public discourse.

In two of the case studies, Just Desserts and the Chinese migrants, the media obviously set out to employ a discourse of moral panic. In the former, an isolated case of violence was cast as a profound societal crisis that imperilled the nation. The papers were in effect declaring, '*We* are not who we used to be.' The city and country were portrayed as under siege by 'Blacks,' 'Jamaicans,' 'illegal immigrants,' who were an imminent threat to White 'civilized,' law-abiding citizens. The press coverage amounted to a signal, a wake-up call to all Canadians (especially politicians) to re-evaluate their ideas about authority, control, policy, and of course race.

The media fomented a similar national crisis around the arrival of 600 Chinese boat people between July and September 1999. Drawing on discourses that have historically been part of Canada's national mythology and nation building, some of the media constructed a discursive crisis that centred on the 'flawed' Canadian immigration and refugee systems. Many newspapers tapped a rich reservoir of core ideas and images, which included often fabricated notions of racialized illegality, objectified identities, amplified migration patterns, health risk, and criminality; in doing so they mobilized politicians, government representatives, and various sectors of the population at large into a frenzy of protest.

In a similar way Diane Francis's coverage of immigration and the *Post*'s over two dozen articles on the threat posed by the Tamil community became part of the moral panic discourse.

Less dramatically, the case studies of employment equity and Avery Haines showed how the media can generate a moral and social crisis. Regarding the former, a policy designed to ensure fairness in the workplace was made out to be a threat of monumental proportions against White, able-bodied males. Regarding both, it can well be argued that the particular event might not have taken on the proportions it did if it hadn't been inflated into a vital issue by the press (Fiske, 1994).

*The Discourse of Tolerance*

Underpinning much of the content in the Canadian print media is the notion that Canadian society is a model of tolerance and accommodation. The emphasis on these values suggests that though one must accept the idiosyncrasies of the *others*, the dominant culture is superior. There is only minimal recognition of difference. The guardians of the dominant culture and social order – which include the media – have created a ceiling of tolerance and stipulated which differences are tolerable (Mirchandani and Tastsoglou, 2000). This ceiling on forbearance and acceptance is woven into media discourse and reflected in the perception that *we* cannot tolerate too much difference because it generates dissent, disruption, and conflict. Many of the editorials and columns included in our analysis of the media articulated the view that paying unnecessary attention to differences leads to division, disharmony, and disorder in society. For example, in the case studies dealing with immigration, minorities were often represented as flagrantly abusing Canada's outstanding record of tolerance.

### The Media's Reproduction of Dominant Cultural Values and Norms

Based on the above discussion, we contend that one of the central problems facing the profession of journalism is a lack of critical self- awareness or reflexivity on the part of many journalists, editors, and publishers. The professional values and norms of newsrooms, and the social, economic, and political forces operating within and outside newsrooms influence how news is produced. Our research findings, our review of the literature, and our own experiences in the media, suggest that the socialization of media professionals in schools of journalism and the corporate culture of media organizations contribute strongly to processes of news making that work without reflection and introspection.[2] The voices and texts of the journalists and editors throughout this book resonate with arrogance, ethnocentrism, and often unrestrained resentment toward minorities; yet these same journalists assert that they are guided by the values of objectivity, professional detachment, and neutrality.

As we have demonstrated through textual analysis, journalists and editors are often not 'objective,' 'detached,' or 'neutral.' They are highly selective when it comes to identifying subjects to cover, and choosing categories and concepts to apply, and in their rhetorical styles forms of argumentation. A journalist's own social location, world view, experiences, and values, and those of his or her editor, publisher, and newspaper owner, filter out alternative perspectives. Also, the interests of other power elites, such as politicians, advertisers, corporate power brokers, and the police, influence how the news is constructed and produced. In the case studies we saw over and over again the strong and pervasive links between the media and the political, economic, and cultural elites, and how those links influenced the ways in which issues and events were examined in the press. In this analysis we provide further support for van Dijk's contention (1993) that the argumentation used in editorials is addressed not only to the unidentified reader, but also more specifically to elites, especially politicians.

In turn, these ideologies and discourses affect the development of public policies. The relationship between the media and the elite is well established in the literature (see van Dijk, 1991, 1998; Fleras and Elliot, 1996; James Winter, 1997; Domke, 2000). There is significant evidence that most news media are owned by corporate interests and are structured to sustain the economic interests of business and government elites. The media's values are inextricably linked to those of the social, political, and economic elite; furthermore, it is in their interest to help produce and generate consensus. We concur with Fleras and Elliot (1996) and van Dijk (1991) that the media have the power to establish the boundaries of public discourse; and that within these boundaries priorities are set and public agendas are established and perpetuated.

### Challenging and Contesting Dominant Discourses: The Discursive Nature of Social Change

The stereotypical images constructed by editors and journalists have enormous strength and resilience. When minorities have relatively little power to control or resist those images, or to produce and disseminate more positive images, these misrepresentations seriously weaken their capacity to participate in mainstream Canadian society, be it culturally, economically, or politically.

Thus, public discourse is a terrain of struggle. Dominant codes and representations are difficult to overturn or subvert. Simply adding more positive images to the largely negative repertoire of dominant cultural representations does not necessarily soften the negative impact of the latter. The binary opposition of *them* and *us* often remains in place. We argue, as does Hall (1997), that offering positive images of sports or entertainment figures does not really challenge the consequences of generations of deleterious stereotypes of Blacks in the mass culture. The occasional positive story about a minority community, or a review on the book pages of a novel by a writer of colour, does little to offset the everyday negative images and opinions that find their way into news stories, editorials and columns as part of the media's discursive practices. The media's everyday, commonsense discourses are crucial in the complex process of attitudinal formation and, more specifically, in the formation and confirmation of racialized belief systems.

One of the more significant barriers to dismantling racialized ideologies and discourses in the media and among the cultural, social, and political elites in other social domains is that the dominant culture has often co-opted the discourses of liberalism, diversity, and equality, while maintaining and preserving hegemonic practices. Dominant discourses provide a rich pool of familiar myths and cherished national narratives that circulate in the public domain through different forms of cultural production (e.g., school curricula, literature, films, advertising, television news and programming). Generally speaking, the mass media reaffirm dominant ideologies, and thereby contribute to how events or situations involving people of colour or minority communities are interpreted or understood. Van Dijk (1991) contends that once the press endorses an ideology that legitimates White group dominance (which is demonstrated in all of our case studies), then any actions taken to challenge this ideological framework are likely to result in a backlash against minorities. The discourses we identified earlier are part of this backlash.

Many scholars contend that as a result of the paradigm shifts that took place in the last decades of the twentieth century, public discourse today is more powerful and influential than ever before (van Dijik, 1998; Winter, 1997; Hackett and Zhao, 1998). And so, it follows, are those who own, control, or have access to the vehicles of discourse. At the same time, minorities are demanding their right to name and replace the discourses and representations that render harm to them and that threaten the possibility of achieving a truly democratic liberal society.

Alternative, resistant discourses can seriously challenge the hegemonic order and disrupt the status quo. The real power of those who have been labelled *others* lies in their capacity to subvert the 'factual' statements of the media. In this regard, further research must be done in Canada with the goal of deconstructing the dominant discourses and ideologies of the social, cultural, and political elites. The everyday discursive practices used by the media and other systems of cultural production and reproduction that help support and reinforce racial inequality in Canadian society must be documented and decoded.

Our research has focused largely on how dominant discourses marginalize and oppress. However, in earlier writings we have shown how minorities are resisting these discourses (Tator et al., 1998). Social change is dialectical and discursive in nature. Diverse ethnoracial communities and networks of individuals are crossing cultural, racial, and other social boundaries in a search for common ground from which to resist the oppressive practices of mainstream cultural producers. They are challenging the dominant discourses employed by White cultural 'authorities.' We see this to some degree in all forms of cultural production: counterdiscourses are slowly being constructed and disseminated. In particular, writers of colour and First Nations writers are being recognized more and more.

In this book we have drawn many examples of oppositional discourse from the words and work of a number of journalists of colour. These individuals have dared to communicate openly and frankly about their experience in the media and have the values and norms of medial culture. This reflects their strong commitment to diversity and equity in the media. These non-dominant voices are struggling to help their colleagues and their readers (from the dominant culture) move past the lure and comfort of the familiar narratives, the reassuring myths, the comforting racialized images and ideas that have done so much to shape everyday dominant discourse.

But it is not just journalists such as Cecil Foster, Haroon Siddiqui, and Irshad Manji who understand the importance of providing oppositional discourses. Communities are also playing a role in discursive resistance. Some good examples: The Tamil community has launched a libel suit against *The National Post.* The Canadian Islamic Congress for the past three years has monitored and analysed newspapers across the country for bias in their coverage of Islam and Muslims. They have put out an annual report card and have met with publishers and editors on a regular basis to press for changes in how the media represent their community and Muslims generally. The Canadian Association of Black Journalists, currently chaired by Hamlin Grange, has done much the same thing for Canada's Black community. First Nations publications are offering important alternatives to the dominant discourse of the mainstream media.

These forms of resistance to marginalization and misrepresentation lead to another point – the ethnic press has a critical role to play in critiquing the positions and perspectives of the mainstream press. Alternative voices are needed that can identify where and how the mainstream media have misrepresented issues and events. The ethnic media are often well positioned to provide the missing social, cultural, historical, and political contexts necessary for understanding complex social realities that White Anglo journalists and editors are unlikely to understand. In this book we have not discussed the ethnic press in any depth. But it seems clear from our study these presses will have an important role to play as marginalized communities struggle to express their alternative perspectives – a struggle that is so necessary for the health of liberal democracies.

We agree with Fiske (1994), Fairlough and Wodak (1997), van Dijk (1991; 1998), and Hall (1997), among others, that social change is dialectical and discursive in nature. According to this view, if social change is ever to be brought about, the everyday discursive practices of systems of representations such as the media must be altered. Critical discourse analysis offers means of understanding how the 'commonsense' of language practices becomes important in sustaining and reproducing power relations (Fairclough, 1992: 3). This is why we selected CDA as our tool for demystifying the mainstream media and for decoding their prevailing ideological messages. CDA can be highly effective in helping illuminate how social power, dominance, and inequality are produced, reproduced, and disseminated by language used as social practice. CDA is premised on the assumption that readers form their attitudes largely through implied propositions, not simply through explicit information (Riggins, 1997).

By drawing on the tools and techniques of CDA, we hope we have demonstrated how the discourse of racism operates in the media and how the media advance the interests of those who have power and privilege in this society. We have tried to point out for the reader some of the words, images, and practices through which inequalities are reinforced, and some of the ways that racial power is applied. As Fiske reminds us: 'Discourse does not represent the world; it acts in and upon the world' (1994: 5). Or as Hackett and Gruneau (2000) comment: 'News is a representation of the world, not a passive reflection of some pre-given reality' (2000: 27). In this work we have provided many examples of how the media did not simply report on an event but actually constructed the event and manufactured the crisis.

**A Final Thought**

This study offers compelling evidence that racism continues to flourish in some of the Canadian print media. Newspapers such as the *Toronto Star*[3] have made significant efforts to be more inclusive in both their coverage and hiring practices; that being said, full access, participation, and equity in the print media continues to elude ethnic minorities in Canada. The interviews with journalists of colour make clear the need for non-biased forms of representation and for policies that promote diversity and equity in media workplaces. Until they enjoy greater access to employment opportunities, people of colour will continue to have almost no influence on how they are represented in the White media. Our interviews, combined with the evidence contained in the case studies and earlier research, make it clear just how much racism influences both the practices and the work environment of journalism.

It is unlikely that media organizations will transform themselves overnight to reflect the culturally pluralistic and racially diverse society that is Canada today. Give that, journalists, editors, and publishers need to practise greater reflexivity. What is missing from the toolkit of many of today's media practitioners – and what schools of journalism should be providing as part of their core curricula – is a greater degree of critical self-awareness. Journalists and editors need to understand how their own social identities, histories, and frames of reference affect their work; and how whiteness acts as a filter, screening out the contradictions and complexities of issues related to race and racism, culture and ethnicity, and other social phenomena. Though operating on the cusp of social change, most of the Canadian print media seem to be sealed into a system of beliefs and values, norms and conventions of the past. As we have shown in this book, this often leads the media to engage in the discourses of colonization and White supremacy, even while they assert their allegiance to liberal values and principles.

This lack of reflexivity leads much of the press to trivialize, minimize, deflect, and dismiss the perspectives and voices of marginalized groups. It also allows journalists and editors to believe, and argue, that their word choices have no measurable consequences. But as the case studies make clear, the language and rhetorical structures and styles of their discourse are often more nuanced than they are straightforward, and more biased than they are neutral. Many journalists regularly engage in discourses that disadvantage and disempower people of colour and other marginalized groups in Canadian society.

John Miller (1998), a journalist and now professor at Ryerson's School of Journalism, observes: 'Newspapers behave as if they are serving themselves, not us ... their motives and agendas ... are hidden from us, when they arrogantly refuse to explain their behaviour or listen to the other side.' Moreover, Miller contends that the media elite have not demonstrated much concern that minorities are habitually constructed as social problems and outsiders who are undermining our way of life.

This study reveals a profound tension in Canadian society: a conflict between the belief that the media are the cornerstone of a democratic liberal society and the key instrument by which its ideals are produced and disseminated, and the actual role of the media as purveyors of racialized discourse, supporters of a powerful White political, economic, and cultural elite, and a vehicle for reinforcing racism Canadian society. A truly democratic liberal society requires a less biased and more inclusive, responsible, and accountable media.

# Glossary

**Aboriginal peoples**   In Canada, status Indians, non–status Indians, Inuit, and Métis.

**acculturation**   A process of adaptation and change whereby a person or an ethnic, social, religious, language, or national group integrates with or adapts to the cultural values and patterns of the majority group.

**affirmative action**   A set of explicit actions or programs designed to eliminate systemic forms of discrimination by increasing the opportunities of individuals and groups who have historically been excluded from full participation in and access to such areas as employment and education.

**anti-racism organizational change**   A process of identifying and eradicating organizational values, policies, procedures, and behaviours that exclude people of colour from full participation as employees, customers, or clients.

**assimilation**   A process by which an individual or group completely adopts – or is absorbed by – the culture, values, and patterns of another social, religious, linguistic, or national group.

**attitude**   A consistent pattern of thought, belief, or emotion toward a fact, concept, situation, or group of people.

**bias**   An opinion, preference, prejudice, or inclination formed without reasonable justification, that then influences an individual's or group's ability to evaluate a particular situation objectively or accurately; an unfounded preference for or against.

**censorship**   The suppression of information and ideas – such as literature, the performing arts, criminal court cases, and ideologies – that are considered unacceptable or dangerous for political, moral, or religious reasons.

**colonialism**   A process by which a foreign power dominates and exploits an indigenous group by appropriating its land and extracting the wealth from it while using the group as cheap labour. Also refers to a specific era of European expansion into overseas territories between the sixteenth and twentieth centuries, during which European states implanted settlements in distant territories, ultimately reaching a position of economic, military, political, and cultural hegemony in much of Asia, Africa, and the Americas.

**commodification**   The process of turning a thing into a commodity or service that can be bought or sold in the marketplace.

**critical discourse analysis (CDA)**   A multidisciplinary study of language use and communication in the context of cultural production. As a type of research it mainly studies how social power, dominance, and inequality are produced, reproduced, and resisted by text and talk in social and political arenas. CDA provides a tool to deconstruct the ideologies and dominant discourses of the mass media and other elite groups. It treats language as a type of social practice used for representation and signification.

**cultural relativism**   A school of thought premised on 'tolerance' for and acceptance of cultural differences. The theory postulates that no hierarchy based on the superiority or inferiority of culture should be presumed to exist within present or past human societies. Cultures are simply different from (i.e. not better than) each other. Geographic, historical, environmental, cognitive, and linguistic differences explain human cultural variation. However, this doctrine does not assume that all cultural expressions are legitimate expressions of the human experience. Fleras and Kunz (2001) accept the hypothesis for the purposes of study and understanding, 'but not necessarily as a basis for living.'

**cultural studies**   The study of cultural practices, of systems of representation and communication, and of the relationship between culture and asymmetrical power relations. It is an interdisciplinary approach that draws from anthropology, sociology, history, semiotics, literary, psychoanalysis, feminism, Third World studies, and literary, art theatre and film criticism, to name a few sources. This approach is used to critically examine the dominant culture and the role that mainstream cultural institutions and the media play in the legitimizing, producing, and entrenching systems of inequality. Cultural studies emphasize the roles of both 'high' and popular culture in transmissing and reproducing values. Cultural studies also examine the processes of resistance by which women, people of colour, and other marginalized groups challenge hegemonic cultural practices.

**culture** The totality of ideas, beliefs, values, knowledge, and language as a learned, shared, and transmitted way of life of a people, group, or nation. For others, culture is a signifying system utilizing knowledge, artifacts, and symbols, through which a social order is communicated, reproduced, and experienced (Williams, 1976 and Grossberg, 1993). In popular discourse, 'high' culture refers to artistic, intellectual development and to the works and activities that are the products of this development.

**deconstructionism** A mode of interpretation based on the assumption that texts/narratives/images do not have fixed meaning. Individual readers and viewers can be said to interpret the meanings of the texts as they read and works of art as they observe and examine them. It follows that there is no absolute 'centre' or system of ideas outside of the text that enables it to be comprehended and interpreted in a predetermined or static manner.

**democratic racism** An ideology that comprises conflicting egalitarian and discriminatory values. One set of values consists of a commitment to a democratic society motivated by egalitarian principles of fairness, justice, and equality. Conflicting with these liberal values are attitudes and behaviours, including negative feelings about people of colour, that carry the potential for differential treatment or discrimination. This conflict between the two ideologies is reflected in the everyday discourses that operate in the media, education, the courts, government, and other mainstream institutional spaces.

**designated groups** Social groups whose members have historically been denied equal access to such areas as employment, accommodation, health care, and education because of their membership in the group. Under employment equity legislation, there are four designated grups: women, visible minorities, Aboriginal peoples, and persons with disabilities.

**disadvantage** Unfavourable and unequal access to resources such as employment, education, and social services.

**discourse**   A repertoire of words, images, ideas and practices through which meanings are circulated and power applied. These discursive formations influence and organize our conception of ourselves, individual and group actions, organizational and institutional policies and procedures (e.g., exclusionary employment and promotion practices, media representations of people of colour, etc.).

**discrimination**   The denial of equal treatment and opportunities to individuals or groups with respect to education, accommodation, health care, employment, and services, goods, and facilities. Discrimination may arise on the basis of race, nationality, gender, age, religion, political affiliation, marital or family status, physical or psychiatric disability, or sexual orientation.

**discursive crisis/ moral panic**   These terms are often used interchangeably to capture the idea that a particular event cannot by seen as contentious without first being 'constructed' in public discourse. In a moral panic, a condition, event or person or group of persons becomes defined as a threat to societal values and national interest, and the dominant culture comes to believe it is experiencing a loss of control and authority. The mass media play a significant role in reinforcing a climate of fear and threat.

**dominant discourses / discourses of democratic racism**   The ways in which society gives voice to racism are often subtle and even invisible to mainstream society because these discourses are often contextualized within the framework of democratic liberal principles and values such as freedom of expression, equal opportunity, colour-blindness, individualism and tolerance. Within these discourses are unchallenged myths and assumptions.

**dominant/majority group**   The group of people in a given society that is largest in number or that successfully shapes or controls other groups through social, economic, cultural, political, or religious power. In Canada, the term has generally referred to White, Anglo-European males.

**employment equity**   A set of practices designed to identify and eliminate discriminatory policies and practices that create unfair or unequal employment opportunities and to provide equitable opportunities in employment for designated groups. Employment equity means more than treating people in the same way (i.e. equal opportunity); it also requires special measures and the accommodation of differences. Thus, equality of results or outcomes, not equality of treatment, is important.

**encoding/decoding**   Terms developed by British cultural studies writer Stuart Hall in an article of the same name. Hall argues that meaning does not simply exist in a media text's code but is the result of a complex relationship between particular audiences and texts.

**equity**   The rights of individuals to an equitable share of the goods and services in society. To ensure equality of outcome, equity programs treat groups differently when the situation in society precludes equal treatment. Equity programs are more inclined to accept the priority of collective rights over individual rights.

**essentialism**   (1) The practice of reducing the complex identity of a particular group to a series of simplified characteristics that deny their individual qualities. (2) The simplistic reduction of an idea or process.

**ethnic/ethnocultural group**   A community maintained by a shared heritage, culture, language, or religion; a group bound together by ties of cultural homogeneity, with a prevailing loyalty and adherence to certain beliefs, attitudes, and customs.

**ethnocentrism**   The tendency to view events, values, beliefs, practices and experiences from the perspective of one's own group/culture; the corresponding tendency to misunderstand or diminish other groups' values and practices, regarding them as inferior.

**Eurocentrism**   A complex system of beliefs that upholds the supremacy of Europe's cultural values, ideas, and peoples. European culture is seen as the vehicle for progress toward liberalism and democracy. Eurocentrism minimizes the role of Europeans in maintaining the oppressive systems of colonialism and racism.

**exclusion**   A process of disempowering, degrading, or disenfranchising a group by discriminatory practices and behaviour.

**harassment**   A persistent and continuing communication (in any form) of negative attitudes, beliefs, or actions toward an individual or group, with the intention of disparaging that person or group. Forms of harassment include name-calling, jokes and slurs, graffiti, insults, threats, discourteous treatment, and written and physical abuse.

**hegemony**   A concept first used by Gramsci in the 1930s taken up in cultural studies. It refers to the ability of dominant classes to maintain power over the economic, political and cultural life of the state. The concept of hegemony is often found in those analyses that seek to show how everyday meanings, representations, and activities are organized and normalized as part of a natural order of domination and subordination.

**identity**   A subjective sense of coherence, consistency, and continuity of self, rooted in both personal and group history.

**ideology**   A complex set of ideas that attempts to explain, justify, legitimate, and perpetuate the circumstances in which a collectivity finds itself. It provides a basis for guiding behaviour, making sense of the world, imparting meaning to life, instilling a common bond among group members, and explaining situations. Ideology provides a framework for organizing legitimizing, and maintaining relations of power and decision making at all levels in institutions and systems.

**inclusion**   Exists when disadvantaged communities and designated group members are incorporated into a pre-existing institutional framework and share power and decision making at all levels in projects, programs, and practices.

**institutions**   Organizational arrangements and practices through which collective actions are taken (e.g., government, business, media, education, cultural institutions such as publishing houses, museums and theatres).

**integration**   The process that allows groups and individuals to become full participants in the social, economic, cultural, and political life of a society while at the same time enabling them to retain their own cultural identity.

**intolerance**   An unwillingness to consider and/or respect the beliefs and practices of others. Racial intolerance prevents members of other racial groups from sharing equally and benefiting fully from the opportunities available in a community, religious intolerance refuses to accept or respect the religious beliefs of others.

**mainstream**   The dominant culture and the political, social, educational, cultural, and economic institutions through which its power is maintained and reproduced.

**marginalization**   The process of restricting an individual, group, or community from participating in the decision-making processes, programmes, activities, benefits, and resources of an institution or society.

**minority group**   A group of people that is either relatively small in number or has little or no access to social, political, or economic power.

**multiculturalism**   (1) A description of the composition of Canada both historically and currently, referring to the cultural and racial diversity of Canadian society. (2) An ideology that holds that racial, cultural, religious, and linguistic diversity is an integral, beneficial, and necessary part of Canadian society and identity. (3) A policy operating in various social institutions and levels of government, including the federal government.

**oppression**   The domination of certain individuals or groups by others through the use of physical, psychological, social, cultural, or economic force.

**othering**   The process by which minorities are portrayed as 'others'; or, the fragmentation into 'we' (the White dominant culture or the culture of the organization) and 'they' (the groups and communities that are the 'other,' and that possess 'different' and undesirable values, beliefs, and norms.

**people of colour** (*See* **racial minority**).

**pluralism**   An approach in which some degree of cultural, linguistic, ethnic, religious, or other group distinction is maintained and valued by individuals.

**postmodernism**   Originally related only to literary and art criticism and to the abandonment of traditional cultural practices in favour of more innovative forms of expression. It also led to the collapse of rigid distinctions between high and popular culture. Later, it became a paradigm for social change. As a philosophy and discourse, it challenged authority and power relations; it also questioned traditional values, as well as the fragmentation of individual identities by social markers of difference such as race, gender, ethnicity, and sexual orientation.

**prejudice**   A mental state or attitude of prejudging, generally unfavourably, by attributing to every member of group characteristics falsely attributed to the group as a whole.

**race**   A socially constructed category used to classify humankind according to common ancestry and that relies on differentiation by such physical characteristics as colour of skin, hair texture, stature, and facial characteristics.

**race relations**   The quality and pattern of interactions between people who are racially different.

**racial discrimination**   Any distinction, exclusion, restriction, or preference based on race that has the purpose of nullifying or impairing the
recognition, enjoyment, or exercise, on an equal footing, of human
rights and fundamental freedoms in the political, economic, social, cultural, or any other field of public life.

**racial incident**   Any incident in which there is an element of racial
motivation, or any incident that includes an allegation of racial motivation made by any person. Racial incidents may involve verbal abuse
(such as banter, jokes, name-calling, harassment, teasing, discourteous
treatment), defacement of property, or physical abuse and assault.

**racial minority**   A group of persons, other than Aboriginal peoples,
who are non-Caucasian in race or non-White in colour, and who so
identify themselves or agree to be so identified. Their minority status is
the result of a lack of access to power, privilege, and prestige in relation
to the White majority group.

**racialized**   Often used interchangeably with racist. The processes by
which race is attributed to particular social practices and discourses in
such a way that they are given special significance and are embedded
within a set of additional meanings (e.g., the 'racialization of crime'
means that criminal activity is often associated with Black people).
*Racialization* is part of a process by which ethno-racial populations are
categorized, constructed, thought inferior, and marginalized.

**racism**   A system in which one group of people exercises power over
another group on the basis of skin colour; an implicit or explicit set of
beliefs, erroneous assumptions, and actions based on an ideology of the
inherent superiority of one racial group over another, and evident in
organizational or institutional structures and programs as well as in individual thought or behaviour patterns. *Individual racism* is a form of
racial discrimination that stems from conscious, personal prejudice.
*Institutional racism and systemic (structual) racism* consists of policies and
practices, entrenched in established institutions and across sectors, that
result in the exclusion or advancement of specific groups of people. It
derives from individuals carrying out the dictates of others who are prejudiced or of a prejudiced society; The latter denies from inequalities,
rooted in the systemwide operation of a society, that exclude substantial
numbers of members of particular groups from significant participation
in major social institutions. *Cultural racism* is deeply embedded in the
ideology of a society. It represents the tacit network of assumptions,
beliefs, and values that encourages and justifies discriminatory actions,

behaviours, and practices. Essed (1990) contends that cultural racism precedes other forms of racism, as it is reflected in everyday language and representations. It is reflected in the images generated by education, media, films, and other forms of cultural production.

**racist**   An individual, institution, or organization whose beliefs, actions, or programs imply or state that certain races have distinctive negative or inferior characteristics.

**racist discourse**   The ways in which society gives voice to racism; it includes explanations, narratives, codes of meaning, accounts, images, and social practices that have the effect of establishing, sustaining, and reinforcing oppressive power relations.

**racist ideology**   The whole range of concepts, ideas, images, and institutions that provide the framework of interpretation and meaning for racial thought in society. It creates and preserves a system of dominance based on race. It communicated and reproduced through agencies of socialization and cultural transmission such as the mass media, schools and universities, religious doctrines, symbols and images, art, music, and literature.

**radical/critical multiculturalism**   A form of multiculturalism that calls for a radical restructuring of the power relations between ethnoracial communities and challenges the hierarchical structure of society. Radical multiculturalism focuses on empowering communities and transforming systems of representation, institutional and structural centres of power, and discourses. Multiculturalism in this context suggests that diversity can be meaningful only within the construct of social justice and equity.

**reflexivity**   Critical thinking and rethinking about issues often taken for granted. Reflexivity also involves deconstructing feelings, events, situations, and experiences by peeling away the various levels of meaning attached to them through the passage of time.

**representation**   The process giving abstract ideological concepts concrete forms (examples: representations of women, workers, Blacks). Representations include all kinds of imagery and discourse, and involve constructions of reality taken from specific points of view. Representation is a social process of making sense within all available signifying systems: speech, writing, print, video, film, tape, and so on.

**semiotics**   The study of the ways in which languages and non-linguistic symbolic systems operate to associate meanings with words, visual images, or objects. Semiotics examines all aspects of communication, focusing on how meaning is created rather than what the meaning is. Semiotics seeks to relate the production of meanings to other kinds of social productions and social relations.

**skin colour**   Skin colour carries with it more than the signification of colour; it also includes a set of meanings attached to the cultural traits of those who are a certain colour.

**stereotype**   A false or generalized conception of a group of people that results in an unconscious or conscious categorization of each member of that group, without regard for individual differences.

**subjectivity**   Encompasses unconscious and subconscious dimensions of the self, such as one's sense of who one is in relation to other people. It is the product of social and cultural systems that magnify differences. This concept has been used widely in literary and film criticism, which holds that narrative texts themselves produce through their codes an ideal 'viewing position,' from which the narrative is experienced by any viewer or reader.

**text**   Any produced work or work of art. 'Text' includes not only books, plays, and poetry, but also media representations, films, and visual art forms.

**textual analysis**   The study of how particular written or verbal cultural artifacts generate meaning, taking into account their social and political contexts.

**universality**   Refers to a level of understanding that transcends all human boundaries of culture and nation. Universalism is a critical quality of expression and comprehension traditionally valued in literature and art. Universality has, however, been defined in specific Eurocentric rather than truly universal terms. The Eurocentrically influenced notion of universality has been disseminated globally through the forces of colonialism.

**whiteness**   A social construction that has created a racial hierarchy that has shaped all of the social, cultural, educational, political, and economic institutions of society. Whiteness is linked to domination and is a form of race privilege that is invisible to White people who are not conscious of its power. Whiteness as defined within a cultural studies perspective is description, symbol, experience, and ideology.

# Notes

## 1: Theoretical Framework

1 Jan Blommaert and Jef Kerschueren (1998); Michel Foucault (1980); Paul Gilroy (1987); bell hooks (1990); Norman Fairclough (1995); Stanley Fish (1995); John Fiske (1994); John Gabriel (1998); Oscar Gandy Jr (1998); Hall (1997, 1991); Ruth Wodak (1999).

2 Critical race theory – a theory and movement led by legal scholars of colour. It was developed to apply to the legal system and first emerged in the United States as a counter-legal discourse of civil rights. It is based on a critique of liberalism and argues that critical legal theory fails to address the racism that is embedded in the fabric of American culture. Later, the theory was expanded to challenge conceptions of antidiscrimination policies that do not take fully into account the complex linkages between race, class, and gender in structuring the everyday racialized experiences of African Americans in other fields such as education and the media (see Billings, 1998).

3 See *Colour of Democracy* for notes on aversive and symbolic racism; and Hall (1981) on inferential racism.

4 The definition of elites by Wodak and Matouschek identifies them in the following way: 'Elites ... may be seen to comprise those who in one form or another dominate public discourse ... Elites are those who initially formulate and evaluate the various issues regarding minority groups. By virtue of their ability to determine an initial set of public discursive parameters, these elites are thus able to formulate an ethnic consensus' (1993: 226).

5 Rick Salutin (*The Globe and Mail* 18 December E1) contends that when a mythology is embedded in culture, it is not really visible. It comes at you from all directions. To discover what a society has as its underlying mythology, you have to ask what kinds of images and ideas we take for granted.

## 2:   Review of the Canadian Literature on Racism in the Print Media

1 The research of scholars working in the United States, the United Kingdom, the Netherlands, Australia, and Austria is woven through the book.
2 The *Toronto Star* continues to be the only Canadian newspaper with public, articulated policy on employment and journalistic diversity and equity.
3 The Oka crisis involved a confrontation between the Mohawks of Kanehsatake (a small community near of Montreal, Quebec) and different levels of government including Oka (the non-Native community adjacent to Kanehsatake settlement), Quebec, and Canada. For seven months in 1990, the Mohawks opposed a municipality developers' plan to expand a golf course onto Mohawk land. The Aboriginal community set up barricades and was surrounded by the Quebec Provincial Police and the Canadian military forces. What at first seemed a relatively limited local conflict ultimately became redefined as a large battleground over which Indian land, cultural, political, and economic rights were contested.
4 In August 2001, Conrad Black sold his interest in the *National Post* to CanWest Global.
5 Herman and Chomsky (1994), Pamela Shoemaker and Stephen Reese, *Mediating the Message: Theories of Influence in Mass Media Content*, 2nd ed. (White Plains, NY: Longman, 1996).

## 4:   The Methodology of Case Studies and Critical Discourse Analysis

1 Though our methods have been influenced by the critical discourse analytic techniques of van Djik, we have not used all of his categorizations.
2 Discourse analysis emerged in the late 1960s and early 1970s from different but related developments in a number of disciplines, including anthropology, ethnography, linguistics, mass communication, history, political science, poetics, and other disciplines interested in the analysis of 'text' and 'talk.' In its approach to discourse analysis it incorporates various dimensions of discourse such as everyday conversations, institutional dialogues, narratives, argumentation, and media discourses (see van Dijk, 1991; Wetherell and Potter, 1992; Fairclough, 1992).
3 A more complete description of these devices can be found in van Dijk, 1991.

## 5:   The Avery Haines Controversy

1 Racist jokes are not innocuous statements. They communicate information,

opinions, and attitudes toward minorities. Racist humour expresses what the in-group in a society thinks about its out-groups. In terms of this form of humour, out-groups are defined by race, colour, culture, gender, and sexual orientation. People find themselves at the periphery of social power because they diverge from those who are traditionally considered part of the 'imagined community' of the nation-state.

### 6:   *Globe and Mail* Editorials on Employment Equity

1 Equitable representation depends on the following factors: the number of designated group members in the working age population in a certain geographic area, the number of trained or skilled members who are employable or can be readily available, and the existence of equal opportunities in each workplace.
2 In March 1987, visible minorities made up 2.7 per cent of the public service and 6.3 per cent of the Canadian population. By March 1996, their share of government employment had risen to 4.5 per cent, but their representation in the population had jumped to 13 per cent. In management, minorities held only 2.3 per cent of the executive positions in the public service (Samuel and Karam, 1996).

### 7:   The *National Post*'s Discourse on Immigration, Refugees, and the Tamils

1 Based on the total figure of 175,000.
2 The photograph was later identified by a FACT member as having been taken during a play enacting the civil war in Sri Lanka.
3 In a letter to the editor signed by a number of faculty of the University of Jaffna, the authors say they wish to express their anger against the reports published by this group. They state that 'the information contained in these reports is based on hearsay and authenticity of the sources from which they are supposed to have been obtained is open to question. The information does not give a true or complete picture of events and seems to be intended to serve only one goal, namely to discredit Liberation Tigers of Tamil Eelam.'

### 8:   News Discourse and the Problematization of Chinese Migration to Canada

1 A modified version of this chapter will appear as 'Constructing a Discursive Crisis: Risk, Problematization, and Illegal Migration to Canada,' in Hier and Greenberg, eds., *Ethnic and Racial Studies*, forthcoming 25(3).

2 On the relationship between globalization, neoliberalism, and changing citizenship discourses, see Brodie (1997), Laquian, Laquian, and McGee (1997), Jensen (1987, 1997), Jensen and Phillips (1996), and Patten (1999).

3 One of these factions is the Canada First Immigration Reform Committee (CFIRC), a racial supremacist organization whose website features critical reviews of refugee and immigration policy, illustrated by such phrases as 'Immigration Can Kill You!' What is of particular concern is the professional relationship that developed between the CFIRC and *National Post* journalist Diane Francis, who in covering the migrants' arrival publicly supported the mandate and points of view of the organization and its leader, Paul Fromm. On the role of Diane Francis in this affair, see Clarkson (2000) and Hier (2000).

4 Throughout this paper we use the terms 'moral panic' and 'discursive crisis' somewhat interchangeably. The former term was coined by Cohen in his study of the Mods and Rockers, and thus serves as a benchmark for our analysis. The latter term has no known point of origin and so provides greater conceptual flexibility. It should be noted, however, that both terms capture the idea that a particular event cannot be seen as contentious without first being 'constructed' in public discourse. We use the term 'crisis' to describe the constellation of failures within the institutions of the state responsible for immigration and refugees; the term 'panic' adequately captures the symptomatic response to this crisis.

5 In Canada, as elsewhere, the rise in prominence of populist political parties such as the Canadian Alliance (formerly, the Reform Party of Canada) has provided a politically legitimate platform for the expression of such commonsense anxieties.

6 Interview with John Bryden, MP and member of the Standing Committee on Citizenship and Immigration (23 May 2000).

7 Critical reaction on the part of the Canadian public and government to the presence of 'boat people' predates the landing of the migrants from Fujian Province. For example, following the arrival of 155 Tamil and 174 East Indian refugees on the coast of Nova Scotia in the summer of 1986 and 1987, respectively, the Canadian government responded with Bills C-55 and C-84 (see Elliot and Fleras, 1994: 246–8). As Beiser (1999) is correct to point out, public discourse often relies on mottoes to encapsulate events. Largely stemming from a representational pattern whereby upwards of 60,000 Southeast Asian refugees entered Canada between 1979 and 1981, the collective epithet 'boat people' has been emblazoned on the minds of the Canadian public. This is an objectifying, depersonalizing ideological mechanism that casts 'boat people' as a static 'phenomenon' necessitating legal and social control.

8 The assertion that social agents are active in the reading of news texts by no means implies that an active reader is by definition a resistant one. The two terms–active and resistant – are often conflated in media studies. This only serves to confuse the relationship between news readers and the ideological contents of news text. By the term 'active,' we mean only to suggest that readers are not at the ideological mercy of whatever happens to appear in the daily news, and that any successful news text must be able to resonate comfortably with the material, social, and cultural experiences of news readers.

9 Hard news consists of those reports that have been subject to the normal journalistic routines of sourcing objective data, interviewing non-partisan sources, and testing for bias and validity. The term is juxtaposed to 'soft news,' which consists of editorials, commentary, and guest columns – types of media reporting that are not bound by these more rigorous and positivistic conventions of news making. On the notion of the journalistic principles of balance and objectivity, see for example P. Schlesinger and H. Tumber (1994).

10 For an analysis of opinion discourse in Canadian newspapers concerning the arrival of the migrants, see Greenberg (2000).

11 The decision to limit the study to four sources was based on material constraints. These particular media were selected on the basis of three criteria: regional location, audience reach, and idiomatic flavour. *The National Post* is generally considered to be a highbrow, 'quality' newspaper catering to the nation's right-wing corporate and intellectual elite, predominantly covering political and financial news from a neoliberal perspective. The *Vancouver Sun* is more of a middlebrow, family newspaper catering to the 'general reader.' It enjoys the highest circulation in British Columbia and reaches both urban and suburban readers. It is noteworthy that Conrad Black's Hollinger Inc. is the controlling owner of both the *Vancouver Sun* and *The National Post.* Both papers tend to give favourable media coverage to elite forces – namely, big business. Other important issues, such as labour relations, are normally represented as disruptive.

Like the *Vancouver Sun,* the *Toronto Sun* is a regionally focused newspaper. Since the events in question did not directly affect Ontarians, it should come as no surprise that this paper carried far less coverage than the others. We sampled the *Toronto Sun* for two reasons: Toronto is the preferred Canadian destination for Asian migrants (Li, 1998); and we wanted to include in the analysis a newspaper with a tabloid format. Alternatively, we could have sampled the more social-liberal *Toronto Star,* which would have provided an interesting contrast with the more right-wing press. We selected the *Toronto Sun* mainly because of its editorial tone: it is a directly antisocialist paper with an appealing but sycophantic populism.

Finally, we sampled all 'hard' news coverage in the Victoria *Times-Colonist*. As the migrants arrived at various points along British Columbia's southern coast, this newspaper provided more coverage than the other three. Like the *Vancouver Sun*, the *Times-Colonist* appeals to the general reader. It is moderately populist, in that it tends to articulate a discourse of discontent in virtually all situations considered to be 'out of the ordinary.' Its discursive style is strongly evaluative and rich in the kinds of ideological effects and connotative characterizations more common among tabloid dailies: essentialism, hyperactivity, and hyperrealism – a dueling logic of objectivity (separation) and subjectivity (closeness), whereby the menacing characteristics of the world are brought into the spheres of personalization and reassurance, where they may be dealt with (Knight, 1998).

12 Attributions of illegality from Table 7.1 include 'Illegal migrants' and 'Illegal aliens,' and the transgressive terms 'Detainees' and 'Other negative.' Attributions of illegality from Table 7.2 include 'Illegal migrants' and 'Illegal aliens, and the transgressive terms 'Detainees,' 'Human cargo,' and 'Other negative.'

13 It is noteworthy that when requested by Canadian authorities to provide contact information for their families in China, the migrants willingly complied. Not one of the 599 migrants was found to have a criminal record in China.

14 The *Times-Colonist* poll failed to demonstrate scientific, objective rigor, yet all news media that reported these results did so under the pretense of objective journalism.

15 From Table 7.1 these terms include 'Boat people,' 'Refugees,' 'Detainees,' and 'Other negative.' From Table 7.2, 'Refugee claimants,' 'Boat people,' 'Refugees,' 'Human cargo,' and 'Other negative.'

16 The *Times-Colonist*, for instance, presented a constant running-head for its coverage of the migrants in three capitalized forms: 'WAVES OF BOAT PEOPLE,' 'MIGRANT INVASION' and 'ILLEGAL MIGRANTS: THE THIRD WAVE.'

17 Toward the end of July 1999, migrants who were being held in detention went on a hunger strike to protest what they saw as poor treatment and poor food. Later, reports surfaced that the migrants were being strip-searched and verbally and physically abused, and were being watched by security officials while they bathed. The authorities' response was to demand the names of the complainants. When none were forthcoming, security was tightened.

18 No migrants were actually reported using the 'weapons' in any threatening manner. In fact, later reports indicated that the tinfoil 'make-shift weapon' was being used for cutting hair.

19 Exactly one year after the arrival of the first boat, *The Globe and Mail* (22 July 2000) ran a full-page story under the headline, 'The Boat People's Big Gam-

ble,' which noted that the cost of processing and incarcerating last year's 'tidal wave of illegal migration' currently stood at $36 million.

20 As of July 2000, 576 of the migrants had claimed refugee status (96 per cent). Of these, 403 had been rejected (67 per cent), 75 were still to be heard, 106 had been deported (18 per cent), 67 had abandoned their claims, and 128 were considered missing (22 July 2000, *The Globe and Mail*). Disturbingly, one month earlier, *The National Post* (22 June 2000) had reported that the immigration department had ordered 100 'Trophy Shirts' (at a cost of $2000), intended for immigration officers who had worked on the migrants' cases. Emblazoned on the front of the shirts was a Vancouver Enforcement Officer crest, with a subtitle reading 'Class of 90,' representing the ninety migrants deported under armed security.

## 9:  The Racialization of Crime

1 The controversy over the musical play *Showboat* in Toronto led to more than 125 articles in the local media alone. A conference of minority writers called 'Writing thru Race,' which took place in Vancouver in 1995, generated nearly as many. See Tator et al. (1998).

2 Prior research has shown that many people in and around Toronto believe there is a relationship between race and crime and that Blacks are, in fact, criminally disposed.

3 This case has already been the subject of sociological and media analysis. See Wortley et al., 1997.

4 As the earlier section indicates, it is very difficult to trace a direct causal relationship between media coverage of an event and its policy and legislative consequences. Most often, that relationship is inferred or implied. In the case of Just Desserts, a direct link is possible. See, Falconer, and Ellis, 1988.

5 Not only was the Just Desserts case often cited as the catalyst for the new legislation, *but specific references to the media's representations of crime and/or immigration were made on twenty-eight occasions* The following media sources were referred to: *The Globe and Mail* (7), the *Toronto Star* (1), *La Presse* (2), the CBC (1), the Canadian Press (1), newspapers (4), news (2), magazines (1), media (5), journalists (2), and clipping services (1).

## 10:  Media Discourse Involving First Nations Peoples

1 Two more articles were published by *The Globe and Mail* over this period. On 25 November, Margaret Wente wrote a piece about the Ramsay case that was designed to raise issues and questions, and did not contain any obvious lin-

guistic or evaluative statements. On 27 November a short article raised the question of the future of Jack Ramsay and suggested that the people of his constituency would be the final judges of his future.

2  Fleras and Kunz (2001) contend that mainstream media coverage of this issue generally missed the key issue of jurisdiction and how to balance Aboriginal and treaty rights to hunt and fish for subsistence with the rights of federal authorities to regulate the environment on behalf of all Canadians. Their analysis also points out that Aboriginal fishers are portrayed as environmental predators, as renegades, as lawless people 'hiding behind the smokescreen of aboriginal rights' (82).

**Conclusion**

1  Democratic racism follows the constructions of 'symbolic racism' (Sears and McConahay, 1973), 'aversive racism' (Gaertner and Dovidio, 1986), and Hall's (1981) notion of 'inferential racism.' Each of these constructions moves away from seeing racism as simply the overt expression of negative, prejudicial attitudes, beliefs, and behaviours of bigoted individuals.

2  A few exceptions to be noted in terms of diversity initiatives currently being implemented in journalism, schools include the Ryerson School of Journalism, where Professor John Miller has demonstrated strong leadership in integrating 'diversity' into the curriculum and research activities. (see www.diversitywatch.ryerson.ca/watch/Media/analysis.html). Another model is provided by the UBC School of Journalism which publishes the *UBC Journalism Review: Thunderbird Online Magazine*, which regularly includes, articles related to the media and ethnoracial issues. Also, the UBC Faculty of Arts has established the Sing Sao School of Journalism, a post-graduate program funded by the Sing Tao newspaper chain.

3  In March 2000 the *Toronto Star* received an award from the Joint Centre of Excellence for Research on Immigration and Settlement (CERIS) for its 'Beyond 2000 Series.' The articles included in this series covered a range of issues, most of which focused on immigration and diversity. As well, it is important to note that the *Star* has distinguished itself from other Canadian newspapers by hiring a large number of journalists of colour in recent years, and by appointing Haroon Siddiqui as editor of the editorial page. Siddiqui continues to write regular columns for the newspaper.

# References

Abella, Rosalie. 1984. *Report of the Commission on Equality in Employment.* Ottawa: Supply and Services Canada

Agocs, Carol, Catharine Burr, et al. 1992. *Employment Equity: Cooperative Strategies for Change.* New York: Prentice-Hall

Ainley, Beulah. 1998. *Black Journalists, White Media.* London: Trentham Books

Allport, Gordon. 1954. *The Nature of Prejudice.* New York: Doubleday

Althusser, Louis. 1971a. 'Ideology and Ideological State: *Philos* Apparatuses.' In *Lenin and Philosophy and Other Essays.* London: Monthly Review

– 1971b. *Lenin and Philosophy and Other Essays.* London: New Left Books

Amit-Talai, Vered, and Caroline Knowles. 1996. *Resituating Identities: The Politics of Race, Ethnicity, and Culture.* Peterborough, ON: Broadview Press

Anderson, Benedict. 1983. *Imagined Communities: Reflections on the Origin and Spread of Nationalism.* London: Verso

Anthias, Floya. 1998. 'The Limits of Ethnic Diversity.' *Patterns of Prejudice.* 32 (4): 6–19

Apple, Michael. 1993. 'Constructing the "Other": Rightist Reconstructions of Common Sense.' In *Race, Identity, and Representation in Education.* Ed. C. McCarthy and W. Crichlow. New York: Routledge

Axon, L., and S. Moyer. 1994. 'An Exploratory Study on the Use of Firearms in Criminal Incidents in Toronto.' Prepared for Department of Justice, Canada

Banton, Michael. 1977. *The Idea of Race.* London: Tavistock

Barahona, Federico. 2001. 'Invisible: Diversity in Canadian Newsrooms.' *UBC Journalism Review: Thunderbird Online Magazine.* April. *http://www.journalism. ubc.ca/thunderbird/2000–01/april/diver sity.html*

Barlow, Maude, and James Winter. 1997. *The Big Black Book: The Essential Views of Conrad Black and Barbara Amiel Black.* Toronto: Stoddart

Barthes, Roland. 1977. *Image-Music-Text.* London: Fontana

Beiser, Morton. 1999. *Strangers at the Gate: The 'Boat People's' First Ten Years.* Toronto: University of Toronto Press

Biagi, S., and M. Kern-Foxworth. 1997. *Facing Difference.* Thousand Oaks, CA: Pine Forge Press

Billings. G.L. 1998. 'Just What Is Critical Race Theory and What's It Doing in a Nice Field like Education.' *Qualitative Education* 11(1): 7–24

Blommaert, Jan, and Jef Kerschueren. 1998. *Analyzing the Discourse of Tolerance.* London and New York: Routledge.

Boyko, John. 1995. *Last Steps to Freedom: The Evolution of Canadian Racism.* Winnipeg: Watson and Dwyer

Brodie, J. 1997. 'Meso-Discourses, State Forms, and the Gendering of Liberal-Democratic Citizenship.' *Citizenship Studies,* 1 (1): xx–xx

Cameron, Dorothy, ed. 1990. *The Feminist Critique of Language.* London: Routledge

Campbell, Christopher. 1995. *Race, Myth and the News.* Thousand Oaks, CA: Sage

Canadian Ethnocultural Council. 1985. 'Brief to the Parliamentary Subcommittee on Equality Rights.' Ottawa

Canadian Islamic Congress. 1999. 'Anti-Islam in the Media: A Six-month Study of Six Top Canadian Newspapers.' *http://www.cicnow.com/docs/media-report/1999/anti-islam.html*

*Canadian Newspaper Association's (CNA) Diversity Committee.* 1994. Editorial Division. April

CCCS (Centre for Contemporary Cultural Studies). 1982. 'The Organic Crisis of British Capitalism and Race.' In CCCS, *The Empire Strikes Back: Race and Racism in 70's Britain.* London: Hutchinson

Center on Crime, Communities and Culture of the Open Society Institute. 2000. *Race, Crime and the Media: A Report for the Center on Crime, Communities and Culture.* New York: Eyal Press

Chan, Wendy, and Kiran Mirchandani, eds. In press. *E-Raced Connections: Racialization and Criminalization in Canada.* Toronto: Broadview

Chouliaraki, Lilie, and Norman Fairclough. 1999. *Discourse in Late Modernity: Rethinking Critical Discourse Analysis.* Edinburgh: Edinburgh University Press

Clarkson, B. 2000. '600 Is too Many: How the Press Used Four Boatloads of Chinese Migrants to Create an Immigration Crisis." *Ryerson Review of Journalism* (spring): 6–9

Cohen, Stanley. 1972. *Folk Devils and Moral Panics: The Creation of the Mods and Rockers.* London: MacKibbon and Kee

Coon Come, Mathew. 2001. 'Respect Rights of First Nations People.' Speech to the University of Toronto Convocation. Quoted in the *Toronto Star,* 22 June 2001, A25

Cottle, Simon, ed. 2000. *Ethnic Minorities and the Media: Changing Cultural Boundaries.* Buckingham, UK: Open University Press

Creese, Gillian. 1993–4. 'The Sociology of British Colombia.' *BC Studies* 100 (winter): 31–42

Curran, J., and M. Gurevitch. 1996. *Mass Media and Society.* New York: Edward Arnold

Dei, George. 1996. *Anti-Racism Education: Theory and Practice.* Halifax: Fernwood

Dellinger, Brett. 1995. 'Critical Discourse Analysis.' *http://users.utu.fi/bredelli/cda.html*

Dines, Gail, and Jean Humez, eds. 1995. *Race, Gender, and Class in the Media: A Text Reader.* Thousand Oaks, CA: Sage

Dirks, Gerald. 1998. 'Factors Underlying Migration and Refugee Issues: Responses and Cooperation among OECD Member States.' *Citizenship Studies* 2 (3): 377–95

Domke, David. 2000. 'Strategic Elites, the Press and Race Relations.' *Journal of Communication* 50(1): 115–48.

Ducharme, Michelle. 1986. 'The Coverage of Canadian Immigration Policy in the *Globe and Mail.*' *Currents: Readings in Race Relations* 3 (3): 6–11

Edelman, Murray. 1988. *Constructing the Political Spectacle.* Chicago: University of Chicago Press

– 1977. *Political Language: Words That Succeed and Policies That Fail.* New York: Academic Press

Entman, Robert, and Andrew Rojecki. 2000. *The Black Image in the White Mind: Media and Race in America.* Chicago: University of Chicago Press

*Equality Now.* 1984. Report of the Special Committee on Visible Minorities in Canadian Society. Ottawa

Ericson, Richard, Patricia Baranek, and Janet Chan. 1987. *Visualizing Deviance: A Study of News Organizations.* Toronto: University of Toronto Press

Essed, Philomena. 1990. *Everyday Racism: Reports from Women of Two Cultures.* Claremont, CA: Hunter House

– 1991. *Understanding Everyday Racism: An Interdisciplinary Theory.* London: Sage

Fairclough, Norman. 1992. *Discourse and Social Change.* Cambridge: Polity Press

– 1995. *Media Discourse.* London: Edward Arnold

Fairclough, Norman, and Ruth Wodak. 1997. 'Critical Discourse Analysis.' In *Discourse Studies: A Multidisciplinary Introduction.* Volume 2. *Discourse as Social Interaction.* Ed. T.A. van Dijk. London: Sage.

Falconer, J., and C. Ellis. 1998. 'Colour Profiling: The Ultimate Just Desserts.' Paper presented at the American Bar Association Meetings, Toronto. August

Feredi, Frank. 1997. *Culture of Fear: Risk-Taking and the Morality of Low Expectation.* London: Cassell

Fine, Michelle, Lois Weis, Linda Powell, and L. Mun Wong. eds. 1997. *Off White: Readings on Race Power and Society.* London: Routledge

Fish, Stanley. 1994. *There's No Such Thing as Free Speech ... And It's a Good Thing Too.* New York and Oxford: Oxford University Press.

Fiske, John. 1994. *Media Matters: Everyday Culture and Political Change.* Minneapolis: University of Minnesota Press

Fleras, Augie. 1994. 'Media and Minorities in a Post-Multicultural Society: Overview and Appraisal.' In *Ethnicity and Culture in Canada.* Ed. J.W. Berry and J.A. LaPonce. Toronto: University of Toronto Press

– 1995. '"Please Adjust Your Set": Media and Minorities in a Multicultural Society.' In *Communications in Canadian Society.* Ed. B. Singer. 4th ed. Scarborough: Nelson: 281–307.

Fleras, Augie, and Jean Elliot. 1992. *Multiculturalism in Canada.* Scarborough: Nelson

– 1994. *Unequal Relations.* Scarborough: Prentice-Hall

– 1996. *Unequal Relations: An Introduction to Race, Ethnic and Aboriginal Dynamics in Canada.* Scarborough: Prentice-Hall

– 1999. *Unequal Relations: An Introduction to Race, Ethnic and Aboriginal Relations.* 2nd ed. Scarborough: Nelson

Fleras, Augie, and Jean Lock Kunz. 2001. *Media and Minorities: Representing Diversity in a Multicultural Canada.* Toronto: Thomson

Foster, Cecil. 1997. 'Colour Barrier Remains.' *Toronto Star.* April 21, A18

Foster, Cecil. 1996. *A Place Called Heaven: The Meaning of Being Black in Canada.* Toronto: HarperCollins

Foucault, Michel. 1977. *Discipline and Punish: The Birth of the Prison.* New York: Random House

– 1978. *The History of Sexuality.* Volume 1. London: Allen Lane

– 1979. 'Governmentality.' *Ideology and Consciousness* 6: 5–21

– 1980. 'Two Lectures.' In *Power/Knowledge: Selected Interview and Other Writings, 1972–1977.* Ed. Colin Gordon. New York: Pantheon

– 1988. 'The Art of Telling the Truth.' In *Politics, Philosophy, Culture: Interviews and Other Writings, 1977–1984.* Ed. Lawrence D. Kritzman. New York: Routledge

Fowler, Roger. 1991. *Language in the News: Discourse and Ideology in the Press.* New York: Routledge

– ed. 1996. *Essays on Style and Language: Linguistic and Critical Literary and Critical Approaches to Literary Style.* London: Routledge and Kegan Paul

Frankenberg, Ruth. 1993. *White Women Race Matters: The Social Construction of Whiteness.* Minneapolis: University of Minnesota Press

Gabriel, John. 1998. *Whitewash: Racialized Politics and the Media.* London: Routledge

Gaertner. Samuel, and John Dovidio. 1986. 'The Aversive Forms of Racism.' In *Prejudice, Discrimination and Racism.* Ed. S.L. Gaertner and J.F. Dovidio. New York: Academic Press

Gandy, Oscar. 1998. *Communication and Race: A Structural Perspective.* London: Arnold

Gellner, Ernst. 1983. *Nations and Nationalism.* Oxford: Blackwell

Gilroy, Paul. 1987. *There Ain't No Black in the Union Jack.* Chicago: University of Chicago Press

Ginzberg, Effie. 1985. *Power without Responsibility: The Press We Don't Deserve.* Toronto: Urban Alliance on Race Relations.

Goldberg, David. ed. 1990. *The Anatomy of Racism.* Minneapolis: University of Minnesota Press

– 1993. *Racist Culture: Philosophy and the Politics of Meaning.* Oxford: Blackwell

Goldberg, Michelle. 1996. 'Can the Government's Discursive Shift Legitimize Its Shift in Equity Definitions?' MA thesis, University of Toronto

Goldfarb, Martin. 1995. *Tapping into a Growing Readership: Visible Minorities Research Project. A Research Report for the Canadian Daily Newspaper Association.* August

Goode, Erich, and Nachman Ben-Yehuda. 1994).*Moral Panics: The Social Construction of Deviance.* Oxford: Blackwell

Gray, Herbert. 1995. *Watching Race: Television and the Struggle for 'Blackness.'* Minneapolis: University of Minnesota Press

Greenberg, Joshua L. 2000. 'Opinion Discourse and Canadian Newspapers: The Case of the Chinese "Boat People".' *Canadian Journal of Communication* 25 (4): 517–37.

Greenberg, Joshua L., and Sean P. Hier 2000. 'Crisis, Mobilization and Collective Problematization: Illegal Migrants and the Canadian News Media.' *Journalism Studies* 2(4): 563–82.

Grenier, Marc, ed. 1992. *A Critical Study of Canadian Mass Media.* Toronto: Butterworths

Grossberg, Lawrence. 1993. 'Cultural Studies and/in New Worlds.' In *Race, Identity, and Representation in Education.* New York: Routledge

Gunther, A.C. 1998. 'The Persuasive Press Inference: Effects of Mass Media on Perceived Public Opinion.' *Communication Research* 25 (6): 486–504

Gunther, A.C., and Christen, C.T. 1999. 'Effects of News Slant and Base Rate Information on Perceived Public Opinion.' *Journalism and Mass Communications Quarterly* 76 (2): 277–92

Hackett, Robert, and Richard Gruneau. 2000. *The Missing News: Filters and Blind Spots in Canada's Press.* Ottawa: Canadian Centre for Policy Alternatives; Toronto: Garamond

Hackett, Robert, and Yuezhi Zhao. 1998. *Sustaining Democracy? Journalism and the Politics of Objectivity.* Toronto: Garamond

Hall, Stuart. 1973. *The Structured Communication of Events.* Birmingham: Centre for Contemporary Cultural Studies

- 1977. 'Culture, the Media and the "Ideological Effect".' In *Mass Communication and Society.* Ed. J. Curran et al. London: Open University Press

- 1978. 'Racism and Reaction.' In *Five Views of Multi-Racial Britain.* London: Commission for Racial Equality

- 1979. 'Culture, the Media and Ideological Effect.' In *Mass Communication and Society.* Ed. James Curran, Michael Gurevitch, and Janet Woollacot. Beverley Hills: Sage

- 1980. 'Encoding/Decoding.' In Centre for Contemporary Cultural Studies, University of Birmingham, *Culture, Media, Language: Working Papers in Cultural Studies, 1972–1979.* London: Hutchinson

- 1981. 'The Whites of Their Eyes: Racist Ideologies and the Media.' In *Silver Linings: Some Strategies for the Eighties.* Ed. G. Bridges and R. Brunt. London: Lawrence and Wishart

- 1983. 'The Great Moving Show.' In *The Politics of Thatcherism.* Ed. S. Hall and M. Jacques. London: Lawrence and Wishart

- 1986. 'Variants of Liberalism.' In *Politics and Ideology.* Ed. J. Donald and S. Hall. Milton Keynes: Open University Press

- 1991. 'The West and the Rest.' In *Culture, Globalization and the World System: Contemporary Conditions for the Representation of Identity.* Ed. A.D. King. Basingstoke: Macmillan

- 1991. 'The West and the Rest: Discourse and Power.' In *Formations of Modernity.* Cambridge: Polity Press/Open University

- 1992. 'The Question of Cultural Identity.' In *Modernity and Its Future.* Ed. S. Hall, D. Held, and T. McGrew. Cambridge: Polity Press in association with Open University

- 1993. 'Encoding, Decoding.' In *The Cultural Studies Reader.* Ed. Simon During. New York: Routledge

- 1996a. 'The Problem of Ideology: Marxism without Guarantees.' In *Critical Dialogues in Cultural Studies.* Ed. Stuart Hall, D. Morley, and Quan-Hsing Chen. London: Routledge

- 1996b. 'The Question of Cultural Identity.' in *Modernity: An Introduction to Modern Societies.* Ed. Stuart Hall, David Held, Don Hubert, and Kenneth Thompson. Oxford: Blackwell

- 1997. *Representation: Cultural Representation and Signifying Practices.* Thousand Oaks, CA: Sage

Hall, Stuart, et al. 1978. *Policing the Crisis: Mugging, the State and Law-and-Order.* London: Macmillan

Hall, Stuart, C. Critcher, T. Jefferson, J. Clarke, and B. Roberts. 1975. 'Newsmaking and Crime.' Paper presented at the NACRO Conference on Crime and the Media. University of Birmingham Centre for Contemporary Cultural Studies

Hall, Stuart, D. Hobson, A. Love, and P. Wilks. 1980. *Culture, Media and Language.* London: Hutchinson

Hannerz, U. 1992. *Cultural Complexity: Studies in Social Meaning.* New York: Columbia University Press

Hay, C. 1994. 'The Structural and Ideological Contradictions of Britain's Post-War Reconstruction.' *Capital and Class* 54: 25–59

– 1995. 'Mobilization through Interpellation: James Bulger, Juvenile Crime and the Construction of a Moral Panic.' *Social and Legal Studies* 4: 197–223

– 1996. 'Narrating Crisis: The Discursive Construction of the "Winter of Discontent."' *Sociology* 30 (2): 253–77

Hebdige, Dick 1993. 'From Culture to Hegemony.' In *The Cultural Studies Reader.* Ed. S. During. London: Routledge

Henry, Frances, and Carol Tator. 1994. 'The Ideology of Racism: Democratic Racism.' *Canadian Ethnic Studies* 26 (2): 1–14

– 2000. *Racist Discourse in Canada's English Print Media.* Toronto: Canadian Race Relations Foundation

Henry, Frances, Carol Tator, Winston Mattis, and Tim Rees. 2000. *The Colour of Democracy: Racism in Canadian Society.* 2nd ed. Toronto: Harcourt Brace

Herman, Edward, and Noam Chomsky. 1994. *Manufacturing Consent: The Political Economy of the Mass Media.* London: Verso

Hier, Sean P. 2000. 'The Contemporary Structure of Canadian Racial Supremacism: Networks, Strategies and New Technologies.' *Canadian Journal of Sociology* 25 (4): 471–94

hooks, bell. 1990. *Yearning: Race, Gender and Cultural Politics.* Boston: South End

hooks, bell. 1990. *Yearning: Race, Gender and Cultural Policies.* Toronto: Between the Lines

Howitt, Dennis. 1998. *Crime, Media and the Law.* Chichester, UK: Wiley

Husbands, Christopher. 1994. 'Crises of National Identity as the "New Moral Panics": Political Agenda-Setting about Definitions of Nationhood.' *New Community* 20 (2): 191–206

Jensen, Jane. 1987. 'Changing Discourse, Changing Agenda.' In *The Women's Movements of the United States and Western Europe: Consciousness, Political Opportunity and Public Policy.* Ed. M. Fainsod-Katzenstein and C. McClurg Mueller. Philadelphia: Temple University Press

- 1997. 'Fated to Live in Interesting Times: Canada's Changing Citizenship Regimes.' *Canadian Journal of Political Science* 4: 627–44

Jensen, Jane, and S. Phillips. 1996. 'Regime Shift: New Citizenship Practices in Canada.' *International Journal of Canadian Studies* 14 (fall): 111–35

Jordan, Glenn, and Weedon, Chris. 1995. *Cultural Politics: Class, Gender, Race and the Postmodern World.* Oxford: Blackwell

Kaplan, Robert. 1990. 'Concluding Essay: On Applied Linguistics and Discourse Analysis.' In *Annual Review of Applied Linguistics.* Volume 2. Ed. Robert Kaplan. New York: Cambridge University Press

Karim Karim. 1993. 'Constructions, Deconstructions and Reconstructions: Competing Canadian Discourses on Ethnocultural Terminology.' *Canadian Journal of Communications* 18 (2): 197–218

- 1997. 'The Historical Resilience of Primary Stereotypes: Core Images of the Muslim Other. In *The Language and Politics of Exclusion: Others in Discourse.* Ed. S. Riggins. Thousand Oaks, CA: Sage

- 2000. *Islamic Peril: Media and Global Violence.* Montreal: Black Rose Books

Kellner, Douglas. 1995. 'Cultural Studies, Multiculturalism and Media Culture.' In *Race, Gender, and Class in the Media: A Text Reader.* Ed. Gail Dines and Jean Humez. Thousand Oaks, CA: Sage

Khaki, A., and K. Prasad. 1988. *Depiction and Perception: Native Indians and Visible Minorities in the Media.* Vancouver: Ad Hoc Media Committee for Better Race Relations

Kidd-Hewitt, David, and Richard Osborne, eds. 1998. *Crime and the Media: The Postmodern Spectacle.* London: Pluto Press.

Knight, Graham. 1998. 'Hegemony, the Press, and Business Discourse: News Coverage of Strikebreakers Reform in Ontario.' *Studies in Political Economy* 55 (spring): 93–125

- 2000. 'Prospecting a Strike: News Narratives and the OPSEU/Harris Government Conflict.' Unpublished manuscript

Kress, Gunter. 1990. 'Critical Discourse Analysis.' In *Annual Review of Applied Linguistics.* Volume 2. Ed. Robert Kaplan. New York: Cambridge University Press

Kulyk Keefer, Janice. 1996. 'Writing, Reading, Teaching Transcultural in Canada.' In *Multiculturalism in North America and Europe: Social Practices – Literary Visions.* Ed. H. Braum and W. Klooss. Trier: Wissenschaftlicher Verlag

Laclau, Ernesto. 1977. *Politics and Ideology in Marxist Theory.* London: New Left Books

Laquian, A., and E. Laquian. 1997. 'Asian Immigration and Racism in Canada: A Search for Policy Options.' In *The Silent Debate: Asian Immigration and Racism in Canada.* Ed. A. Laquian, E. Laquian, and T. McGee. Vancouver: University of British Columbia Institute of Asian Research

Laquian, A., E. Laquian, and T. McGee, eds. 1998. *The Silent Debate: Asian Immigration and Racism in Canada*. Vancouver: University of British Columbia Institute of Asian Research

Lawrence, Erroll. 1982. 'Just Plain Common Sense: The "Roots" of Racism.' In CCCS, *The Empire Strikes Back: Race and Racism in 70's Britain*. London: Hutchinson

Lawrence, Erroll. 1982. *The Empire Strikes Back*, Centre for Contemporary Cultural Studies. London: Hutchinson

Li, Peter. 1994. 'Unneighbourly Houses or Unwelcome Chinese: The Social Construction of Race in the Battle over "Monster Homes" in Vancouver, Canada.' *International Journal of Comparative Race and Ethnic Studies* 1 (1): 14–33

– 1996. *The Making of Post-War Canada*. Toronto: Oxford University Press

– 1998. *Chinese in Canada*. Toronto: Oxford University Press

– 1999. *Race and Ethnic Relations*. 2nd ed. Toronto: Oxford University Press

Li, Peter, and B. Singh Bolaria. 1988. *Racial Oppression in Canada*. Toronto: Garamond

Linklater, Kenneth. 1986. 'Setting the Record Straight: The Press and Native People.' *Currents: Readings in Race Relations* 3 (3): 16–17.

Ma, J., and K. Hildebrant. 1993. 'Canadian Press Coverage of the Ethnic Chinese Community: A Content Analysis of the *Toronto Star* and *Vancouver Sun*.' *Canadian Journal of Communications* 18 (4): xx–xx.

Mackey, Eva. 1995. 'Postmodernism and Cultural Politics in a Multicultural Nation: Contests over Truth in the *Into the Heart of Africa* Controversy.' *Public Culture*. 7 (2): 403–31

– 1996. 'Managing and Imagining Diversity: Multiculturalism and the Construction of National Identity in Canada.' D.Phil., University of Sussex.

Manji, Irshad. 1995. 'Racism in the Media.' Toronto: Municipality of Metropolitan Toronto, Access and Equity Unit

Manji, Irshad. 1995. Metro Report on Racial Minorities in the Media, Municipality of Metropolitan Toronto

Manji, Irshad. 1995. Presentation on Racism in the Media. Conference on Racism in the Media. Report. published by the Municipality of Metropolitan Toronto, Access and Equity Unit

Marx, Karl. 1976. *Capital*, Volume 1. Harmondsworth: Penguin

Marx, Karl, and Friedrich Engels. 1978. 'Manifesto of the Communist Party.' In *The Marx–Engels Reader*. Ed. R. Tucker. New York: Norton

Mayers, A. 1986. 'Minorities in Ontario Newsrooms.' MBA thesis, McMaster University

McConahay, J.B., and J.C. Hough, Jr. 1976. 'Symbolic Racism.' *Journal of Social Issues* 32 (2): 23–45

McQuail, Denis. 1994. *Mass Communications Theory.* London: Sage

Miles, Robert. 1989. *Racism.* London: Routledge.

Miles, Robert, and Victor Satzewich. 1990. 'Migration, Racism and "Postmodern" Capitalism.' *Economy and Society* 19 (3): 334–58

Miller, David, and J. Kitzinger, et al. 1998. *Circuit of Mass Communication: Media Representation and Audience Receptions in the Aids Crisis.* London: Sage

Miller, John. 1998. *Yesterday's News: Why Canada's Daily Newspapers Are Failing Us.* Halifax: Fernwood

Miller, John, and Prince, K. 1994. *The Imperfect Mirror: Analysis of Minority Pictures and News in Six Canadian Newspapers.* Toronto: School of Journalism, Ryerson Polytechnic University

Mirchandani, Kiran, and Evangelia Tastsoglou. 2000. 'Toward a Diversity beyond Tolerance.' *Journal of Status in Political Economy* (spring): 49–78

Morley, David. 1992. *Television, Audiences and Cultural Studies.* London: Routledge

Mosher, Clayton James. 1998. *Discrimination and Denial: Systemic Racism in Ontario's Legal and Criminal Justice Systems, 1892–1961.* Toronto: University of Toronto Press

Mouammar, Mary. 1986. 'When Cartoons Aren't Funny.' *Currents: Readings in Race Relations* 3: 20–1

Parekh, Bhiru. 1986. 'The New Right and the Politics of Nationhood.' In *The New Right: Image and Reality.* London: Runnymede Trust

Patten, S. 1999. 'Citizenship, the New Right and Social Justice: Examining the Reform Party's Discourse on Citizenship.' *Socialist Studies Bulletin* 57–8: 25–51

Pearson, G. 1985. 'Lawlessness, Modernity and Social Change: A Historical Appraisal.' *Theory, Culture and Society* 2 (3): 15–35

Perigoe, R., and B. Lazar. 1992 'Visible Minorities and News.' In *Critical Studies of Canadian Mass Media.* Ed. M. Grenier. Toronto: Butterworths

Pieterse, Neverdeen Jan. 1992. *White on Black: Images of Africa and Blacks in Western Popular Culture.* New Haven, CT: Yale University Press

Razack, Sherene. 1998. *Looking White People in the Eye: Gender, Race, and Culture in Courtrooms and Classrooms.* Toronto: University of Toronto Press

Rex, John. 1983. *Race Relations in Sociological Theory.* 2nd ed. London: Routledge and Kegan Paul

Ridington, R. 1986. 'Texts That Harm: Journalism in British Columbia.' *Currents: Readings in Race Relations.* 3 (4): 6–12

Riggins, Stephen. ed. 1997. *The Language and Politics of Exclusion: Others in Discourse.* Thousand Oaks, CA: Sage

– In progress. 'Asian Minorities and the Canadian Press: Representing Identities in a Multi-ethnic Society.'

Roman, Leslie. 1993. 'White Is a Color! White Defensiveness, Postmodernism, and Anti-Racist Pedagogy.' In *Race, Identity, and Representation in Education*. Ed. C. McCarthy and W. Crichlow. New York: Routledge

Rosenfeld, S., and M. Spina. 1977. *All the News That's Fit to Print: A Study of the Toronto Press Coverage of Immigration, Ethnic Communities, and Racism*. Toronto: Cross-Cultural Communications Centre

Roth, Lorna, Beverley Nelson, and Marie David Kasennahaw. 1995. 'Three Women, a Mouse, a Microphone and a Telephone: Information (Mis)Management during the Mohawk/Canadian Governments' Conflict of 1990.' In ed. *Feminism, Multiculturalism and the Media: Global Perspectives*. Ed. Angharad Valdivia. Thousand Oakes, CA: Sage

Said, Edward. 1978. *Orientalism*. New York: Vintage Books.

Said, Edward. 1978. *Orientalism*. New York: Pantheon.

Samuel, John, and Aly Karam, 1996. 'Employment Equity and Visible Minorities in the Federal Workforce.' Paper presented to Symposium on Immigration and Integration. Winnipeg. 25–7 October

Saussure, Ferdinand de. 1974 [1916]. *Course in General Linguistics*. London: Fontana

Schelesinger, Philip, and Howard Tumber. 1994. *Reporting Crime: The Media Politics of Criminal Justice*. Oxford: Clarendon Press

Schissel, Bernard. 1997 *Blaming Children: Youth Crime, Moral Panics and the Politics of Hate*. Halifax: Fernwood

Schramm, W., and W.E. Porter. 1982. *Men, Women, Messages and Media*. New York: Harper and Row

Sears, David, and John McConahay. 1973. *The Politics of Violence: The New Urban Blacks and the Watts Riot*. Boston: Houghton Mifflin.

Shohat, Ella, and Robert Stam. 1994. *Unthinking Eurocentrism: Multiculturalism and the Media*. London: Routledge.

Siddiqui, Haroon. 2001. 'Media Out of Touch with New Pluralistic Canada.' *Toronto Star*. 22 April

Siddiqui, Haroon. 1993. 'Media and Race: Failing to Mix the Message.' *Toronto Star*, 24 April, D1, 5

Simmons, Alan. 1997. 'Globalization and Backlash Racism in the 1990s.' In *The Silent Debate: Asian Immigration and Racism in Canada*. Ed. A. Laquian, E. Laquian, and T. McGee. Vancouver: University of British Columbia Institute of Asian Research

Skea, W.H. 1993–4. 'The Canadian Newspaper Industry's Portrayal of the Oka Crisis.' *Native Studies Review* 9 (1): 15–27.

Small, S. 1994. 'The Contours of Racialization: Private Structures, Representations and Resistance in the U.S.' In *Race, Identity and Citizenship: A Reader.* Ed. R. Torres, J. Inda, and L. Miron. Madden MA: Blackwell

Social Planning Council of Winnipeg. 1996. *Media Watch: A Study of How Visible Minorities and Aboriginal Peoples Are Portrayed in Winnipeg's Two Major Papers and the Effect of These Portrayals.* Winnipeg: publisher

Solomon, Norman. 1998. 'Diversity Fatigue in the New Media.' 10 April. *http:// aspin.asu.edu/hpn/archives/Apr98/128.html*

Standing Committee on Citizenship and Immigration. 2000. 'Refugee Protection and Border Security.' March

Surette Richard. 1998. *Media Crime and Criminal Justice: Images and Realities.* Belmont, CA: Wadsworth

Switzer, Maurice. 1998 *Aboriginal Voices* 5 (6): 8

Szuchewycz, Bohdan, and Jeannette Sloniowski, eds. 1999. *Canadian Communications: Issues in Contemporary Media and Culture.* Scarborough: Prentice-Hall

Tator, Carol, Frances Henry, and Winston Mattis. 1998. *Challenging Racism in the Arts: Case Studies of Controversy and Conflict.* Toronto: University of Toronto Press

t'Hart, P. 1993. 'Symbols, Rituals and Power: The Lost Dimensions of Crisis Management.' *Journal of Contingencies and Crisis Management* 1 (1): 36–50

Thompson, John B. 1990. *Ideology and Modern Culture.* Cambridge: Polity Press

Tolson, Andrew. 1996. *Mediations: Text and Discourse in Media Studies.* London: Arnold

Torpey, J. 2000. *The Invention of the Passport: Surveillance, Citizenship and the State.* Cambridge: Cambridge University Press

Valdivia, Angharad, ed. 1995. *Feminism, Multiculturalism, and the Media: Global Diversities.* Thousand Oaks, CA: Sage

van Dijk, Teun. 1986. *News Analysis. Case Studies of International and National News in the Press: Lebanon, Ethnic Minorities and Squatters.* Amsterdam: University of Amsterdam

– 1987. *Communicating Racism: Ethnic Prejudice in Thought and Talk.* Newbury Park, CA: Sage

– 1988a. 'How They Hit the Headlines: Ethnic Minorities in the Press.' In G. Smitherman-Donaldson and T. A. van Dijk, *Discourse and Discrimination.* Detroit: Wayne State University Press

– 1988b. 'News as Discourse.' In G. Smitherman Donaldson and T. van Dijk, *Discourse and Discrimination.* Detroit: Wayne State University Press

– 1988c. *News as Discourse.* Hillsdale: Lawrence Erlbaum

– 1991. *Racism and the Press.* New York: Routledge

– 1993. *Elite Discourse and Racism.* Newbury Park, CA: Sage

– 1994. *Racism and the Press.* New York: Routledge

- 1996a. 'Discourse, Power and Access.' In *Texts and Practices: Readings in Critical Discourse Analysis*. Ed. C.R. Caldas-Coulthard and M. Coulthard. London: Routledge
- 1996b. 'Opinions and Ideologies in Editorials.' http:www.let.uva.nl/~teun/editoria.html p,14; second draft, March. www.hum.uva.nl.teun.editoria.htm
- 1998. *Ideology: A Multidisciplinary Approach.* London: Sage
- 2001. 'Critical Discourse Analysis.' In *The Handbook of Discourse Analysis*. Ed. D. Schiffrin, D. Tannen, and Heidi Hamilton. Oxford: Blackwell
Wellman, David. 1977. *Portraits of White Racism.* Cambridge: Cambridge University Press
West, Candice, Michelle Lazar, and Cheris Kramarae. 1997. 'Gender in Discourse.' In *Discourse Studies: A Multidisciplinary Introduction*. Ed. Teun van Dijk London: Sage.
Wetherell, Margaret, and Jonathan Potter. 1992. *Mapping the Language of Racism.* New York: Columbia University Press
Whitaker, Reg. 1998. 'Refugees: The Security Factor.' *Citizenship Studies* 2 (3): 413–34
Williams, Raymond. 1976. *Keywords.* London: Fontana
Winant, H. 1997. 'Behind Blue Eyes: Whiteness and Contemporary U.S. Racial Politics.' In *Off White: Readings on Race, Power and Society.* Ed. M. Fine, et al. New York: Routledge
Winter, James. 1997. *Democracy's Oxygen: How the Corporations Control the News.* Montreal: Black Rose Books
Wodak, Ruth. 1996. *Disorders and Discourse.* London: Longman.
- 1997. *Gender and Discourse.* London: Sage.
Wodak, Ruth, Rudolph de Cillia, Martin Reisigl, and Karin Liebhart. 1999. *The Discursive Construction of National Identity.* Edinburgh: Edinburgh University Press
Wodak, Ruth, and Bernd Matouschek. 1993. "We Are Dealing with People Whose Origins One Can Clearly Tell Just by Looking": Critical Discourse Analysis and the Study of Neo-racism in Contemporary Australia.' *Discourse and Society* 4 (2): 225–48.
Wortley, S., J. Hagan, and R. Macmillan. 1997. 'Just Desserts: The Racial Polarization of Criminal Justice.' *Law and Society Review* 31 (4): 637–76
Yon, Dan. 1995. 'Unstable Terrain: Explorations in Identity, Race and Culture in a Toronto High School.' PhD dissertation, York University
- 2000. *Elusive Culture: Schooling, Race and Identity in Global Times.* Albany, NY: SUNY Press

# Index

vagueness, 77, 99, 101, 102, 186, 187, 221. *See also* argumentation

Valpy, Michael, on Just Desserts shooting, 170–3, 176, 181–5, 190, 196

*Vancouver Sun*, 45, 203, 255–6 n 11; coverage of Chinese migration to Canada, 143–57

van Dijk, Teun, 110, 233, 238; and critical discourse analysis, 12, 16, 19, 35, 71–2, 74, 76, 252 nn 1, 2, 3; on editorials, 75, 93–4, 185, 235; on elites, 26; on headlines, 121–2, 144; on ideology, 5, 20, 227; on incoherence, 114; on language, 25; on media, 4, 5, 36, 226, 236; on 'new racism,' 23; on subject of immigration, 109; on 'text' and talk,' 23, 35, 71, 93, 109

*Victoria Times Colonist*: coverage of Chinese migration to Canada, 3, 143–57, 256 n 11

Vienneau, David, 191

Vietnamese/Vietnamese Canadian and racialization of crime, 79, 167–8, 198, 199, 200. *See also* Asians/ Asian Canadians

*The View*, 81, 90

visible minorities. *See* racial minorities

'visual evidence,' 142–3

Vo, Tommy (Chanh Thong Vo), 196, 198–201, 229

Wallin, Pamela, 87

Walters, Barbara, 81, 90

Weedon, Chris, and Glenn Jordan, 8

Wellman, David, 36

Wente, Margaret, 80, 83, 87, 88, 89, 257 n 1

Wetherell, Margaret, and Jonathan Potter, 19, 35, 36, 71, 107, 252 n 2

White(s), 9–10, 34; Amiel on, 52; attitudes toward daily newspapers, 46; as dominant culture, 9, 40–1, 93, 117, 216, 227, 230, 231, 236; and employment equity, 98; as experts, 66; and the media, 7, 55, 57, 64, 66, 67, 226, 227, 239; race classification, 9–10; refugees, 113; superiority/supremacy, 43, 215, 239, 254 n 3; White elite, 7, 76; White gaze, 76, 215, 230; White victimization, 175, 230–1; Whiteness, 9–10, 41, 107

Whyte, Ken, 120

*Windsor Evening Record*, 41

*Winnipeg Free Press*, 45, 57

*Winnipeg Sun*, 45

Winter, James, 52–53, 235, 236; and Barlow, 51; *The Big Black Box*, 51

Wodak, Ruth, 251 n 1; and critical discourse analysis (CDA), 35, 72; and Norman Fairclough, 16, 72, 238; and Bernd Matouschek, 251 n 4

'Writing thru Race,' 257 n 1

Yon, Dan, 37–8

young offenders, 170, 171–2, 173, 175–80, 182, 195

Young Offender's Act, 175, 180

Zerbisias, Antonia, 89

Zhao, Yuezhi, and Robert Hackett, 5, 53, 236

Ziemba, Elaine, 101